THE WORLDS OF RICHARD III

A. J. Pollard

TEMPUS

First published 2001

PUBLISHED IN THE UNITED KINGDOM BY:

Tempus Publishing Ltd
The Mill, Brimscombe Port
Stroud, Gloucestershire GL5 2QG
www.tempus-publishing.com

PUBLISHED IN THE UNITED STATES OF AMERICA BY:

Tempus Publishing Inc.
2 Cumberland Street
Charleston, SC 29401
(Tel: 1-888-313-2665)
www.arcadiapublishing.com

Tempus books are available in France, Germany from the following addresses:

Tempus Publishing Group   Tempus Publishing Group
21 Avenue de la République   Gustav-Adolf-Straße 3
37300 Joué-lès-Tours   99084 Erfurt
FRANCE   GERMANY

Copyright © A.J. Pollard, 2001

The right of Professor A.J. Pollard to be identified as the Author of this work has been
asserted by him in accordance with the Copyrights, Designs and Patents Act 1988.

All rights reserved. No part of this book may be reprinted or reproduced or utilised in
any form or by any electronic, mechanical or other means, now known or hereafter
invented, including photocopying and recording, or in any information storage or
retrieval system, without the permission in writing from the Publishers.

British Library Cataloguing in Publication Data.
A catalogue record for this book is available from the British Library.

ISBN 0 7524 1985 4

Typesetting and origination by Tempus Publishing.
PRINTED AND BOUND IN GREAT BRITAIN.

CONTENTS

Acknowledgements

I am grateful to the following for permission to reprint the various chapters of this book: Elsevier Science for Chapter 1, reprinted from the *Journal of Medieval History* 3, pp 147-166, © North-Holland Publishing Company (1977); the University of Nottingham for Chapter 2 reprinted from *Nottingham Medieval Studies*, vol. xxxviii (1994), pp. 152-63. The Richard III Society for Chapter 3 reprinted from *The Ricardian*, vol. v, no. 74 (1981), pp. 384-9; Sutton Publishing for Chapter 4 reprinted from *Patronage, Pedigree and Power in Later Medieval England*, ed. Charles Ross (1979), pp. 37-59 and Chapter 9 reprinted from *Kings and Nobles in the Later Middle Ages,* eds R.A. Griffiths and J.W. Sherborne (1986), pp. 109-29; Peter Hibbard, The Old School Arts Workshop for Chapter 6 (1983); the North Yorkshire County Record Office for Chapter 7 reprinted from *The North Yorkshire County Record Office Journal*, 6 (1978), pp. 5-24; the Yorkshire Archaeological Society for Chapter 8 reprinted from *The Yorkshire Archaeological Journal,* vol. 50 (1978), pp. 152-68; and the Richmond Civic Society for Chapter 8 reprinted from *The Richmond Review*, 15 (1992), pp. 13-18.

I would also like to express my gratitude to Geoffrey Wheeler for gathering together the illustrations and coping with the vagaries of a scanned text; to Jonathan Reeve for his patient assistance as we struggled to sort these out; and to my wife, Sandra, for picking up yet more oddities at proof stage. No doubt one or two transpositions have escaped all detection, for which I crave the reader's tolerance.

La Bournelie Basse
15 August 2001

Introduction

I first encountered Richard III when writing an essay as a first year undergraduate on the question: 'Was Richard III the malignant monster of tradition?' I have no memory of how well I tackled it, but it did engage my interest (which lay dormant until I returned more seriously to the topic a decade or so later). Since then, I seem to have been entangled almost perpetually with Richard III, his friends and enemies, then and now. The essays and occasional pieces in this collection were written between 1975 and 1998; all but one have been previously published. To a significant extent, they may be seen as preliminary and supplementary sketches for two books, *North-Eastern England during the Wars of the Roses* and *Richard III and the Princes in the Tower*, published in 1990 and 1991.[1] The worlds of Richard III which I have visited in them might broadly be described as the literary world of historical representation and myth making, for as well as against this controversial king (where I began), and the down-to-earth world of the fifteenth-century north in his time (where I came to live). They are, however, overlapping worlds and all the essays in one way or another relate to both, not least because any historian's writings are representations of an imagined past. They are broadly of two kinds: those which sought to develop broader conclusions and those that dealt with particular individuals, families and places. They are reproduced below unchanged except for corrections of fact and typography.

It was Charles Ross who set that first essay, and it was he also who instigated my interest in Richard III and the north. I had begun to explore northern gentry society as a result of the fortuitous discovery of a portion of a list of Middleham retainers dating from the late 1450s, which had been sewn into the Clervaux Cartulary.[2] Charles was at that time writing his study of Richard III. I remember discussing with him, characteristically in the White Hart on Park Row in Bristol, the significance of the fees paid to retainers from Middleham by successive late fifteenth-century lords and especially the importance of the north to Richard III and the role played by northerners during his reign. It now seems extraordinary, but in the early 1970s this was still a relatively unexplored and little recognized dimension to his career. Since then, of course, not only Ross but also several other historians have fully explored the association between Richard III and the north. Thirty years later, the theme is not only fully established in the historiography, but has also fallen into the danger of being blown out of all proportion.[3]

One should not suppose, however, that the 'northern-ness' of Richard III was completely overlooked before the late twentieth century. Early northern historians of the reign were embarrassed by the evident close association between their region and the malignant monster. They took refuge in denial. 'The dreadful machinations,' wrote William Hutchinson, 'by which Richard duke of Gloucester was opening his passage to the throne do not seem to have had any particular influence on the north parts of the realm'. Only George Buck, idiosyncratically for his age, endorsed Richard of Gloucester as a true son of the north, concluding that 'he was so much in the good liking of the north countries as that he desired only to finish his days there and in the condition of a subject and a servant to the king'. Nineteenth-century writers were responsible for permanently implanting the perception that he was a northerner, perhaps inspired by the Caroline Halsted's two volume encomium of 1844. Fifteen years later James Raine Jnr declared, largely on the basis of a much-quoted obituary notice preserved in the minutes of the York city council, 'Rarely, if ever has there been a prince in the north so universally beloved as Richard III'. It soon became established that the Richard III of northern tradition was a virtuous hero maligned by Tudors and southerners alike. All that was needed was P.M. Kendall's subsequent endorsement of the oneness of man and region, 'the native country of his soul'.[4]

The first three essays all explore themes related to the early shaping of the historical reputation of Richard III and the creation of the perception of him as a tyrant, especially a tyrant from the north, whence, of course, all evil comes. The first foray into the field, and perhaps the most rash, was 'The Tyranny of Richard III'. The portrait presented here of the plantation of the south is crude and simplistic. It was subsequently toned down and modified in *North-Eastern England*, reflecting my own reconsideration as well as the important reassessment by Rosemary Horrox.[5] The discussion of kingship and tyranny has also been superseded[6] and I would no longer wish to stress in the same way, although it now has a curiously postmodern air to it, that the tradition itself was inextricably part of the historical truth. Nevertheless, I understand that it had its vogue as a controversial piece, especially when recommended to undergraduates, and I have to admit that the title, shamelessly borrowed from Caroline Barron,[7] was designed to be provocative.

The essay on Dominic Mancini's narrative of the events of 1483 was first given to a conference organised by the Richard III Society and then elaborated a few years later on the encouragement of the editor, Michael Jones, for *Nottingham Medieval Studies*. This piece arose out of my dissatisfaction with the treatment of the very first account of the occupation of the throne by Richard III as an authoritative account just because it was written almost immediately and well before Henry VII became king. What I hope I was able to show is that it is a complex work drawn from several different sources available to the author in the summer of 1483 which happened to come from the same perspective as that dominant after 1485, and that it was, therefore, in essence as one-sided as the 'official' Tudor version. It is, of course, a matter for great regret that no similar version of events, written between 1483 and 1485 from the point of view of the other side, has survived. One can reasonably reconstruct what this might have been (and reasonably suppose it would have been no more reliable), but its absence has always made it more difficult to deny by historical argument that Richard III was the 'malignant monster'. This does not mean that he was. As Horace Walpole (at least initially) so elegantly argued, it is beyond reason to suppose so.[8] It would be accurate to say that I have arrived at the position where sceptically I distrust both traditions about Richard III and have retreated to cynical agnosticism.

The short essay on 'North, South and Richard III' was also first delivered to a Ricardian audience in 1981. Here too I have moved on, first in *North-Eastern England* and then in an essay on 'The Characteristics of the Fifteenth-Century North', published in 1996 at the same time as an introduction to a collection of essays delivered at a third Richard III Society conference entitled *Richard III and the North of England*.[9] The issue concerning Richard III is caught up in a wider debate concerning the notion of a north-south divide in English history, to which one particularly enticing contribution was the proposal that for a brief while, 1483-5 one assumes,

1. Edward Prince of Wales (later Edward V), from the Royal Window, Canterbury Cathedral.
2. Richard Neville, Earl of Warwick, 'Warwick the Kingmaker'. Victorian glass, Cardiff Castle.

England was ruled from Wensleydale. Would that it had been true.[10] Sadly Richard III was well on the way to becoming a southerner again when he was overthrown.

'The Richmondshire Community of Gentry', was an early detailed study in which I sought to flesh out the northern associations. It too owed its title to a fellow historian, Michael Bennett, who had recently published his article on Cheshire and whose ideas deeply influenced me in the construction of the piece.[11] It was done initially for a symposium of younger scholars organised by Charles Ross at Bristol in 1978, the first of many that have since been held. Its proceedings too were one of the first volumes on fifteenth-century history to be published by Alan Sutton. Also giving papers were Margaret Condon, Keith Dockray, Michael Hicks and Rosemary Horrox (that given by Margaret Condon having best survived the passage of time, now being a classic on the reign of Henry VII).[12]

In retrospect I wondered for a time whether the words 'community of' might have been best left out of the title, but perhaps they too have stood the test of time. The piece explored the network of gentry associations within the honour of Richmond in north-west Yorkshire. It highlighted the manner in which the resident gentry looked to and were dominated by the lords of Middleham who were, for most of the fifteenth century, also the grantees of the comital rights of Richmond. Richmondshire, a contemporary term describing the five wapentakes of north-western Yorkshire which formed a feudal liberty, was a shire within the county.

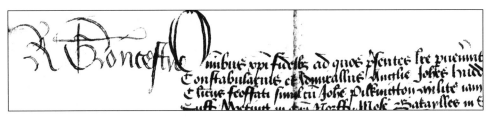

3. Signature of Richard, Duke of Gloucester, endorsing one of the foundation documents for Middleham College. (North Yorkshire Record Office)

In 1979 I assumed that one could attach the concept of county community to it. As was pointed out in one review, however, it represented something of a conceptual contradiction: a sub-county community shaped by a baronial affinity.[13] However, further work has begun to modify perceptions of county communities in the fifteenth century as quasi-autonomous political bodies. Whilst the matter is still controversial, one view is that baronial affinities, which did not necessarily coincide with royal administrative boundaries, formed the essential informal political association in late medieval England.[14] The social networks of the resident gentry of Richmondshire and their political gravitation towards the great lord of the district seated at Middleham were to a large extent shaped by the feudal liberty. The baronial affinity and gentry community thus coincided within an older legal and administrative unit. The homogeneity this created strengthened the hand of successive lords, and helps explain the prominence of Middleham and Richmondshire in the politics of the Wars of the Roses.

Edward IV certainly had cause to fear commotion in Richmondshire fostered by Warwick the Kingmaker in 1469-71.[15] That the fear of marauding northerners became a feature of late fifteenth-century propaganda, to be deployed systematically against Richard III and his regime by the Tudors, cannot be denied. But I have argued elsewhere that this was as much a literary and cultural con-vention as a reflection of any fundamental social and economic divide within the realm of England. I am not convinced that there was such a regional division, let alone a distinctive northern conscious-ness in late-fifteenth century England. Southerners, that is to say those who chose to define them-selves as southerners, had certain preconceptions about northerners which it was convenient for successive governments, especially Henry VII at the beginning of his reign, to exploit.[16]

I have over the years thus changed my views quite considerably. Indeed I would no longer write, as I did in 1990, that the north, in particular the north-east, was more difficult for histor-ical, legal and institutional reasons for Westminster to control.[17] Then, and to some extent in my piece on Richard III and the county palatine of Durham entitled 'St Cuthbert and the Hog' (published in 1986), I underestimated the extent to which the county palatine provided the opportunity, at one remove, for the crown to exercise its authority in the region through its servant, the bishop of Durham and the administrative and legal powers vested in him. This is as apparent during the pontificate of Thomas Langley (1406-1437) as it was under Richard Fox (1494-1501) and thereafter. Richard III, as duke of Gloucester succeeded, through the pliant William Dudley, to suborn palatine authority for his own ends, but as king was equally able after 1483 to reassert royal control. Thus I have come to conclude that the weakness of the crown in the north-east, as one or two of my critics pointed out, was as much the consequence of the failure of royal will in the face of Neville aggrandisement in the mid-fifteenth century

4. Tomb of Thomas Langley, (d.1407), Durham Cathedral.

as of institutional weakness as such. This is a matter I endeavoured to put right in my discussion in 1996 of the election of Robert Neville as bishop of Durham in 1437.[18]

I write here of the north-east away from the Scottish border. But even in terms of the protection of the border in the far north there was much to be said for Lancastrian and Yorkist entrustment of defence and the enforcement of truces to magnates who had resources and roots in the region in preference to the meddling and under cutting of local authority by the early Tudors. Richard III in his short reign kept tight personal control of the north; whether had he ruled longer he would have reverted to the traditional practice of delegation to trusted local magnates, or like Henry VII sought to keep control through a policy of divide and rule which undermined the defence of the north, will never be known.[19]

The more detailed studies of individual persons, families and places sought to show, among other things, how northern society readily adapted to changes of regime. For them, as the late medieval history of the Burghs of Brough shows, Richard III was but a passing phenomenon; his career advantageous while it lasted, but not the alpha and omega of the world as they knew it. Omega came for the Burghs in the early sixteenth century with a disputed inheritance. The detailed study of Richard Clervaux was made possible by the unique collection of documents brought together by him in his cartulary. They demonstrate, among other things, how the River Tees did not represent an impenetrable social or economic boundary. A few further documents have come to light since the piece was written, which show the great difficulty Clervaux faced towards the end of his life in collecting rents in Darlington and reveal his embroilment in a dispute with Roger Conyers of Wynyard, Co. Durham over the compensation due following the death of his daughter Isabel, who died before her marriage with Conyers' son Thomas was consummated. The same proceedings before the Durham justices also reveal that Clervaux died between 1 January and 25 March 1491, for he was still alive when the last hearings considering his plea were held in the Lent session of 1491. The year of death given on his tomb is, of course, old calendar.[20]

It was Bill Chaytor, Clervaux's descendent at Croft, who introduced me to the Cartulary. The shorter paper on Richmond was first delivered to a meeting of the Richmond Civic Society in March 1992. The town of Richmond, like Richard Clervaux and the Burghs who had significant interest in the town, was equally adept at flowing with the political tide. The townsmen perhaps had more pressing need than their gentle neighbours to secure royal favour in 1485. The economic decline and contraction of their town in the later Middle Ages left them with little choice but to welcome their returning earl with open arms.

The genesis of 'The Middleham Connection' was a public lecture delivered at the University of York on 11 June 1983, subsequently published in connection with a small exhibition which I helped mount with Peter Hibbard at the Old School Arts Workshop as part of the celebration of the quincentenary of Richard III's accession. Middleham has most sucessfully marketed itself as a heritage centre on the back of its association with Richard III. This little pamphlet sought to do its bit. However, the emphasis I then gave to the particular association between Richard III and Middleham is to some extent misleading. It is arguable that Middleham was more important as a focal point and centre of power for both Richard, earl of Salisbury and Warwick the Kingmaker than it was for Richard III. It was during the lordship of either father or son that the castle was 'modernised' and its top storey added.[21] More evidence has survived of both of them residing there than of Richard of Gloucester. The duke, on the other hand, seems at first to have preferred both Pontefract and Barnard Castle. Not perhaps until after 1478, when his son and heir known as Edward of Middleham was resident there, and after which he upgraded the parish church to collegiate status and sought to revive the flagging commercial prosperity of the town, does Richard appear to have become particularly close to the place.[22] It was perhaps the decision to base the household of his son there which, for a short while, made Middleham central to the Duke of Gloucester's interests. There is every sign, after his accession and following Edward's death, that Middleham, along with the king's other ducal estates in the north, was relegated to a source of ancillary royal finance.[23]

Even before 1483 a significant portion of the resources of Middleham, under all three of its late fifteenth century lords, was diverted to pay the fees of indentured retainers. This is not evidence of the canker of bastard feudalism, especially as it fuelled the feuds between Neville and Percy. Retaining on this scale was undertaken specifically, and under royal licence, to provide the mobile reserves which successive lords of Middleham, as wardens of the west march, could call out on the outbreak of war with Scotland. The permanent garrison at Carlisle was maintained on a peace-time footing only. In time of war it had to be rapidly reinforced by the calling out of the warden's retainers and county levies. The men of Richmondshire were not retained by Richard of Gloucester and his predecessors merely to enhance his power and prestige; they had a specific military role to play in the defence of the kingdom.

This is not say that these retainers did not also on other occasions turn out for their lords in time of civil war. One may suppose, although the evidence is indirect, that several of them responded to their lord's summons twice in 1483.[24] The last essay, not previously published, focuses on the summer of that year when Richard III made himself king. It goes down a byway, as it were, seeking from a fragmentary source to reconstruct what happened back in Middleham after Richard took the fateful high road to London. Besides throwing ancillary light on the events themselves, as others have fully recognised, the remnant of the Middleham estate papers on which it is based offers a glimpse of the 'normal' life of a noble boy of the royal blood in the two months before he was suddenly thrust into the public world as prince of Wales.

The north remained as important to Richard III during the first year of his reign as it had been before he became king. One has, however, to be cautious in estimating that importance and careful not to exaggerate or romanticise the association. Before he was king Richard did not rule the north. He was no viceroy. The powers of lieutenant given to him were temporary and for the prosecution of war against the Scots. It is unclear as to whether Edward IV encouraged Gloucester to concentrate his interests in the region, or whether Gloucester took more for himself than his brother the king intended.[25] We should not assume either that Gloucester was universally beloved by northerners. As rifts within the ruling elite of York and pub gossip there reveal, he had his enemies as well as his friends.[26] Northerners, one suspects, asked not what they could do for him, but what he could do for them.[27]

One needs also to be cautious about what one means by Richard III's north. The essays collected here all deal with the north-east, and several with one district, Richmondshire, in particular. But what of the north-west, the counties of Cumberland and Westmorland? Until recently the assumption has tended to be made that, because of the wardenship of the west march and the possession of Penrith, this district was equally tied into the Ricardian hegemony.[28] However, Dr Booth has plausibly argued that on the other side of the Pennines Gloucester was not all dominant and that he shared pre-eminence with the controller of the king's household, Sir William Parr.[29] It was perhaps not until the very end of Edward IV's reign, with the creation for him of a county palatine based on the wardenship of the march and to be forged by conquest in south-west Scotland, that his interest shifted in that direction. Richard of Gloucester, the younger brother of a king who had not been granted his own patrimony by his father, was a restless man. We should not assume that even had events taken a different course he would have remained as closely identified with the north-east of England as he was during the comparatively short period of 1471 to 1483. At the beginning of 1483, a new patrimony the other side of the Pennines appeared an attractive new prospect. A few months later, the throne itself beckoned. Richard III's interests in the north-east of England were perhaps as fleeting as in the event was the north-east's association with him.

So too is my involvement in the history of the last Plantagenet. The compilation of this collection provides a fitting moment at which to draw a line under my long running engagement in print with the subject of Richard III. It will have become apparent that in the process I have incurred a considerable body of debt. First of all there is the Richard III Society with which I have worked for many years. Several of these pieces began with or for the Society. I have also jousted with many fellow members, most particularly the late Jeremy Potter. Although we rode on different sides of the barrier, we remained friends. And so it has been with many Ricardians, in England, the USA and Australasia. Readers will also have noticed that several pieces to which I have referred, including two here, were published by Alan Sutton, who few remember began his publishing career on Richard III and fifteenth-century history. It is therefore especially a pleasure for me that he has been willing to publish this volume. There are many others. My own understanding has been enhanced and enriched by the complementary work and encouragement of Lorraine Attreed, Michael Bennett, Barrie Dobson, Ralph Griffiths, Peter Hammond, Bill Hampton, Michael Hicks, Rosemary Horrox, Michael K. Jones, David Palliser, Colin Richmond, Anne Sutton and, by whom I was first introduced to the malignant monster, Charles Ross. But above all I would like to acknowledge my debt to Keith Dockray who began working on the late fifteenth-century gentry of Yorkshire long before I stumbled upon them. He has never published as much as he should of his early studies,[30] but from the beginning he generously made the results available to me. If I have been able over these years to make a small contribution to an understanding of the worlds of Richard III, as much is owed to Keith's unselfishness as to my own endeavours.

1

THE TYRANNY OF
RICHARD III

'Although he did evil, yet in his tyme were many good actes made.' This comment made by
the mayor and aldermen of London to Cardinal Wolsey in 1525 has become something of a text
for recent interpretations of the reign of Richard III (Myers 1954: 521).[1] It sums up what may
be called the 'balanced' view which has received more or less general acceptance over the past
twenty years. 'That there was a sound constructive side to Richard III', we are assured by the
Oxford historian of the fifteenth century, 'is undoubted. He was very far from being the
distorted villain of tradition'.[2] The whole weight of twentieth-century scholarship has been
marshalled against the notorious interpretation of Richard's first, early-Tudor historians, whose
works, because of the unreliability of their information and because of the inevitable antagonistic bias of their outlook, are now said to be more of a barrier than a path to understanding.
As Professor A.R. Myers has put it recently (1968: 201):

> most academic historians have lost his [Gairdner's] faith in the value of the Tudor
> historical tradition as a guide to the problem.

This piece sets out to question recent interpretation and to suggest that Gairdner's faith may
not have been so misplaced. Its argument is that, used with caution, the Tudor tradition is still
an important guide. That tradition had at its heart the notion that Richard III had been a tyrant.
The thesis presented here is that the early historians believed that Richard had, according to
their own understanding of the term, acted tyrannically; that, moreover, some of Richard's acts
gave them good grounds for this belief; and that, finally, the value of the tradition can only
properly be appreciated if it is seen to have had its roots in the experiences and memories of
the southern counties of England.

In his preface to his *Richard III*, Gairdner wrote (1898: xi-xii):

> The attempt to discard tradition in the examination of original sources in history is,
> in fact, like the attempt to learn an unknown language without a teacher. We lose the
> benefit of a living interpreter who may indeed misapprehend, to some extent, the
> author whom we wish to read; but at least he would save us from innumerable
> mistakes if we followed his guidance in the first instance.

Gairdner, it is no doubt true, misapprehended more than he realized; but it is equally true that
serious misinterpretation of the reign of Richard III can be avoided if we follow both his

5. Self-portrait of John Rous, chaplain of Guy's Cliff Warwick, from his Rous Roll 'History of the Earls of Warwick', (Latin version).

guidance and that of the tradition more closely. The trouble has perhaps stemmed from the fact that Gairdner accepted the tradition too literally. The result has been that recent historians, quite rightly, have concentrated their attentions on the weaknesses and inaccuracies of the early histories, without paying due attention to their overriding aims and underlying assumptions. It is now incontrovertible that in many points of detail, More and Vergil, let alone John Rous and Bernard André, were imprecise, ignorant or credulous. Richard III is indeed unlikely to have fitted the lurid physical description first put forward by John Rous, although strangely enough John Burton, schoolmaster of St Leonard's, York, was reported to have said during a tavern row that 'King Richard was a hypocrite, a crouchback' (Raine 1941: 72). He is unlikely to have committed the long list of crimes assigned to him before his accession. On the contrary, he showed himself a loyal and competent helper of his elder brother for many years. These revisions were all necessary and help us towards a more exact assessment of his career and character. But the accuracy of specific details was not considered of such importance in the sixteenth century. History also had a higher function: it delivered universal truths and carried moral lessons for its audience. The historian thus approached the past from a different direction: he wrote with a clear moral and didactic purpose (Hay 1952: 162-6; Smith-Fussner 1970: ch. 5). In this case it was to demonstrate the tyranny of the late King Richard III. In writing, he was guided by a preconceived notion of what a tyrant was and presented the 'facts' in such a way as to achieve this. The result is that the picture of Richard III has much in common with an ideal type of evil king. This philosophy of history can be seen at work in the writings of both of the principal creators of the Tudor tradition – Polydore Vergil and Sir Thomas More.

History, wrote Vergil in his dedication to Henry VIII of his *Anglica Historia*, 'displays eternally to the living those events which should be an example and those which should be a warning' (Hay 1952: 153). In the work itself, and especially in the books on the fifteenth century, he is

6. Engraving of Queen Anne Neville, Richard III and their son Edward, Prince of Wales, from the Rous Roll, (English version, British Library)

constantly returning to the theme of the role of fate and divine retribution in the lives of princes (1952: 139-43). It is most marked in his treatment of Richard III, where he sets out the divine retribution awaiting the tyrant. Commenting on the coronation, he writes:

> Thus Richard, without the assent of the commonaltie, by might and will of certaine noblemen of his faction, enjoyned the realme, contrary to the law of God and man.

And at the end, after giving his account of the king's death, he adds:

> And so the myserable man had suddaynly such an end as wont ys to happen to them that have right and law both of God and man in lyke estimation as will, impyetie, and wickedness (Ellis 1844: 187, 226).

More's portrait of Richard is the more colourful and justifiably the more famous. This is the work that has received most vituperation from Ricardian apologists, perhaps because of the single-mindedness with which it pursues its theme of tyranny. According to Erasmus, More had a particular loathing for tyranny. There is certainly evidence from his *Epigrammata*, written during the same period as the *History*, that he was then preoccupied with the question. In the *History* too, as Professor R.S. Sylvester has demonstrated, More drew heavily on the first six

7. Modern inn sign of the 'King's Arms', Ouse Bridge, York, showing Richard's portrait, testifying to the affection in which he is still held in the city.

books of Tacitus' *Annals*, then newly discovered, which depict the tyranny of Tiberius. Using this and other classical models, More shaped his history into a work which is more than just a history, but also a drama and a political treatise. His portrait goes beyond empiricism: as Sylvester puts it,[3]

> His Richard is no mere usurper, but a grand villain whose figure draws much of
> its strength from the similarity it bears to the tyrants of tradition: the usurping
> protector is seen in terms of a broad historical metaphor that allows More to
> emphasize the moral patterns implicit in his story. The truth about Richard III,
> as More saw it, was not so much a matter of the facts of his reign; rather it
> resides in the timeless correspondence between events of the past and the
> immediate situation in which men found themselves involved.

The details, then, are subordinated to the over-riding and controlling aim of presenting Richard as the quintessence of tyranny.

Thus the important question concerning the tradition and the early historians who formed it is not the accuracy of their detail, but their shared assumption that Richard was a tyrant. How did they arrive at this? It is now accepted that neither Vergil nor More was a mere propagandist. Both, as recent studies have clearly demonstrated, had purposes which went beyond merely bolstering up the Tudor dynasty. And in writing their accounts, they drew upon a whole array of information both from men who had been prominent fellow exiles of Henry VII, and from men who had experienced Richard III's reign at first hand. They were men of affairs who gave both authors the benefit of their informed opinion. Coloured it inevitably was, but it is to be doubted that it was deliberately falsified (Hay 1952: 93, 154, 171; Sylvester 1963: lxvii-lxix, lxxxii, xcix; Hanham 1975: 126-9, ch. 7). Moreover, where Vergil's and More's accounts can be compared with contemporary and near-contemporary accounts uninfluenced by the full flood of Tudor propaganda, striking confirmation of their tone and interpretation can be found. Dominic Mancini's *De Occupatione* written in December 1483 as an 'eye-witness' account, is uncannily similar in tone and detail to all later versions of the usurpation. And on the reign as

THE
HISTORIE
OF THE PITIFVLL
Life, and unfortunate Death
of *Edward* the fifth , and
the then Duke of *Yorke*
his brother:

With the troublesome and
tyrannical government of Usvr-
ping *Richard* the third, and
his miserable end

Written by the Right Honor-
able Sir *Thomas Moore*
sometimes LordChanc-
cellor of England.

LONDON,

Printed by *Thomas Payne* for
the Company of *Stationers*, and
are to be sold by *Mich: Young*,
at his shop in *Bedford-street* in
Covent-Garden, neere the
new Exchange.1640.

AD INVICTISSIMVM
ANGLIÆ, FRANCIÆ, HYBERNIÆ-
QVE REGEM
Fidei defenforem ,
HENRICUM VIII.
POLYDORI VIRGILII
URBINATIS

In Anglicam Hiftoriam fuam prooemium.

AM INDE *ab initio rerum humanarum, cunctis mortalibus ,* HENRICE *Rex maxime , gloriam virtutis , rerumque geftarum memoriam perpetuandi, commune ftudium fuit : hinc fanc urbes conditæ, illisque conditorum nomina impofita : hinc ftatuæ repertæ , hinc pyramidum moles , multaque id genus magnificaopera extructa funt : hinc item fuere femper, qui n...i dubitarint , patriæ tuendæ caufa , etiam immaturam opetere mortem. Ea tamen omnia cùm temporis curriculo partim corruerent, partim oblivione obfcurarentur , deinde homines cæperunt & ipfa opera & facinora celebrare literis , quæ ufque eò fempiterna reddiderunt omnia, ut poft ea pro fe quifque benefacta pariter imitanda , atq, malefacta multò diligentiffime declinanda curavit : quando hiftoria ut hominum laudes*
A 2 *loqui-*

8. *(left) Page from Thomas More's 'History of Richard III'.*
9. *Page from an early printed edition of Polydore Vergil's 'Anglica Historia'.*

a whole, the history of the Yorkist dynasty known as the second continuation of the Croyland Chronicle is even more revealing.

   Although the identity of the author and date of composition of the Croyland continuation have still not been satisfactorily resolved, it can be established beyond doubt that the author was a man who had been one of Edward IV's senior councillors and it can be shown from internal evidence that it was indeed written in April 1486, as the author claims.[4] The author's view of the reign commands respect because of his concern, in the new spirit of the Renaissance, to be objective. He avows at the start that he will set forth the events 'in as brief terms and in as unprejudiced a manner as we possibly can' and at the end he again avows that he has set down a history,

> so far as the truthful recital of the facts suggested itself to our mind, without knowingly intermingling therewith any untruthfulness, hatred, or favour whatsoever?[5]

And it is clear also that he had a fairly detached and sophisticated view of recent politics; 'the affairs of England' were, he commented, 'a thing that everyday experience too well teaches us, are subject to many changes and vicissitudes' (Riley 1854:454). With one notable exception, the author appears to have achieved his aim. The exception, of great importance for our purpose, is a very strong prejudice against northerners, which keeps re-appearing and is summed up in this comment on the disturbances in Yorkshire at Eastertide 1486, 'a sedition was set on foot by those ingrates in the North, whence every evil takes its rise'.[6] On Edward IV himself he is more objective, being generally favourable to him but critical of certain aspects of his reign. But his disapproval of the usurpation, and most of Richard III's reign, is very apparent: it leads him to welcome Henry VII in these glowing terms:

> he began to receive the praises of all, as though he had been an angel sent down from heaven, through whom God had deigned to visit His people and to deliver it from the evils with which it had hitherto, beyond measure, been afflicted (Riley 1854: 504-5).

In a poem on the kings named Richard, transcribed along with the Croyland continuation in our only surviving text, (which may or may not have been composed by the same author), we find these lines (1854: 504-5):

> Edward's vast hoards of wealth consumed, the Third
> Was not content therewith, but must destroy
> His brother's progeny, and then proscribe their
> Partisans. Two years had he usurp'd
> The throne, when, meeting these, he lost his life
> And ill-gained crown, upon the battlefield.

It is clear that he too concluded that Richard was an undeserving king.

Thus an entirely independent account, written shortly after the events by a man who lived through them, lends substantial support to the opinion of Henry VII's own partisans. And if, as has recently been suggested (Hanham 1975: 135-42), Polydore Vergil did indeed have access to and used a copy of the History, the origins of the Tudor tradition in the experience of the reign stand out even more clearly. In short, the assumption that Richard was a tyrant was derived, directly and indirectly, from the informed opinion of those who had experienced his reign. It is surely conceivable that this was based not on a mindless partisanship for the house of Tudor, but on a deeper hostility towards the king that was Richard III for offending against certain fundamental rules of kingship?

Such an attitude towards Richard III might well have been adopted in the light of a quite unambiguous and uncontroversial definition of the difference between kingship and tyranny. The nature of kingship in fifteenth-century England was summed up in Sir John Fortescue's description of England as a *dominium regale et politicum*, that blending of absolutism and limited monarchy which he believed was peculiar to his native land. According to Fortescue, the king had absolute power but was not above the law; for it was the law which made him ruler, and the maintenance of laws and property was his *raison d'être*. 'A king', wrote Fortescue (Chrimes 1942: 31-3),

> who is head of the body politic is unable to change the laws of that body, or to deprive that same people of their own substance uninvited or against their wills.

The exercise of his absolute power by the king of England was thus limited in practice by the need for the assent of his subjects. The significance of Fortescue's *dominium regale et politicum* lies in the fact that it was not an abstract theory, but a statement of the constitutional practice of his day (Chrimes 1934: 130-6, 143-6; Jacob 1961: 314-6).

In essence, Fortescue's description of the English constitution puts it in line both with the typical medieval theory of kingship and tyranny and later English opinion. Marsilius of Padua, writing in the early fourteenth century, concluded (Gewirth 1956: 27-8):

> A Kingly Monarchy then is a temperate government wherein the ruler is a single man who rules for the common benefit and in accordance with the will or consent of his subjects. Tyranny, its opposite, is a diseased government wherein the ruler is a single man who rules for his own private benefit apart from the will of his subjects.

These notions of kingship and tyranny are also reflected in Sir Thomas Smith's comments in Chapter 7 of his *De Republica Anglorum* (1583), headed 'the definition of a king and a tyrant', which sums up the commonplace view of the English gentry of his day:[7]

> Where one person beareth the rule they define that to be the estate of a king, who by succession or election commeth with the good will of the people to that government, and doth administer the common wealth by the lawes of the same and by equitie, and doth seeke the profit of the people as much as his owne. A tyraunt they name him, who by force commeth to the Monarchy against the will of the people, breaketh lawes alreadie made at his pleasure, maketh other without the advise and consent of the people, and regardeth not the wealth of his communes but the advancement of himselfe, his faction, & kindred. These definitions do containe three differences: the obtaining of the authoritie, the maner of administration thereof, & the butte or marke whereunto it doth tend and shoote.

We may expect therefore that any fifteenth or sixteenth-century king of England who relied merely on his *dominium regale* ran the risk of being deemed a tyrant.

It is clear that in fifteenth-century England, considerable importance was attached to the limiting aspects of the *dominium politicum*. Now, when Fortescue and others wrote of the 'will', 'profit', 'consent', or 'assent' of the people, they were not of course thinking in modern democratic terms, nor indeed exclusively in terms of representative assemblies. For a start, the will and consent of the people at large was held to be subsumed in the will and consent of their natural rulers – those of gentle and noble blood. This was made abundantly clear by Bishop John Russell in the sermon he drafted for the opening of Edward V's planned first parliament. In his intended plea to the Lords for social peace and harmony, he was to have reminded them that (Nichols 185: xiii-xiv):

> The cause why lordys and nobille men ought more to be persuadid to accord, and eche amyabilly to herken apon other, then the hole generalite of the people,

is playne and evident inowe, considerynge how the polityk rule of every region well ordeigned stondithe in the nobles.

This was the case in ancient Rome, he continued, and in old-testament Israel,

> Lyke as in theys dayes in every region where is a monarchie and one prince (the semblable) policie is observed... Ye be like to Moyses and Aaron, whych escend unto the mount where the lawe ys geuen. The peuple must stond aforr, and not passe the lymittes; ye speke with the prince... as they did with God mouthe to mouthe; but hyt sufisith the peuple to recyve with due obeissance the prince's commandementes by the direccion of hys wyse ministers and offycers.

The people then, whose good will and consent the English king had in practice to keep, was that of the community of those of gentle and noble blood. And one of the most important customary aspects of the English constitution was that the day-to-day rule and government of the shires of England lay in the hands of these magnates and gentry. This was a vital part of the political dominion which limited the absolute power of the English king. A king who intervened too thoroughly in this local autonomy, or attempted to displace the local county rulers, could easily be seen as one ruling without the consent and good will of his people.

Such, briefly, was the notion of tyranny by which Richard III might well have been judged both by his contemporaries and by his early historians. If it were believed that he came to the throne by force and without right, then he would have been judged a tyrant; or if it were believed that he governed without the consent of, or in fact acted against the material interests and political rights of the county gentry and nobility, then he would also have been judged a tyrant. In such circumstances Richard would be a tyrant, as Smith put it, both by 'the obtaining of authoritie' and by 'the manner of administration thereof'. What then is the evidence of Richard's brief reign?

The question of Richard III's title and right to the kingdom need not detain us long. There can be very little doubt that Richard was in fact a usurper and not a lawful king. The justification put forward by him, that the sons of Edward IV were bastards on account of a precontract of marriage undertaken in the early 1460s, remains, as the Croyland Continuator later described it, 'the colour for this act of usurpation' (Riley 1854: 489). As Mortimer Levine concludes a judicious discussion of the question (1959: 401):

> The most telling arguments against the truth of the precontract remain: it was the first made public; the parties to it were both dead and when a powerful uncle was in a position to displace a helpless nephew on the throne; no proof of the precontract was produced nor was its authenticity ruled on by a court which properly had jurisdiction over matrimonial causes.

Dominic Mancini's account of the events of May and June 1483, to which he was witness, makes it clear that no-one in London believed for one moment that Richard had a right to the throne. Richard, he wrote, 'rushed headlong into crime' driven on by 'an insane lust for power'. In the last days of the protectorship, when he exhibited himself through the streets of the city he was scarcely watched by anybody, rather did they curse him with a fate worthy of his crimes, since none now doubted at what he was now aiming.

At the same time, men began to fear for the lives of the boy king and his brother:

> I have seen my men burst forth into tears and lamentations when mention was made of him after his removal from men's sight; and already there was a suspicion that he had been done away with (Armstrong 1969: 20-1, 91, 92, 9).

The crime stood out so markedly because Richard was the king's own uncle and had been charged with his protection. And it appeared all the more wicked because the king was reckoned still to be an innocent child. This, as Mr Armstrong has suggested, probably explains the deep aversion and widespread compassion immediately aroused by the fate of the princes. Robert Fabyan, who lived through the usurpation, may appropriately be allowed the last word on the matter:[8]

> Had he contynuyd styll protectour and have suffyrd the childyr to have prosperid accordyng to his alegeaunce & ffydelyte he shuld have been honourably laudyd ovyr all, where as now his (ffame is) dyrkyd & dyshonowrid as fferre as he was knowyn.

The question of whether Richard could be said to be a tyrant 'by administration' is considerably more complex. The most substantial argument put forward by the apologists is that, although one might concede that he was a usurper, nevertheless in his short spell as king 'Richard could claim to have been shaping well' (Woodward 1972: 20). In his reign, we are assured, he proved himself an enlightened and capable administrator. In particular we are directed to the constructive legislation of the parliament of 1484, especially the Statute against Benevolences, the establishment of the Council of the North, the making of peace with Scotland, and even a long needed programme of 'moral rearmament'.[9] Professor Kendall would have us believe, relying perhaps too much on the testimony of the partisan Thomas Langton, bishop of St David's, that:

> In the course of a mere eighteen months, crowded with cares and problems, he laid down a coherent programme of legal enactments, maintained an orderly society, and actively promoted the well-being of his subjects.[10]

This surely is to claim too much. But there is still no reason to doubt Richard's energy and efficiency, which was certainly more consistently applied than his brother's. Much also has been made of Richard's popularity with the city of York and with the north as a whole. Edward Hall, paraphrasing Polydore Vergil, assured his readers that the people of the north 'entirely loved and highly favoured him' (Ellis 1809: 424-5). And Vergil himself, in telling the story of Henry VII's first visit to York in the spring of 1486 comments that Henry 'did not know whence he could gather a reliable force in a town so little devoted to his interests, which hitherto had

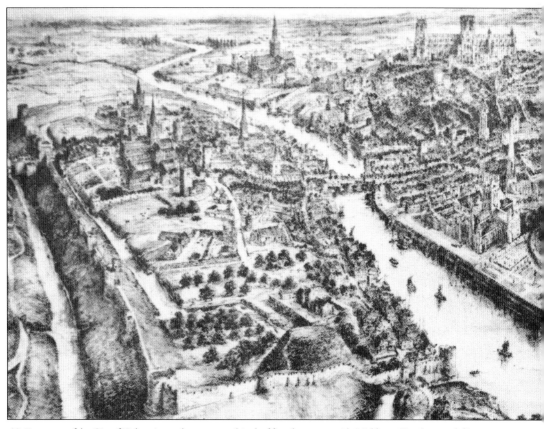

10. Panorama of the City of York as it may have appeared in the fifteenth century, with Micklegate Bar (extreme left),

cherished the name of Richard' (Hay 1950: 11). On the basis of comments such as this and surviving city records (especially the minuted epitaph: 'Pitiously slane and murderd, to the great heavyness of this citie')[11], it has been possible for historians to argue that in the north Richard was genuinely and generally popular.

But, one wonders, have recent historians taken the words of Vergil, and some of the city records a little too much at face value? Richard's strength and support undoubtedly lay in the north, but do we not need to ask more sceptically what the nature of the relationship between royal duke and county gentry and city fathers actually was? What the York records reveal is quintessentially the relationship between client and patron. Richard proved himself to be a most assiduous and, what is more important, successful patron of the city council. He was, as the council wrote effusively but correctly in 1477, 'our tul tendre and especiall gude lorde'.[12] But in return Richard expected and received actual military assistance – not only in the Scottish wars, but also no less than three times during his reign. It was always provided, if perhaps with growing reluctance.[13] Looked at from Richard's point of view this was, in short, a classic 'bastard' feudal relationship, the only difference being that in this case the client was a corporation not an individual. As far as Richard was concerned, the city of York represented one of the more important strands in the web of political power he was spinning over the north of England in the decade before his brother's death. Another

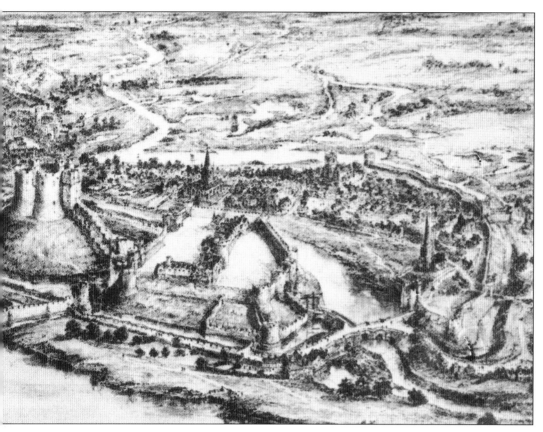

the Minster (centre background) and the Castle (now Clifford's Tower) in the foreground. E.L. Ridsdale Tate

was Henry Percy, earl of Northumberland, with whom Richard established a close working relationship. Their agreement, thrashed out in 1473 and 1474, was that they would in effect retain independent spheres of interest (Northumberland's were his titular county and the former East Riding of Yorkshire); that they and their retainers would serve together on royal commissions and in royal government; but that Richard would have personal pre-eminence as established through a contract of retainer. It was, as it has been put, a 'condominion' over the north. But it was undoubtedly one in which Richard took the lead (Jacob 1961: 368; Ross 1974: 199-203). Equally significant, but less remarked upon, is the manner in which Richard, as the heir to the junior branch of the Neville family seated at Middleham, patched up the quarrel with the senior branch, the earls of Westmorland, seated at Raby in County Durham. For Ralph, Lord Neville, the earl's nephew and heir, became one of his followers too. The second earl of Westmorland (died 1484) was never politically active; it was left to his brothers to take advantage of the civil war of 1459-61 to renew their quarrel with the more favoured junior branch of the family headed by the earls of Salisbury and Warwick. Ralph's father, John, Lord Neville, had been killed at Towton, was attainted and had his lands forfeited in 1461. Ralph's cousin, Sir Humphrey Neville of Bywell, had subsequently maintained an unrepentant opposition to Edward IV and Warwick until his execution in September 1469. After Warwick's fall the way was open for the reconciliation of the senior branch of the family with the Yorkist regime. On 6 October 1472, the attainder was reversed and Ralph, now sixteen, was restored to his father's title and lands. In April 1475 he was knighted. When the young man entered Richard of Gloucester's service is not known, but in June 1483 Richard wrote to him in these terms, 'and, my good lord, do me now gode service, *as ye have always before done*' (my italics). Ralph was subsequently to benefit materially from Richard's reign (*Complete Peerage* 12, 2: 551; Ross 1974: 58-9; Gairdner 1875: 306; Pugh 1972:111-12).

Richard thus successfully ended the two great feuds which had split the higher nobility of the north, and had indeed done much to hasten the recent civil wars. In the 1470s and early 1480s, with lesser peers such as John, Lord Scrope of Castle Bolton; Humphrey, Lord Dacre of Gilsland; Ralph, Lord Greystoke, and Henry, Lord FitzHugh of Ravensworth also in his affinity, or like the Cliffords of Skipton displaced by him, Richard united the northern families into one combined political force. With his own wealth in Yorkshire being constantly enhanced by royal grants, with his appointment in 1482 as King's Lieutenant in the North, and ultimately, in January 1483, with the creation of a huge new hereditary county palatinate for him carved out of whatever parts of south-west Scotland he could conquer, he was on the way to creating what was in effect an almost independent duchy for himself in the north(Ross 1974: 199-203). In terms of wealth, in terms of status, in terms of followers and allies, Richard was by 1483 the most over-mighty subject yet seen in an age of over-mighty subjects.

Richard may indeed have won the hearts of the people of the north but there is no proving this. What is certain, and more to the point, is that they gave him power. This seems to have been grasped by the Croyland Continuator. Writing of the rumours circulating around court and in London in early 1485 that Richard was planning to marry his niece Elizabeth, he tells how the king called a meeting of his council to deny them and how Sir Richard Ratcliffe and William Catesby told him to his face (Riley 1854: 499):

> that if he did not abandon his intended purpose… opposition would not be offered to him by merely the warnings of the voice; for all the people of the north, in whom he placed the greatest reliance, would rise in rebellion against him, and impute to him the death of the queen, the daughter and one of the heirs of the Earl of Warwick, through whom he had first gained his present high position.

This puts it in a nutshell. Richard by stepping into the dead earl of Warwick's shoes had built up an unassailable position in the north. The benefit of Richard's assiduous cultivation of the north was fully revealed during the crises of 1483. His northern followers stood threateningly in the wings during the usurpation. Force was not needed because Richard was able to exploit the divisions amongst Edward's courtiers and the resentments which certain barons, most significantly the duke of Buckingham, had built up against the whole Edwardian régime. Yet a northern army was brought on stage as an added precaution to police the coronation.[14] It was only when Buckingham and the southern counties rebelled in October 1483 that the northerners came to the fore. A northern army suppressed the southwestern risings. And in the aftermath Richard's most trusted northern followers were given a significantly novel role. The risings brought home to Richard the weakness of his hold on the southern counties. In the settlement that followed he determined to control them through his own men. Again it is the Croyland Continuator who puts his finger on it (Riley1854: 496);

11. Raby Castle, Co. Durham, the birthplace of Richard's mother, Cecily Neville.

> While at the same time [the Parliament of January 1484] attainders were made of
> so many lords and men of high rank, besides peers and commoners, as well as three
> bishops, that we do not read of the like being issued by the Triumvirate even of
> Octavianus, Antony and Lepidus. What immense estates and patrimonies were
> collected into the king's treasury in consequence of this measure! All of which he
> distributed among his northern adherents who he planted in every spot throughout
> his dominions to the disgrace and lasting sorrow of all the people in the south who
> daily longed more and more for the hoped for return of their ancient rulers, rather
> than the present tyranny of these people.

Here lies the basis of his charge of tyranny: that by redistribution of the forfeitures brought by
the attainders Richard planted his northern followers in the rebellious south. If this can be
substantiated perhaps much of the hostility towards Richard both before and after 1485 can be
properly explained.

How harsh were the attainders passed by the parliament of January 1484? One hundred and
three persons were in fact attainted and their estates forfeited. Numerous as this was, it was less
than the number of attainders imposed in Edward IV's first parliament. Nor were there many men
of high rank. Indeed nearly three-quarters were of the rank of esquire or below; proportionately
more of lower rank than in Edward's attainders. But Edward had allowed almost as many
prominent opponents to escape as he had prosecuted, and the severity of his treatment of those he
did prosecute was softened by his subsequent leniency. Furthermore these attainders came in the
aftermath of a civil war and a change of dynasty; Richard's merely followed rebellion. This contrast
and the higher proportion of victims of more humble status suggest that his behaviour was indeed
more ruthless.[15] He reigned for too short a time for us to know whether he would have shown
leniency later on, but the chronicler's outrage may perhaps reflect the belief that the attainders
were intended to be permanent. In so far as the handling of the confiscated property is concerned,
it is not true that only northerners benefited, nor indeed, as the passage implies, that all of
Richard's closest adherents were from the north. Lavish rewards were heaped into the welcoming

12. Effigy of Ralph Neville, 2nd earl of Westmorland (d.1484), and his wife, Brancepeth, Co. Durham. From the Yorkist livery collar around his neck, the white boar badge of Richard III once hung as a pendant (missing since the 1920s). These effigies were destroyed by fire in 1998.

arms of the duke of Norfolk, his son the earl of Surrey as well as the earl of Nottingham and the earl of Lincoln, whose fortunes Richard's accession had already greatly enhanced. Also among those who benefited were Viscount Lovell, William Catesby and Sir James Tyrrell, three of his most trusted associates and all from elsewhere. The exaggeration may perhaps be explained by the author's antagonism towards northerners in general, which has already been noted. On the other hand, a study of royal grants and commissions in the eighteen months following November 1483 gives substance to the accusation.

The evidence of the Patent Rolls and the Signet Docket Book, BL MS. Harley 433, confirms that a large number of grants of offices, lands and annuities were made, primarily from forfeited estates, to some forty northerners, mostly Yorkshiremen, who were already prominent in the service of either Richard or the earl of Northumberland. The heaviest concentration of grants to northerners was indeed in those southern counties where there had been risings in the autumn of 1483 and where there was the likelihood that Henry of Richmond would attempt a landing. In some of these grants the necessity of satisfying the demands of some prominent and not entirely reliable supporters was paramount. The earl of Northumberland was allowed to make good his claim to the disputed Bryan and Bure estates from the marquis of Dorset's patrimony. Lord Stanley received lands to the value of nearly £700 for a reserved rent of just £50 per annum.[16] But a good many of the grants seem to have had the additional purpose of putting the defence of the south coast and the rule of the dissident southern counties into the hands of Richard's trusted northern retainers. These men were given the constableships of strategic castles, made sheriffs, placed on the commissions of the peace and given the leadership of the commissions of array through which the counties were to be defended against the anticipated Tudor invasion. To give them the necessary local footing, to support them, and to reward them they were granted forfeited estates.

In the settlement, the southern counties were dealt with as three regions: the south-east, the central south and the south-west. In the south-east (Essex, Kent, Surrey and Sussex) Richard's principal lieutenants were Sir Robert Brackenbury of Denton and Selaby, County Durham, his constable of the Tower; Sir Robert Percy of Scotton, near Knaresborough, controller of the household, and a distant kinsman of the great family; Sir Ralph Ashton of Fryton-in-Ryedale in North Yorkshire, a long-standing councillor who had been appointed vice-constable of England when the news of Buckingham's rebellion broke; and Sir Marmaduke Constable of Flamborough, East Riding, one of the earl of Northumberland's most trusted retainers but now a Knight of the Body. Brackenbury was appointed sheriff of Kent and constable of Tonbridge Castle, and was granted forfeited lands worth approximately £400 per annum. He was also appointed receiver of all the income from the forfeited estates which the king did not grant out in Sussex, Kent and Surrey.[17] Ashton became the lieutenant of the elderly and inactive earl of Arundel in the key strategic posts of constable of Dover Castle and warden of the Cinque Ports. He received lands in Kent worth £116 per annum.[18] Sir Robert Percy was made sheriff of Essex and Herts. and amongst other rewards was granted the stewardship of Kennington, Surrey.[19] Constable was granted the honour of Tonbridge and lordships of Penshurst, Brasted, Hadlow and Yalding in Kent. An order dated 22 January 1484 which was sent from the Signet Office to the inhabitants of these places is worth citing in detail as it demonstrates clearly the role assigned by the king to Constable and his like. The king informs his subjects that:[20]

> we… have deputed and ordained him to make his abode among you and to have the rule within our honour and lordships aforesaid. We therefore will and straightly charge ye nor any of you in no wise presume to take clothing or be retained with any man, person or persons whatsoever he or they be but that ye be ready to attend wholly upon our said Knight at all times that ye by him shall be commanded to do us service.

In other words, the men of this part of Kent were subjected to the compulsory lordship of this particular 'trusty and right well-beloved' Yorkshire knight. It goes without saying that Constable and the others became justices of the peace in the counties where they were granted lands and served on the commissions of array of May and December 1484.[21]

In the central south (Berkshire, Hampshire and Wiltshire) Richard's principal men were John Hoton and William Mirfield, veterans from his own service, and Sir John Saville of Thornhill, Yorkshire, from the long-serving Yorkist family. Hoton was made constable of Southampton and Christchurch and rewarded with the keepership of the New Forest and the manors of Ringwood, Christchurch and Bitterne. Mirfield became keeper of Portchester Castle and governor of Portsmouth and received lands in Wiltshire and Hampshire worth 100 marks per annum; Saville took over the lieutenancy of the Isle of Wight, for which he received a fee of £200 per annum and was also granted lands in Hampshire and Wiltshire. Saville and Hoton became justices and commissioners in Hampshire, where Richard in 1485 expected Richmond to land.[22]

It was in the four southwestern counties (Cornwall, Devon, Dorset and Somerset) where disaffection in the autumn of 1483 had proved most widespread, that forfeited estates were most numerous. It was here too, perhaps, that the 'plantations' were most outrageous. Military command of the region was given to Richard's Yorkshire neighbour and cousin, John, Lord Scrope of Castle

Bolton. He was given the commission to crush the rebellion in Devon and Cornwall on 13 November 1483. Subsequently, he took over the constableship of the castles of Barnstaple and Exeter and was granted the stewardship of the temporalities of the see of Exeter as well as estates in Devon, Cornwall and Somerset worth just over £200 per annum. He also lent his weight to all the royal commissions in the two southwestern counties.[23] Edward Redman of Harewood, whose family had served the lords of Middleham since 1462, also played a prominent governmental role. He was associated with Scrope on a commission of 13 November 1483 charged to arrest the south-western rebels and to confiscate their possessions; was a commissioner of array in Wiltshire and Dorset; and became sheriff of Somerset and Dorset. He received grants of lands worth approximately £80 per annum.[24] But in this region, grants of lands alone were more frequent. As examples one may cite Thomas Tunstall, a retainer of the king since 1471, who was entrusted with the command of the castles of North Wales but amongst his rewards was granted the manor of Totnes in Devon; Robert and Gilbert Manners, Northumberland gentry who shared the Cornish estates of the marquis of Dorset and Sir Giles Daubeney; Sir Thomas Everingham, who received the lands of Sir Roger Tocotes in Devon and Somerset; Richard, Lord Fitzhugh, who gained lands to the value of nearly £140 per annum in Somerset, Dorset and Wiltshire; Ralph, Lord Neville, who was granted the Somerset estates of Daubeney and the countess of Richmond, worth approaching £200 per annum;[25] and Sir Thomas Markenfield of Markenfield near Ripon, who had been retained for life by Richard in December 1471 and now received lands in Somerset to the value of £100 per annum. Markenfield is an interesting case in that although he was placed on the Somerset bench in December 1483 and joined the commission of array for the county in 1484, later in that year he became sheriff of his native county. And amongst his various rewards he was also gratified by an increase in his fee (drawn on the revenues of Middleham) from the reasonable figure of £10 to the staggeringly generous sum of 100 marks per annum.[26] But the most remarkable case of all is that of Richard's confidant, Sir Richard Ratcliffe, whose own North Yorkshire estate of Sedbury-in-Gilling was relatively modest. He was granted on 6 September 1484 lands, principally in Devon, Dorset and Somerset, drawn mainly from the patrimony of the earls of Devon, to the value of approximately £650 per annum?[27] In one step he rose into the greater landowning class and filled the vacuum left in west country politics by the flight of the earl of Devon.

It would be wrong to suppose that these grants, and others like them, entirely substituted a foreign for a native ruling élite in the southern counties. For a start Richard could still count on the support of some leading families everywhere, even in the west country where four members of the Powderham branch of the Courtenay family; John, Lord Dinham; and John, Lord Zouche (Scrope's cousin, and Ratcliffe and Catesby's brother-in-law) all worked for him.[28] Nor could the new men have formed anything more than a small minority of the landed classes of the counties in which they were planted. Not even on the commissions of the peace and of array did they form a majority. But their importance far outweighed their numbers. They took the lead in these counties and occupied the key royal offices. Moreover their very presence enabled the king to keep a watchful eye on potential malcontents and was a permanent reminder to them of the likely consequences of further rebellion. One can well understand, therefore, how from early 1484 onwards the mass of the lesser gentry of the south could have longed more and more for the hoped-for return of their ancient rulers rather than the present tyranny.

Rhetoric and exaggeration notwithstanding the Croyland Continuator's comments do carry conviction. It is easy to see how Richard's policy towards those southern counties already unwilling

13. Effigy of Edmund Redman (d.1510), All Saints Church, Harewood, South Yorkshire.

to accept his régime could well have created bitter animosity, especially if the settlement imposed during 1484 was believed to be permanent. As far as the gentry of the south were concerned, this was tyranny; for it transgressed the constitutional convention that local rule should lie in their hands. Richard's tyranny lay in calling upon the power of his northern following to rule the dissident parts of his kingdom. It is important not to forget, however, that this was only a southern reaction. Richard was in no way regarded as a tyrant in the north where indeed, as Lovell's rising in 1486, Scrope's rising in 1487 and perhaps even the murder of the earl of Northumberland in 1489 show (Hay 1950: 11, 39; Raine 1941: 9-10; Hicks 1971: 69-71), support for his cause lingered on amongst the remnant of his affinity until the end of the decade.

In fact this points to a final, important, but little remarked on, aspect of the Tudor tradition. It was of strictly southern origin. It was drawn in part from the opinions and memories of Londoners, who we have seen were hostile to Richard from the outset; and in part from prominent early Tudor politicians, who, in addition to having vested interests in the survival of the new régime, were also members of the southern gentry whose hoped-for return had been desired. It finds corroboration from the Croyland Continuator, who as we have already noted had a virulent dislike of northerners. Indeed the fear and hatred of northerners may have been widespread in the southern and eastern parts of the country in the decades following Queen Margaret's infamous march to the gates of London in 1461. Not only did Abbot John Whethamstede of St Albans share the Croyland Continuator's opinion but so also did Clement Paston.[29] Was there, one may wonder, an under-current of regional animosity to the political and dynastic conflicts of late fifteenth-century England which came to the surface in the 1480s? If so, recognition of its existence may help reconcile the traditional and apologetic interpretations of Richard III's reign. Tudor tradition reflects the opinion and experience of only half the kingdom. It enshrines not only the official attitude of the victorious dynasty to the last Yorkist, but also the animosity of the dominant southern half towards the northerners on whom Richard had relied.

The Tudor tradition should surely not be discarded; handled cautiously it is still a valuable guide. It is firmly rooted in the experience of Richard III's reign. It arose from the memory that Richard rode rough-shod over the sentiments and interests of a substantial part of the English political nation in two ways; for by his usurpation he committed a moral offence, and by his rule in the southern counties he committed a constitutional offence. Richard was deemed guilty of an act of tyranny in his treatment in the south just as on later occasions Charles I, Oliver Cromwell and James II were deemed guilty of the same. He thus was taken for a tyrant both by his entry and by his administration. Whatever his other qualities, whatever his record before the fateful summer of 1483, whatever his popularity and following in the north, in the event he was seen to put self before duty, self before the well-being and rights of his wards, and self before the 'wealth of his communes'. Where the tradition has no doubt let us down is in its refusal to treat the plight and dilemma of the man with sympathy, in its failure to look beyond the experience and outlook of the southern half of the kingdom, and in its determination to turn history into a morality tale. In this respect tradition has been partisan. The historian may nevertheless conclude that Richard III by his acts gave a considerable number of his contemporaries and near contemporaries good cause for their severe judgement upon him.

2

DOMINIC MANCINI'S NARRATIVE OF THE EVENTS OF 1483

There can be no doubt that Dominic Mancini's *De Occupatione Regni Anglie per Ricardum Tercium* is the most important source for the events of the summer of 1483.[1] It is the only account written before 22 August 1485, and therefore the only surviving source to be entirely free of Tudor influence and authorial hindsight coloured by knowledge of the ultimate fate of Richard III. Indeed it was written before the end of 1483, by one who had been present in London during the revolution he describes. It is thus an immediate, first-hand account of the kind fifteenth-century historians rarely have available. It is true that it has its drawbacks. The author was an Italian who had not been to England before, did not know the English well and probably did not speak or understand their language. Mancini's memory of the precise chronology is shaky and his knowledge of English geography and topography weak. However, the fact that in substance his story confirms the later, Tudor version of what happened has given it a powerful authenticity. Charles Ross suggested that it supplies, 'direct contemporary evidence that Richard III's ruthless progress to the throne earned widespread mistrust and dislike'.[2] And Alison Hanham has asserted that it is 'a reliable yardstick against which to judge the accuracy of other writers'.[3]

This comfortable, and comforting, view that Mancini's text, only rediscovered in 1934, corroborates the essential truth of the Crowland Continuator, Vergil and More has remained largely unchallenged until the recent publication of Michael Hicks' *Richard III: the Man behind the Myth*. Hicks, however, has trenchantly argued that Mancini's account cannot be taken at face value. It too incorporates propaganda and the material that he so rigorously analysed was not everything he thought.[4] In particular, he has drawn attention to the manner in which Mancini, as 'an innocent newcomer' absorbed and repeated Richard III's own successful propaganda campaign of the summer of 1483 which discredited Edward IV's régime, vilified the Woodvilles and advanced himself as a man of integrity. Thus, paradoxically, Mancini's analysis of the situation at Edward IV's death is highly favourable to Richard because it highlights the difficulties Edward IV left behind him and because it presents a complex web of long-standing problems calling for drastic solutions.[5] In drawing attention to the success of Richard III's propaganda in 1483, and in claiming that in the process Richard invented himself as the 'Good Lord of the North', Professor Hicks has put the cat among the Ricardian pigeons. But he has also opened a necessary debate about the nature and value of a text which is far from being a reliable yardstick against which to judge all other writers.

Mancini's biography, what we know of it, is familiar and uncontroversial. He was born in Rome in the late 1430s. He was probably an Augustinian friar. He was a humanist and moved in humanist

14. *This anonymous woodcut, c.1500, shows a cleric writing in his study, suggestive of the Italian humanist Dominic Mancini at work on his account of Richard III's usurpation for his patron, Angelo Cato.*

circles. And by 1482 he was living in Paris, probably already in the service of Angelo Cato, fellow Italian, archbishop of Vienne and physician to Louis XI. It is not known why he came to England at the end of 1482. The fact that, as he reports, he was recalled to France by Cato in July 1483 suggests that he was in his employment.[6] Physicians, as confidantes of kings, princes and magnates were frequently involved in their master's most sensitive and secret affairs.[7] For this reason, it is possible that he was sent to England at a particularly sensitive moment in Anglo-French relations to discover, if he could, whether, after the Treaty of Arras, an English invasion of France was likely. He might, in short, have been a spy. However, the initial purpose of his visit, whatever it was, was superseded by the death of Edward IV on 9 April and the drama that subsequently unfolded. And after he returned to France it was the story of Richard III's accession to the throne of England which intrigued him.

Mancini was an educated and cultured man, in his own words, an 'eloquent orator and poet laureate' at the centre of French literary circles.[8] The *De Occupatione Regni Anglie* is, as Antonia Gransden pointed out, a,

> combination of two contemporary literary genres, that of contemporary humanist historiography and that of the diplomatic newsletter.[9]

The classical influence is apparent in both the vocabulary, style and structure of the work. Echoes of Sallust and Suetonius have been detected.[10] In this he points the way for both Vergil and More, whose accounts of Henry VII and Richard III were based on classical models. Mancini did not go as far as Vergil who adopted Vespasian as his pattern for Henry VII, or More who drew heavily upon the figure of Tiberius for Richard III, but like them, he viewed history as a literary art. But Mancini was also writing for an immediate purpose: to inform others, Angelo Cato and Cato's first patron, Federico, prince of Taranto, who subsequently succeeded to the throne of Naples, of recent events in a neighbouring country. Written so soon after the event it is a newsletter; a self-consciously literary piece of journalism written by the equivalent of a very able foreign correspondent.[11] It is setting out to tell European leaders in European courts a story in which they would have a natural interest: how power had recently changed hands in England.

Like journalists the world over, Mancini relied heavily on the accuracy of his informants, his 'usually reliable sources'. His account is only as good as the quality of the information he received. And like a journalist too, Mancini was 'filing a story'. C.P. Scott might famously have proclaimed that facts were sacred, opinion free, but Mancini, like all journalists and historians who have ever lived, could only offer what was at best an informed interpretation. Inevitably Mancini takes a line. His line, his interpretation, is also unavoidably coloured not only by the accuracy and partisanship of the information he received, but also by how he saw it in literary and moral terms. Thus successfully to evaluate his text we need to identify his contacts and detect where their vested interests lay; we need also to lay bare the story line and to discover what it was that so fascinated him about the events he witnessed in London in May, June and July 1483.

It is possible to identify from the text at least five different sources of information drawn upon by Mancini. The first and most certain is Dr John Argentine, a member of Edward V's household, the only informant whom Mancini names: 'The physician Argentine, the last of his attendants whose services the king enjoyed'.[12] He was an early English humanist who had visited Italy in the 1470s and may have been known to Angelo Cato. It is conceivable that Mancini arrived in England with letters of introduction from his patron. Be that as it may, there are several pieces of information that one may confidently assign to this source. From Argentine, his physician, surely comes the information that Edward V as prince of Wales devoted himself to horses and dogs and other youthful exercises, 'in order to invigorate his body'[13] by doctor's orders one might suppose. He too, with his medical interest, is likely to have supplied the detail that Edward IV customarily took an emetic for the delight of gorging his stomach once more.[14] From him, too, Mancini surely heard of the letters sent by the dukes of Buckingham and Gloucester to the young king at Ludlow assuring him of their loyalty.[15] And who else would have provided the detailed and seemingly eyewitness account of the two dukes' reception by the king at Stony Stratford? Who else would have observed that they were exhibiting mournful countenances when they presented themselves to their monarch following the arrest of Rivers, Grey and Vaughan, or given Mancini a full report of the conversation between king and dukes that followed?[16] Again the detail that, after the royal household's arrival in London, the two dukes alternated in maintaining a strong guard about his residence for fear lest he should escape or be rescued, is surely the point of view of someone who believed himself to have been imprisoned in the bishop of London's palace.[17] And lastly we have the report that Edward V himself,

> like a victim prepared for sacrifice, sought remission for his sins by daily confession
> and penance, because he believed that death was facing him[18]

15. Brass to John Argentine, Provost of King's College, Cambridge and physician to Edward V he was probably one of Dominic Mancini's prime sources of information.

16. Engraving by Georges Vertue. Portrait of Edward IV, based on the original (c.1534-40) in the Royal Collection, Windsor.

which is directly accredited to Argentine and is immediately followed by a eulogy of the young prince. John Argentine is one unequivocal source which provided Mancini with a unique view of events from the point of view of the young Edward V's entourage.

The second of Mancini's usually reliable sources is more difficult to identify. But it would seem that he benefited from a leak, or a series of leaks, from within the council. He received details, if somewhat garbled, of the debates in April 1483 about the appropriate form of government for the king's minority. Dorset's boast that he and his faction were so important that even without the king's uncle (Gloucester) they could make and enforce decisions possibly came from this source.[19] Mancini was similarly informed about the council debate which took place before the removal of the duke of York from sanctuary in June.[20] The same source may well have supplied the technical information, unlikely to have been known to an outsider, but understood correctly to have important implications, that even after Hastings' execution 'all private deeds and official documents continued to bear the titles and name of Edward V' and that it was not until Richard was assured of the throne that:

> acts in the name of Edward V since the death of his father were repealed or were suspended, seals and titles changed and everything confirmed and carried on in the name of Richard III.[21]

Mancini's informant may have been his fellow Italian, Pietro Carmeliano, who had come to England in 1480 and found employment as a chancery clerk, handling official documents and close enough to the business of government to have had some knowledge of what was being said in the council chamber.[22]

The third, and no longer exclusive, source was public announcement: open letters, proclamations and speeches. The manner in which Mancini cites in detail a letter sent to the council by the duke of Gloucester in April 1483 putting his case for pre-eminence in the new government, the text of which was subsequently published, presumably by Gloucester's agents, reveals that he had the content translated for him.[23] Similarly, he summarizes the contents of two letters written to the council and the mayor of London justifying the 'rescue' of the prince of Wales at Stony Stratford which were, he reports, read aloud in the council chamber and to the people.[24] Again he cites the proclamations made after Hastings' execution, as well as the sermons and speeches made to advance Richard's claim to the throne.[25] Other information, or disinformation, might have come Mancini's way as a result of Gloucester's skilfully conducted campaign of propaganda. The duke might have been the originator of the common belief that Edward IV's treasure was divided between the queen, the marquis of Dorset and Edward Woodville as justification for denouncing Edward as an enemy of the state.[26]

But common belief, gossip, rumour and 'general report' were a fourth, frequently tapped and probably unreliable source. As a well-trained humanist, Mancini no doubt understood the classical art of authentication by association with rumour; but it is also likely that he genuinely heard any amount of rumour and gossip – just as George Cely did.[27] Thus 'the story runs' that Edward IV threatened Elizabeth Woodville with a dagger in his effort to have his wicked way with her. He might even have heard this one before he set foot in England.[28] More recently, he reported, Gloucester 'was overheard to say' in 1478 that he would one day avenge Clarence's death; a much used authenticating preamble to mere speculation.[29] But general report is also cited for events and details after Edward IV's death, when Mancini himself was in London. Thus, the weight of Edward IV's treasure 'was said to be immense'; it was commonly believed that it was divided between the queen, the marquis of Dorset and Sir Edward Woodville.[30] Some say that the dead king had appointed Gloucester Protector before he died; 'according to common report' Hastings divulged all the deliberations of the April council to Gloucester; 'it was reported' that Hastings advised the duke to hasten to the capital; and there was 'a sinister rumour' that the duke had brought his nephew under his control to gain the crown for himself.[31]

The question arises as to how Mancini came by this body of general report if, as is supposed, his command of English was so weak. There were two communities, within which, it is reasonable to assume, he moved. One was the community of clerks, including men like Argentine and Carmeliano, for whom Latin was a natural medium of communication. From this community perhaps derived the general high regard in which senior clergymen – Archbishop Rotherham of York, Bishop Morton of Ely and Bishop Russell of Lincoln – were held.[32] The other community was that of the Italian merchants resident in London. We know that he had connections with the Genoese because of his lengthy description of how a Genoan captain, himself or one of his crew his informant, brought most of the royal fleet back to London.[33] The Genoese had regular contact with London citizens. Even if Mancini did not talk to Londoners himself, he did talk to Italians trading in London. It is not unreasonable to suppose that Mancini frequently discussed the unfolding events of the early summer of 1483, which were, after all, somewhat exciting, with his clerical and Italian acquaintances.

The fifth and final source identifiable from the text is the author's own observation. He himself, he wrote, had

> seen many men burst forth into tears and lamentations when mention was made of him (Edward V) after his removal from men's sight.[34]

This statement also suggests that he had some understanding of what was being said in English. There are other descriptions which, if not acknowledged, might also have derived from direct observation. The descriptions of Gloucester's public appearances, with much pomp and circumstance, between 16 and 22 June, suggest an eye-witness. The duke abandoned mourning and donned purple. He surrounded himself with a large retinue, yet he was scarcely watched by anyone. All these are observable details which do not depend on an intermediary.[35] And, it seems, he had a close view of Edward IV. Was Mancini speaking from direct experience when he wrote of the late king:

> he was so genial in his greeting, that if he saw a newcomer bewildered at his appearance and royal magnificence, he would give him courage to speak by laying a kindly hand upon his shoulder.[36]

Mancini's narrative is thus drawn from several interwoven strands. Bearing in mind the time-lag that occurred before he put pen to parchment, it should not be surprising that he was not very critical of his sources. The account is an amalgam of hearsay, propaganda and selective, partisan, inside information. It is neither entirely accurate, nor impartial, nor consistent. Lack of accuracy can be demonstrated at many levels, from the author's ignorance of where Richard of Gloucester's estates lay, through the major error in chronology of placing the seizure of the duke of York from sanctuary before the execution of Hastings rather than three days later, to significant mistakes of interpretation and fact which can be corrected by reference to record sources. One such mistake concerns the 'immense treasure' left by Edward IV which was supposedly stolen by the queen and her kinsmen. Recent analysis of the royal finances in 1483 has shown that there was in fact very little in the royal coffers on the accession of Edward V, and that his personal store of plate and jewels remained firmly in control of his father's executors.[37] Likewise, Mancini is demonstrably wrong in stating that Gloucester withdrew from court following the execution of his brother the duke of Clarence in 1478. It is true that he spent more of his time in the north after 1478 than he did before, partly because of the demands of war against Scotland after 1480. However, the charter rolls clearly reveal that he remained *persona grata* at court throughout the last five years of his brother's reign, for he lent his name to every royal charter issued between February 1478 and January 1483.[38]

The origins of Mancini's misconceptions about such matters as the state of the royal finances and the duke of Gloucester's position at court cannot be identified with certainty. One possibility is that he simply picked up the ill-informed gossip of his associates in London. Wealth is frequently exaggerated; people in positions of power are frequently suspected of putting their fingers in the till; the rifts between politicians are the very stuff of tittle-tattle. A more sinister explanation, not at all implausible, is that both these stories were deliberately put about as part of a systematic propaganda campaign launched by the duke of Gloucester to

17. The tomb and mutilated effigy of John Morton, Archbishop of Canterbury, in the crypt of Canterbury Cathedral. Decorated with numerous heraldic Tudor badges, of the crowned roses and portcullis, as well as his own badge of an eagle on a barrel or 'tun'.

blacken the queen and her family. It was, Mancini wrote, because the queen's adherents had stolen the treasure that royal finances were in such a parlous state; it was because of the evil influence of the queen and her faction that Gloucester had honourably withdrawn from court.[39] Did Mancini repeat 'popular' opinion or absorb Ricardian propaganda.

There is no doubt that the whole text contains a major strand that is deeply antagonistic to the queen, her family and creatures who are portrayed as greedy, factious and immoral, as having virtually taken over the rule of the kingdom after 1478, and as being universally disliked.[40] Yet Mancini also takes great care to make an exception of Anthony, Earl Rivers. He identifies four kinsmen of the queen: her two sons, Thomas, marquis of Dorset and Sir Richard Grey and her two brothers, Sir Edward Woodville and Earl Rivers. He has nothing good to say of the first three; but for Rivers there is nothing but praise. He:

> was always considered a kind, serious, and just man, and one tested by every vicissitude of life. Whatever his prosperity he had injured nobody, though bene-
> fiting many; and therefore he had entrusted to him the care and direction of the king's eldest son.[41]

It may well be that Mancini's hostility to the queen and three of her kinsmen did indeed derive from Gloucester's vilification. But it is all the more remarkable, therefore, that Rivers, the most powerful and politically important of the Woodvilles is not also tarred with the same brush. He, whom Gloucester accused of plotting his death as the justification for his arrest on 30 April, was the Woodville he most feared and surely had the greatest desire to vilify. The most likely explanation of Mancini's contradictory assessment of the Woodvilles is that he received his opinion of them from two sources. For the queen and her kinsmen at court he relied upon the common gossip, or the duke of Gloucester's smear campaign; for Rivers he drew upon the testimony of one who had served closely with him in the household of Edward V – John Argentine. The eulogy of the earl as one who had been given the responsibility for the upbringing of the prince of Wales because of his unbelievable virtue points inescapably to Argentine.

The inconsistent approach to the Woodvilles reveals that Mancini not only wove the narrative from different sources, but that he also incorporated the contradictory opinions of his informants. Nevertheless, it would be entirely wrong to suppose that he was completely unaware of partisanship. He might have repeated as if it were fact much of the malicious gossip about the queen and her associates, but he also knew that they were being vilified by both the dukes of Gloucester and Buckingham. Not everything was believed. In discussing the reasons why Richard claimed the throne Mancini states that 'he proclaimed that he was harassed by the ignoble family of the queen'.[42] He tells how the dukes sent four cart loads of weapons up to London as 'proof' of a planned coup, which their agents proclaimed were to have been used in the attempt. Yet, he comments, 'many knew these charges to be false'. Indeed the whole charade was got up because:

> these two dukes were seeking at every turn to arouse hatred against the queen's kin, and to estrange public opinion from them.[43]

Mancini could not be more explicit. Thus, paradoxically, while he appears to have been fully aware of a propaganda campaign being waged by the duke of Gloucester, he still seems to have been willing to repeat elements of it in his written account. This suggests that Mancini had formed the opinion not only that the queen and her friends at court were unpopular but also that Richard, who 'sought in every way to procure the good will of the people', shamelessly exploited public opinion to his own advantage.[44]

Mancini's narrative is complex and to some extent inconsistent and contradictory partly because of the differences of opinion carried by his sources and partly because he was writing from memory. But from his memory he crafted a powerful story. Like Thomas More's History, *De Occupatione Regni Anglie* makes gripping drama. He has shaped his evidence into a tale of treachery on a grand scale. The story, it is made clear from the very beginning, is the tale of the 'machinations' by which Richard III, 'actuated by ambition and lust for power', attained the high degree of kingship,[45] the means by which he destroyed Edward IV's children and the manner by which he then seized the throne. The victim of this crime, the boy king, twice described as a noble and accomplished youth, is an innocent prepared for sacrifice and doomed to death.[46] The villain, the boy's trusted uncle, is duplicity itself. At almost his first entry we are told that he is better at concealing his thoughts than his brother Clarence. After Clarence's death, however, he is so overwhelmed with grief that he cannot dissimulate so well. All his actions and words from the moment of Edward IV's death are dishonest and deceiving. When he assures the council that he would 'expose his life to every danger that the children might endure in their father's realm', the reader knows that he intends the very opposite. The point is made explicit in the comment on the report of Gloucester's assurance of his good intentions to the mayor and council of London:

> most praised the duke for his dutifulness, some however, who *understood his ambition and deceit* [my italics], always suspected where the enterprise would lead.[47]

When Mancini came to tell his story in the knowledge of its outcome, he turned much of Richard of Gloucester's own propaganda against its begetter. That is why he remembered it and repeated it. Gloucester's high reputation before Edward IV's death was a sham and part of this duplicity. Between 1478 and 1483, when he withdrew from court to escape the queen's jealousy, he deliberately set out to win the loyalty of his people through favour and justice so that one day he could avenge his brother's death. By these machinations too he made himself popular.[48] After Edward IV's death Gloucester continued to manipulate popular opinion. His letters to the mayor and council, Mancini tells, turned the minds of the people, who, as they had previously favoured the duke from a belief in his probity, began to support him openly and aloud.[49]

Accordingly, only a few astute observers knew from the beginning what was really happening. 'Mistrust', however, was 'exceedingly augmented' when the dukes of Gloucester and Buckingham claimed that the arms collected by the Woodvilles for the war against Scotland were to be used in an attack on them. Despite the manipulation by the dukes, therefore, public opinion gradually came to realise what was going on. At first the 'ignorant crowd' believed the proclamation put out after Hastings' execution, but the real truth was on the lips of many, namely that the plot had been feigned. The few of early May became the many by mid-June. Finally, when Gloucester made his open bid for the throne, the many became practically everyone:

> he was scarce watched by anybody, rather did they curse him with a fate worthy
> of his crimes, since no-one now doubted at what he was aiming.[50]

Thus only when it was too late did the ignorant crowd, the chorus in this tragedy, ultimately understand the scale of the villain's duplicity, known all along to a few discerning commentators.

The reputed vice of the queen and her kinsmen at court are likewise incorporated into the structure of the drama. They provide a secondary motive; Richard was spurred on not only by ambition but also by a desire to seek vengeance on the queen and her family. The dukes of Gloucester and Buckingham claimed that their lives were in danger from them; they sought at every turn to arouse hatred against them.[51] Their claims are given plausibility by what the author tells us about the queen. We thus see how many people, even respected and experienced noblemen such as Hastings, were duped. Of course, all this was shaped with the benefit of hindsight. We have no way of knowing what Mancini thought at the time it was happening; and it is pointless to speculate. What is clear, however, is that he moulded it into a coherent story, which he had already recounted many times before he wrote it down.

The account given by Mancini is a story. And it is also a commonly recurring story: the story of a trusted guardian who turns on and destroys his or her innocent wards.[52] It might not be 'literary' in the narrow technical sense of the rhetorical mode of Renaissance historical writing, but it is a skilfully constructed narrative. It is no mere record of a sequence of events. And the moral stance of the author is explicit. The central character is actuated by a lust for power, spurred on by a desire for revenge, who from the moment of Edward IV's death had his designs upon the throne and 'rushed headlong into crime'.[53] It is a warning against excessive ambition. 'Whom will insane lust for power spare, if it dares violate the ties of kinship and friendship.'[54] A moral judgement is being made, one that Mancini and his clerical friends would be expected to make, that there are bounds beyond which political behaviour should not stray. The author is no Machiavelli, who, one imagines, would have have been indifferent to the notion of crime and treated the story somewhat differently. *De Occupatione Regni Anglie* is not, like More's later work on the same history, a moral tract against tyranny, but nevertheless Mancini's deep disapproval of what Richard III did shines through.[55]

It follows that Mancini was probably reflecting the disapproval of some of his informants. It is unlikely that the colouring and shape of his interpretation of the events came entirely unprompted. And indeed the informants who shaped his overview are likely to be identifiable as the few credited as being astute enough to know what was really going on from the very beginning. Who these few were we are unlikely to know; and indeed it might only have been in retrospect that they claimed to have foreseen what would happen. But one of the few is likely to have been John Argentine. For surely the story line adopted by Mancini is exactly the perspective that one would expect from within the young king's household. The idea that Gloucester's supposed probity was pure hypocrisy seems to be consistent with the point of view of someone who was seeking to explain a completely unexpected out-turn of events from an unforeseen direction. The last person expected to be a threat to Edward V in April 1483 was Richard of Gloucester, yet he ruthlessly deposed him.

It follows that a man who had truly earned the honourable reputation he enjoyed at the beginning of 1483 could not have behaved the way he did. From Argentine's point of view, therefore, deliberate deceit and duplicity were self-evident. Every assurance of loyalty had been dishonoured. How else was the course of events to be explained apart from Gloucester deliberately plotting his seizure of the throne from the moment he heard of Edward IV's death? Is it too fanciful to suggest that the shape of the story derives from Argentine? Does this explain why *De Occupatione Regni Anglie* is so profoundly partisan, so much the story from the perspective of Edward V's entourage?

In the light of this analysis it is hard to see how *De Occupatione Regni Anglie* is, even inadvertently, 'highly favourable' to Richard III. And in so far as Mancini carries echoes of Richard III's own propaganda of 1483, it is also clear that he is aware of it. There may indeed be good reason to believe that Richard deliberately created for public consumption the image of himself as the good lord of the north, the loyal dependable brother of the king, an honest, blunt soldier, excluded from influence by a group of embezzlers, lecherers, sorcerers and traitors.[56] What report and record we have of Richard's statements between April and July 1483, in the pages of Mancini and elsewhere, lend credence to that idea. But Mancini is no unwitting agent of Richard's public relations exercise. At the time of writing, he wants his readers to know that he understood what Richard had been up to; that he did not believe all the stories put out; and that he knew that much of it had been propaganda. Indeed one might even argue that Mancini was the first to put in writing the idea that: 'For much of his adult life Richard had the best press possible because he had the best of public relations officers: himself.'[50] As far as the truth of the allegation that Richard III was the inventor of himself as the good lord of the north goes, in effect an accusation also carried by Mancini himself, the resolution is not to be found in his text. Rather, it is to be sought in sources deriving from Richard's years as duke of Gloucester before his brother died. And these are ambivalent: some reveal a man who offered justice, redress for the wronged and the successful restoration of peace and order in the north; others reveal a man ruthlessly in pursuit of his own aggrandisement, often at the expense of the defenceless.[58] But of these matters Mancini himself knew little.

Mancini presciently wrote in his incipit:

> I shall undoubtedly expose myself in writing to the criticism of my readers. Wherefore you should not expect from me the names of individual men and places, nor that this account should be complete in all details: rather shall it resemble the effigy of a man, which lacks some of the limbs, and yet a beholder delineates for himself a man's form.[59]

And so the reader does. What is remarkable is that this form is the same form that shaped Tudor and nearly all historical interpretations of Richard III until the twentieth century. Although details vary, the accounts of Vergil, More and ultimately Shakespeare are all versions of the same story of cunning duplicity and an insane lust for power destroying the innocent princes.[60] How is it that Mancini, who laid down his pen in December 1483, told the same story as became established after 1485? The most likely answer is that they all come from the same common root; the memories of the ousted servants of Edward V, who became the victors of Bosworth. Even Argentine, it is worth recalling, later became physician to Prince Arthur and Provost of King's College, Cambridge. He lived until 1508. He had ample opportunity to reminisce with others at court or college about the times he had seen, even perhaps with Thomas More and Polydore Vergil.[61] While, as Thomas More himself wrote, 'whoso divineth upon conjectures may as well shoot too far as too short',[62] there is nevertheless reason to suppose that, although he was untouched by Tudor propaganda, Mancini saw the events from exactly the same standpoint. This is not only frustrating for the historian, but it also means that, despite its immediacy, his account is not necessarily any more, or any less, reliable than those written after the death of Richard III.

3

North, South and Richard III[1]

Traditional accounts of Richard III have tended (among other things) to give too little attention to the regional divisions within England which characterise his short reign. Only recently have historians begun to draw attention to the King's reliance on his trusted northern followers to rule a dissident south after the autumn risings of 1483. It is now apparent that much hostility was created by this plantation of men of the north.

The exact nature of Richard's régime after Buckingham's revolt is a topic currently being examined in detail elsewhere[2], but an equally important aspect is the effect that the memory of it had on opinions of the King after his downfall. The King's policy was not quickly forgotten by southerners: as late as 1594 an old Dorset man told of the time recalled by his father 'when King Richard drove Cheyney out of the land'.[3] But even before Richard's reign southerners feared and distrusted men from the north. It is likely that there was an undercurrent of regional animosity running beneath the political and dynastic conflicts of the late fifteenth century which came to the surface in the 1480s. Moreover, it is possible that this animosity, given dramatic focus by the events of 1483-85, has played an important part in shaping, and continuing to shape, attitudes towards the last Plantagenet. This paper explores that possibility.

That there was a strand of antagonistic feeling towards the north and northerners among southern opinion in the late fifteenth century can be readily demonstrated. Whether it pre-existed or was created by the infamous Lancastrian campaign of 1461 is neither here nor there. The fact is that Margaret of Anjou marched south, with a large, and apparently poorly disciplined, army of northern and Scottish levies early in that year, inspired a fear and distrust of northerners which the inhabitants of the south-east of England long retained. There is a tone of hysteria in many contemporary and near-contemporary reports, the most quoted of which is the colourful passage composed by the Prior of Croyland in the late 1460s.[4] It would seem that this was initially generated by a heady mixture of propaganda and rumour. The propaganda can be seen in the letters sent out from London by Warwick and the privy council rallying support before the second battle of St Albans; in this they laid on with a trowel the danger threatened by 'the misruled and outrageous people in the north parties of this realm' coming 'towards these parties to the destruction thereof, of you, and subversion of all our land'. Warwick, of course, also drew much of his personal support from the north. Presumably his followers were well-ruled and peace loving.

The rumour is to be seen at work in the letter sent by Clement Paston to his brother John on 23 January, 1461:

18. Medal of Margaret of Anjou, Queen of Henry VI by Pietro Di Milano, 1463.
19. Commemorative medal celebrating the marriage of Henry VII to Elizabeth of York, January 1486.

the pepill in the northe robbe and styll and ben apoynted to pill all thys contre, and gyffe away menys goods and lufflods in all the southe country.[5]

Such views were subsequently to be enshrined in the poem known as 'The Rose of Rouen' which celebrated Edward IV's triumph at Towton. It is worth quoting several verses:[6]

> Be-twix Cristmas and Candelmas, a litel before the Lent,
> Alle the lordes of the northe thei wrought by oon assent,
> For to stroy the sowthe cuntre their did alle hur entent,
> Had not the Rose of Rone be, al Englond had be shent.
>
> The northen men made her bost, whan thei had done that dede,
> 'We wol dwelle in the southe cuntry, and take al that we nede;
> These wifes and hur doughtres, oure purpose shal thei spede',
> Than seid the Rose of Rone, 'Nay, that werk shal I for-bede'.
>
> The northen party made hem strong with spere and with shelde,
> On Palme sonday, affter the none, their met us in the felde,
> Within an owre thei were right fain to fle, and eke to yelde,
> Twenty-six thousand the Rose kyld in the felde.
>
> The Rose wan the victorye, the felde, and also the chace,
> Now may the housband in the southe dwelle in his owne place,
> His wif and eke his faire doughtre, and al the goode he has,
> Suche menys hath the Rose made, by vertu and by grace.

An echo of the hysteria of 1461 is to be heard in 1483 in the alarm of the University of Cambridge at the reported approach '*virorum borealum*' on the way to London at the time of Richard III's coronation.[7] A more pervasive influence is to be found in the memoirs of a Yorkist councillor known as the Second Continuation of the Croyland Chronicle. The author, whosoever he was, was a southerner who had experienced the 'great scare' of 1461 and had no love at all for the men of the north. There can be little doubt that these memoirs were written, as the author states, at Croyland during the last ten days of April 1486.[8] At the time of writing he knew that a rebellion had occurred in Yorkshire against Henry VII, but he had not heard what the outcome was. It is easy for us, with our knowledge of the ultimate success of the Tudor dynasty, to dismiss this rising as of little significance. But to the author, in April 1486, the situation seemed critical and fraught with danger. And his apprehension is reflected in his work. Much emphasis is given to the role played in recent politics by the men of the north with whose support, he knew, Richard III had first seized and then held the throne, and who now threatened to overthrow the man who only six months ago had, in his view, rescued the kingdom from their tyranny. It is no wonder that in his anxiety he wrote the following comment as a postscript to the story which he had originally intended only to take up to the death of Richard III:[9]

> And although by these means (the marriage of Henry VII and Elizabeth of York) peace was graciously restored, still, the rage of some of the malignants was not averted, but immediately after Easter a sedition was set on foot by these ingrates in the north, whence every evil takes its rise, and this even although the king was staying in those parts.

This antagonism towards the north and northerners was taken up some twenty years later by Polydore Vergil. 'The folk of the north' were, he commented, 'savage and more eager than others for upheaval'.[10] And from Vergil the antagonism ran into the mainstream of the Tudor tradition concerning Richard III.

The ill-will shown by the Croyland Continuator towards the northerners is perhaps, in part, a reflection of real regional differences. Compared with the south-east, the north was economically backward. It was less densely populated. At a very rough guess only 15 per cent of the population lived in the six northern counties of Cumberland, Northumberland, Westmorland, Durham, Lancashire and Yorkshire which made up a quarter of the area of the Kingdom. In both 1334 and the reign of Henry VIII, Lancashire, the North Riding and the West Riding were in terms of taxable wealth per square mile the poorest in the realm (the four most northerly counties were not taxed).[11] One must not have the impression that the whole of the region was uniformly impoverished. Rather, the region was characterised by marked contrasts between the densely populated and rich lowland areas, especially the Vale of York and the East Riding, and the vast acres of open moorland and fell. Nevertheless, there is evidence to suggest that the north was becoming poorer between the early fourteenth and early sixteenth centuries, both absolutely and relatively to the south-east (see Map 3).

Current research suggests that early in the fourteenth century there was a marked decline in wealth in the upper reaches of the Yorkshire dales and along the north-eastern coast of the county.[12] It would appear that there was a process of contraction to the more favoured and sheltered lands. This process of contraction would seem to be reflected in urban decline after 1377. Recent work in urban history has revealed a profound shift in the balance of urban wealth away from the north and east towards the south and west and, in particular, an absolute decline of towns sited on, or looking towards, the eastern sea-board north of the Wash: towns such as Beverley, Hull, Scarborough, and,

20. Berwick Castle. Almost all the remains were destroyed over 100 years ago to make way for the railway station.

above all, York. The decline of York, as Professor Palliser has shown, was especially marked after 1450: 'York', he concludes, 'undoubtedly experienced a serious economic recession under the Yorkists and early Tudors'.[13] The cumulative evidence now seems to be pointing to the conclusion that during the second half of the fifteenth century the contrast between the impoverished and declining north and the prosperous and growing south-east was becoming ever more striking. One wonders whether an awareness of such an imbalance of wealth lay behind the ready credence given to the idea that northerners were itching for the chance to rob and pillage in the south.

If the distant north were poor and becoming relatively poorer, one might have expected that it would have played an insignificant and increasingly peripheral part in the politics of a kingdom which, by the second half of the fifteenth century, clearly had its centre of gravity in London. In fact the very reverse was the case; the north had a political significance out of all proportion to its wealth, and it played a central role in politics between 1450 and 1490. This, of course, was entirely due to the Scottish border, to the development of Anglo-Scottish relations from the reign of Edward I and to the measures adopted by successive English kings for the defence of the border while they pursued their ambitions in France.

The story of how the power of the great families of the north, the Percys and Nevilles especially, was built up, and of the development of the wardenships of the marches which they monopolised, has been told elsewhere.[14] It may be that kings who felt impelled to fight in France had no choice but to develop such a system. Certainly it seems that the monarchs from Edward III to Henry V were aware of the inherent dangers in the policy and endeavoured, usually successfully, to pursue the time honoured course of divide and rule in their relationships with the northern powers. But under the slack hand of Henry VI, uncontrolled rivalry led directly to open conflict. There is no need to reiterate that the feud between Percy and Neville was of central importance in the collapse of the Lancastrian dynasty.[15] By the same token, the victory of Edward IV was also the victory of Neville over Percy. In the 1460s Edward had no option but to allow the north to be ruled by one man, Warwick, a circumstance all previous kings had managed to avoid. In 1470 he paid the price: he was run out of his kingdom by an overmighty subject who turned his northern power against the king.

It is perhaps characteristic of Edward IV that after he had fortuitously regained his throne and destroyed Warwick he should by his own choice repeat the mistake of placing the north in the hands of another, even mightier subject – his own brother. Of course, it was Edward's policy to rule the kingdom through a select band of close friends and relations.[16] It was a policy that worked as long as he lived, but proved disastrous as soon as he died. In 1483 Edward's son was dispossessed by an overmighty subject who, like Warwick before him, turned his northern power against his king. The concentration of northern power into the hands of Richard of Gloucester was the ultimate consequence of English royal policy towards Scotland and the north over two centuries. It was not inevitable that this should have happened; Edward IV need not have so favoured his brother; but that is what he did. Thus under Henry VI and Edward IV, for different reasons, the north became progressively more important in the politics of the kingdom until it reached its apogee in the brief reign of Richard III.

Richard III was a king from the north. It is not surprising that the disapproval of him expressed by southerners, such as the Croyland Continuator or the Londoners who discussed current events with Dominic Mancini in the summer of 1483, was matched by the approval expressed by one or two northerners. Bishop Langton came from Appleby in Westmorland and was in the process of benefiting from the King's patronage when he wrote in 1483 that 'God has sent him to us for the weal of us all'.[17] This could perhaps be taken as an authoritative statement of northern opinion. Richard, as Duke of Gloucester, would appear to have successfully established himself with the leaders of northern society. His campaigns against Scotland, however much they offended the Croyland Continuator and apparently irked the king, would appear to have been popular with the northern aristocracy and gentry.[18] A grand raid as far as Edinburgh and the recapture of Berwick in 1482 were significant achievements in the eyes of northern society. Richard had also willingly responded to the pleas for assistance from the citizens of York facing serious economic decline. It is quite understandable why, in October 1485, the city council considered him to be 'the most famous prince of blessed memory'.[19]

The high opinion in which Richard III was held in the north, for obvious reasons, found its way only as an aside into the early histories and the later sixteenth-century interpretation of the man and his reign. But an echo of it is to be heard in the first systematic defence of Richard's reputation – Buck's *History*. Thanks to Dr. Kincaid's painstaking reconstruction of the original text we can now accord this work its proper place in the historiography of the subject.[20] As the late Professor Myers observed it is 'a work of pietas to vindicate the memory of a king for whom his [the author's] great-grandfather had laid down his life'.[21] But it was more than this. Buck came from a long line of Yorkshire gentry, who had served the house of York for at least three generations before 1485. There are passages in the text which quite clearly connect Buck's pride in his northern ancestry with his desire to vindicate the memory of the king who was so closely associated with the north. Early in the first book there lies the following, not entirely accurate, digression on Gloucester and the north:[22]

> But for the most part the employment of this Duke of Gloucester was in the north parts, where he much lived and did good service according to his charge and duty. For he was Lord Warden of all the marches, eastern, middle and western, and earl and governor, or captain (as they then said) of Carlisle. And he liked well to live in parts of the north for sundry good causes. For besides that Yorkshire was his native country; and that is clear to every man, and most esteemed, for the birth in any place

breedeth espectal love and affection to the place, and that by a natural instinct, as the poet said well: '*Natale solum dulcedine cunctos mulcet*'.

And for that they were the native country both of the duke his father and of the duchess his mother, and by whom he had most noble alliance and very many great friends, and much love in those parts. And certainly he was generally well beloved and honoured of all the northern people, his countrymen, not only for his greatness and alliance, but also (and chiefly) because he was a valiant, wise, and a bountiful and liberal prince, and a good and magnificent housekeeper, and the which bringeth not the least love of the people, but rather the most and greatest good will, for they and all men love and admire liberality and good hospitality. And thirdly he liked best to live in these parts because his appenage and patrimony was there chiefly and he had besides goodly possessions and lordships by hereditary right of the duchess his wife in the north parts.

And for these many good causes, he was so much in the good liking of the north countries as that he desired only to finish his days there and in the condition of a subject and of a servant to the king. And his ambition and other worldly aims extended no further. And he governed very wisely and justly both in time of peace and of war and preserved the concord and amity between the Scots and English so much as he could.

Buck is expressing a line of argument used by apologists ever since, but he is also reflecting an opinion which stretches back to northern society in the late fifteenth century.

It is arguable, therefore, that both the opposing traditions concerning Richard III have their distinctive regional roots in the late fifteenth century. Certain southerners, those in particular who wrote, or supplied information for histories, feared and disliked northerners. Since Richard III was a king who seized the throne with northern backing; who held it after the autumn risings of 1483 with the substantial aid of men drawn from his northern affinity; and who finally sought to save it with northern arms on the field of Bosworth in 1485, it is hardly surprising that in the mind of an influential early historian such as the Croyland Continuator the view of the King is coloured by an animosity felt towards all things northern. All that we know of northern opinion shows, on the other hand, that in his home country he was highly regarded. The significant point about the isolated favourable remarks concerning Richard is surely not that they were contemporary, but that they were northern.

Nor should it be forgotten that all our principal narrative sources for the late fifteenth century are southern, indeed specifically south-eastern, in origin. In fact, in one way or another they tend to lead back to London. Thus the 'official' history of Richard III is seen through metropolitan eyes. Alison Hanham has argued with force that the dominant image of Richard III was created not simply as propaganda for the Tudor régime, but more sophisticatedly as a literary exercise; in effect what in late twentieth century jargon was called a 'faction'.[23] To this one might add that the dominant image also developed out of the specific perception of south-easterners. Richard the malignant monster is not so much Tudor propaganda as metropolitan 'faction'. Thus there remain two Richards of tradition: a noble Richard and a monstrous Richard – a northern Richard and a southern Richard. Which of the two is correct is, of course, another question.

4

THE RICHMONDSHIRE COMMUNITY OF GENTRY DURING THE WARS OF THE ROSES

In April 1486, when Henry VII was making his first and critical visit to the city of York, 'the folk of the North', according to Polydore Vergil, 'savage and more eager than others for upheaval', were reported to be gathering together a little beyond Middleham.[1] This chapter is about those savages and the neighbourhood of Middleham from which they came. In one respect the topic is intensely local: it is a study of the community of gentry in that part of north-west Yorkshire made up of the wapentakes of Gilling East and West, Hang East and West, and Hallikeld which formed the feudal Honour of Richmond and the nucleus of the Archdeaconry of Richmond (see Map 1). Richmondshire as it was known then, and still is known, was the jungle in which Vergil's savages lived. But Vergil had heard correctly of their reputation for rebelliousness. In the thirty years before Henry VII's visit to York their rebellions had several times shaken the throne of England. The people of Richmondshire had an importance in national politics out of all proportion to their wealth and location. This national importance seems to me to justify a close examination of the social and political structure of the community of this remote corner of England.

Before moving into this analysis it is worth reminding ourselves of some of the occasions on which the people of Richmondshire rose in rebellion. Especially noticeable is their involvement in the events of 1469-71. According to Warkworth, Robin of Redesdale was Sir William Conyers. It has been customary on the strength of W.A.J. Archbald's article in the the *Dictionary of National Biography* to argue that it was in fact Sir John Conyers and not his brother. He based his case on information in the Chronicle of the Lincolnshire Rebellion that Sir John submitted to Edward IV at York in March 1470. But, as we shall see, it is clear in the text that this relates to a rising then and not nine months earlier.[2] It seems, therefore, that there is no reason not to take Warkworth at face value and identify Robin of Redesdale as William Conyers of Marske in Swaledale. With William Conyers in this rising were John Conyers, his nephew and son and heir of Sir John, Sir Henry Neville, son and heir of Lord Latimer and a Richard Nicholson of Hornby, the Conyers seat, all of whom were killed on the winning side at the battle of Edgecote.[3] There can be little doubt, therefore, that the leadership of Robin of Redesdale's rising in the summer of 1469 was drawn from the Richmondshire gentry.

In the spring of 1470 they were in arms again. The Chronicle of the Lincolnshire Rebellion tells the story:

> In this season (12 March, just after the defeat of the rebels at Loosecoat field) the king, understonding that the commocion in moving people in Richmondshire by the stirring of the Lorde Scrope and othere, sent by the saide Duc (Clarence) and erle (Warwick) there for that cause with many lettres, his highness sent into Northomberland and Westmoreland to arredre certain filaship to afilowed uppon theym if they had com forwarde and to Markes Montague, with his filaship to have countred theym in theire faces; thay (Scrope etc) understandıng and havyng tithinges also (of) the kinges victorie, and, as divers gentilmen of that felaship said, thinkyng, by the maner of the saide erle of Warrewike writing sent thidre in his own name oonly to arreise the people, that theire stirring shulde be ayenst the king, and fering his spedy comyng unto their parties with his oost, left theire gadering and satt still.[4]

In a later passage the author refers to Warwick's hopes of,

> oute of Yorkshire to (have) assembled so gret a puyssaunce that thay might have be able to have fought with the kinges highnes in plein felde.[5]

But, finally, when the king was at York between 22 and 26 March,

> there com to the king the Lorde Scrope, Sir John Conyers, young Hilyard of Holdernes and others which had laboured specially provoced and stirred the people in their parties to have (made) commocion ayeinst the king, wherein they frely submitted them to the kinges grace and mercy . . . and also of ther fre willes, unconstreyned and undesired, they clerely confessed that so to make commocions they were specially laboured and desired by the said duc and erle.[6]

Nowhere else are our sources so specific in identifying the participants in these northern risings as the gentry and people of Richmondshire. Nevertheless, it is clear that it was they who were in arms again four months later. In July and August, as Sir John Paston reported, 'ther be many ffolkes uppe in the northe' under the leadership of Lord FitzHugh.[7] In fact, as the lists of pardons in the patent rolls show, there were at least twenty of the gentry of Richmondshire, including two more of the irrepressible Conyers family, who were suspected of coming out with FitzHugh and drew Edward IV north, so allowing Warwick to land unopposed in the south.[8] And finally, after Edward IV's dramatic return to England in the spring of 1471 and his victories at Barnet and Tewkesbury, there was, according to the Arrivall, a last forlorn rising in the north which quickly collapsed on hearing of the Lancastrian defeat and that Edward was marching north, and because they did not have 'any of Warwick's or Neville's blood unto whom they might have rested, as they had done afor'.[9]

This is not to imply that the gentry and people of Richmondshire were the only ones to be so rebellious between 1469 and 1471, even in the north. Of course people from other parts of Yorkshire and Cumbria participated. Nevertheless, Richmondshire was the nucleus of the northern rebellions. The reason for this, as Edward IV knew and as the author of the 'official' Chronicle of

21. Sixteenth-century portrait of the chronicler, John Warkworth, with his manuscript 'Chronicle of the First Thirteen Years of the Reign of King Edward IV'. (Peterhouse College, Cambridge)

the Lincolnshire rebellion knew, was that Richmondshire, dominated by his lordship of Middleham, was the engine room of Warwick's political power. That political power was stoked by the gentry of Richmondshire. Thus, an analysis of the community of Richmondshire is of some significance in explaining why not only Warwick, but also his successor Richard of Gloucester, were able to wield such power in Yorkist England. Such an analysis draws on collections of family papers, some published, some unpublished;[10] wills proved in the probate court of the diocese of York, mostly those published by Canon Raine in *Testamenta Eboracensia*; the register of the Archdeaconry, published by A.H. Thompson some years ago;[11] and ancillary public records. There are no private letters. It is particularly interesting that the correspondence of the Plumpton family, who lived only just south of Richmondshire, is of very little use for this study. All the relevant sources are in the last resort concerned with property. This obviously makes the analysis one-sided. But on the other hand, it does reflect the fundamental shared interest of the gentry, for it was the possession, protection and extension of property which bound them together as a social group.

How many landowners were there in Richmondshire and what authority and wealth did they possess? As the basis of the answer to this first question I have adopted the controversial procedure of counting manors. It is a severely limited method. The ownership of manors was not the same as the ownership of land. The pattern of landownership was in fact much more complex. Gentry families owned the odd tenement and a few shillings of rent in widely scattered communities. Rarely did a lord of a manor own all the land in it. In most villages, there were several different landowners besides the lord. In Brompton-on-Swale, for instance, where the Abbey of St Agatha's, Easby held the manor, land was additionally owned by Lord Scrope of Bolton, William Burgh, Richard Conyers, Thomas Metcalfe, Thomas Swaldale and Richard Brian.[12] Such holdings were often parcels of land which changed hands through marriage settlements, provision for younger children and endowments for charity. But in a rough and ready way this complexity cancelled itself out. As a rule of thumb, the more manors he owned, the more land a gentleman possessed wherever it was. Moreover the calculation is based on the *Victoria County History of the North Riding* which, though comprehensive, is not entirely reliable.[13] Nevertheless, in the absence of relevant tax returns, there is no other way of reaching an overall view of the pattern of landowning and authority in the district (see Map 2).

Eight peers held land in Richmondshire. The largest property owner was the lord of Middleham. He owned some twenty-seven manors, including grants to him from the Honour of Richmond, as well as parks and great stretches of forest. The total yield was almost £1,000 p.a.[14] His local authority was enhanced by the grant of the castle of Richmond, knights' fees, and castleward from the Honour of Richmond. Next to the Nevilles came Scrope of Bolton and FitzHugh, with some two dozen manors each, the former based in Teesdale, the latter in Wensleydale. Their estates were worth well over £500 p.a.[15] Scrope of Masham held eleven manors concentrated in the southern corner of the district. The other peers had much smaller estates. Neville of Latimer, at Snape and Well, had lands worth £100 and over.[16] Lovell at Bedale and nearby had about the same.[17] Both of these, especially Lovell, had holdings elsewhere, as did Greystoke (two in Richmondshire) and the earl of Westmorland (one in Richmondshire). The Percys did not have any property in the district. There were two gentry families whose holdings and wealth nearly matched Scrope of Masham. Pre-eminent were the Conyers of Hornby who held the equivalent of eight manors in Richmondshire, and others in neighbouring Allertonshire. The Mountfords of Hackforth also held the equivalent of nearly eight manors. There were at least ten other gentry families, either with holdings concentrated in Richmondshire, or more widely spread in neighbouring districts FitzRandall, Ingleby, Lascelles, Laton, Markenfield, Metham, Norton, Pigot, Saltmarsh, Strangways and Wandesford, whose holdings were worth approximately £200 a year. A late fifteenth-century valor of the Wandesford estates, for instance, shows an income of £185 from rents in twenty-three separate places.[18] All these gentry had greater wealth locally than either Neville of Latimer or Lovell. One then comes to the great bulk of the local squirearchy with one or two manors, and property worth anything from £20 to £100 p.a. There were some forty-eight families in this category. Typical of them were William Burgh of Brough, near Catterick, lord of the manor of Brough, with lands there and elsewhere,[19] and Richard Clervaux of Croft-on-Tees, lord of East Cowton, owner of most of Croft and with lands in six other places,[20] both of whom enjoyed incomes of £50 p.a. or more. The manorial squirearchy by no means exhausts the gentry for beneath them in the social hierarchy existed all those styled merely gentlemen, lords of no manors but possessing lands producing at least £10 clear income a year, about whom Garter King of Arms admitted in 1530 that:

> those not vile born or rebels might be admitted to be ennobled to have arms having lands and possessions of free tenure to the yearly value of ten pounds sterling.[21]

This was the grey area which merged into that of the yeomanry. How many there were of this status in Richmondshire we have no way of knowing. Only occasionally are their names thrown up by our sources. One such family was that of Stockdale. William Stockdale of Richmondshire, yeoman, was a commissioner for taking the oath against maintenance in 1434 and Thomas Stockdale, retained for life, by Richard Neville, earl of Salisbury, was for nineteen years his attorney at the Exchequer. A member of the next generation of the family, John Stockdale, gentleman, was a Yorkshire elector in 1467 and, styled yeoman, took out a pardon after FitzHugh's revolt in 1470.[22]

22 & 23. Easby Abbey near Richmond and Fountains Abbey, Yorkshire.

Another 'service' family, as it were, was that of Weltden, of whom Christopher and John were successively feodaries and under-stewards of the lords of Middleham, who married into the local gentry families and eventually established themselves at Colburn.[23] Others in this social group were submanorial gentry such as the Colvilles, Lockwoods, Swaldales and Vincents and prosperous townsmen like William Clerionet of Richmond, Thomas Otter of Middleham and John Thomson of Bedale. But these are but a few names from amongst what must have been a large number of 'mere' gentlemen.

There is one other important category of landowner to be considered, namely the Church. Fifteen religious houses owned the equivalent of thirty six manors and a dozen granges in the district.[24] The biggest was Jervaulx, with at least eight manors and as many granges, which produced the greater part of its £235 net annual income at the Dissolution.[25] The next largest were St Mary's, York, Fountains, Coverham and St Agatha's, Easby. Of these, only Easby was principally a Richmondshire house and it enjoyed a net income of £112 at the Dissolution.[26] Although there were many religious houses, most of them were small. In terms of manorial holdings they owned only 20 per cent of Richmondshire. This certainly represents an underestimate of the clerical wealth in the district. For one, in the case of religious houses especially, the counting of manors conceals the extent to which in almost every community one or more of the local houses owned a few shillings of rent.[27] Secondly, our figures do not include ecclesiastical livings especially the very valuable Archdeaconry of Richmond and Prebend of Masham, worth something of the order of £300 per annum between them in the late fifteenth century.[28] And after 1475 there was a spate of chantry foundations in Richmondshire which transferred more wealth from lay to clerical hands.[29] But, even making allowance for this, it is hard to equate this picture of Richmondshire with Dr Schofield's calculation that in 1515 almost two-thirds of the assessed taxable wealth in the North Riding was clerical.[30] Allowing for the rough and ready basis of the estimates of wealth and land-holding, it seems to be the case that in Richmondshire there was a greater concentration of wealth and property in lay hands than elsewhere in the North Riding. The impression that the district was densely populated by gentry seems to be confirmed by comparison with calculations for other parts of England based on taxation returns. One is, of course, not comparing like with like. In taxation returns, men were taxed, and therefore listed, on the basis of their principal holding. Several of our gentry in Richmondshire would therefore be taxed elsewhere. On the other hand, taxation returns were by no means comprehensive. There were, however, approximately fifty gentry families with incomes of £20 and over who were resident in Richmondshire. This compares, for instance, with the fifty-four, a handful of whom were esquires of ancient blood but slender means, who were assessed in the whole of Lincolnshire, one of the richest counties of England, for the income tax of 1436.[31] This is an imprecise and impressionistic analysis. Nevertheless, the general conclusion that there were many gentry as well as three powerful noble families in Richmondshire in the fifteenth century seems to be inescapable. Here then, in sheer numbers and collective wealth, lies the first of the characteristics of the Neville political strength drawn from Richmondshire. The second lies in the social cohesion of the landowning class in Richmondshire.

Of all the social institutions and customs which bound the gentry together, marriage was the most important.[32] Constant intermarriage between the families tied them into a close-knit kinship group. Marriage was, of course, a business transaction. But besides being a property deal, marriage was also a means of social preservation or advancement. Through their marriage alliances one with another the gentry families constantly reaffirmed and strengthened their social positions, while for

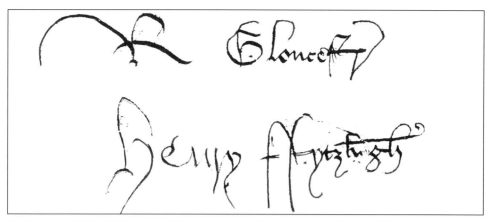

24. Signatures of Richard Gloucester and Henry Fitzhugh, leader of the small rebellion in Yorkshire against Edward IV in 1470. (Redrawn from the 'Fitzhugh Chronicle', Corpus Christi College, Cambridge)

individual families marriage offered one way into the group and one way of advancement in the pecking order within it. There was a marked tendency for the children of Richmondshire gentry to marry the children of other Richmondshire gentry. Elder sons had a greater propensity to marry outside the district. Three generations of eldest sons of the Clervaux, for instance, married daughters of Lumley of County Durham, Vavasour of Haslewood in the West Riding, and Hussey of Sleeford, Lincs. On the other hand, five generations of eldest sons of Burgh in the fifteenth century all married into North Riding families, four of which – Aske, Lascelles, Conyers and Metcalfe – were Richmond-shire neighbours.[33] Younger sons and daughters usually followed the pattern of the Burgh heirs. William Burgh III, who died in 1492, had daughters who married sons of Catterick, Saltmarsh and Weltden and a sister who married his neighbour Alan Fulthorpe.[34] Daughters of Sir James Strangways married sons of Aske, Clervaux and Ingleby. Richard Clervaux's younger children married, in addition to Strangways, children of Aske, FitzHenry, Laton and Conyers of Wynyard, County Durham.[35] And in fact the husband in the last case, William Conyers, was the nephew of Sir John. The Conyers family itself it perhaps the best example of this intermarrying, if only because it was the most prolific. Christopher, who died in *c*.1465, had twenty-four children by two marriages. Four of his younger sons married daughters of Wycliffe, Frank, Cleseby and Langton of Wynyard. His daughters married sons of Aske (two of them), Burgh, Lascelles, FitzRandall, Pickering, Pudsay (two again) and Wycliffe. Sir John Conyers in the next generation could only manage twelve children, but amongst their marriages were alliances with Aske, Claxton (of Claxton, Co. Durham), Fitzwilliam of Sprotburgh in the West Riding, Markenfield, Mountford and Place. The Conyers are also the finest example of a family advancing itself through marriage. Heiresses which came the way of this grasping family were Elizabeth Cleseby, which set up Sir John's brother William at Marske in Swaledale and Sybil Langton which set up his brother Roger at Wynyard. Other marriages brought noble blood into the Conyers veins. Sir John was married to one of the joint heiresses of Lord Darcy, his own eldest son was matched with one of the heiresses of William Neville, Lord Fauconberg, and his grandson and eventual heir William was married to Mary, daughter of John, fifth Lord Scrope of Bolton.[36] In fact, the occasional marriage between the less substantial gentry families and the lesser peerage,

25. (right) Memorial brass inscription to Christopher Conyers (d. 1465) and his first wife, Ellen (d. 1443) with indents of shields and crests, or pair of hands, holding hearts, Hornby Church, Yorkshire. His grandson, Sir John Conyers (wrongly said to be 'Robin of Redesdale') was probably also buried in the church.

26. (below left) Stained glass portrait of Judge Richard Pigot in his purple ceremonial robes, Long Melford Church, Suffolk.

27. Memorial brass to William Fitzwilliam (d. 1474), Sprotborough, Yorkshire.

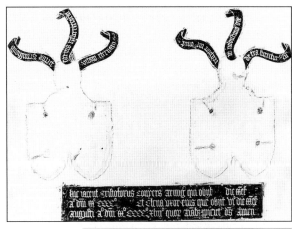

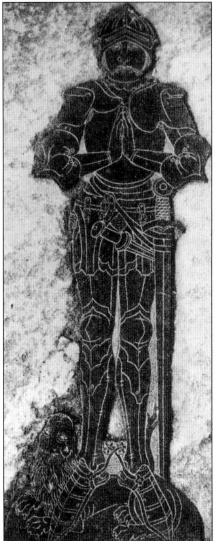

such as that between Agnes daughter of Henry, fourth Lord Scrope of Bolton and Sir Christopher Boynton of Sedbury,[37] shows that there was no rigid barrier between gentry and peerage.

One could continue to catalogue examples of intermarriage, but it would be merely repetitious to do so. The fact is that in the later fifteenth century a member of the gentry of Richmondshire could count practically all the gentry of the district amongst his cousins. This kinship inevitably drew them together, not necessarily always amicably, as a group with common interests. Most important of these was the protection of titles to land. Thus it is that they were constantly associating themselves one with another as feoffees in land settlements or as executors of wills, and calling upon each other to witness these transactions. A typical enfeoffment is that organised by John Wandesford to ease the passage of his property to his son. Initially he placed it in the hands of William Burgh, James Strangways, Christopher Conyers and Randolph Pigot. On 4 April 1463 they passed their charge to a younger group of Thomas Mountford, John Pigot and Richard Pigot.[38] Strangways and both Christopher and Sir John Conyers, as dominant landowners, were frequently employed as feoffees, by gentry families such as the Wandesfords and Inglebys and by the peerage as represented, for example, by Lord Latimer in 1469.[39] Local lawyers, especially Sir Robert Danby and Richard Pigot were much in demand, both in enfeoffments and to execute wills. Danby was an executor of the will of William Burgh in 1465 as well as of Richard Neville, earl of Salisbury. Pigot was an executor for Burgh and Thomas Witham in 1475.[40]

The witnessing of deeds was another important function carried out on one another's behalf by these gentry. At a time when titles were often uncertain and there was no system of registration the evidence of witnesses, especially witnesses of substance, could be crucial. On 11 January 1465, for instance, Sir James Strangways, an aged Christopher Conyers, Christopher Boynton, Thomas Surtees of Dinsdale in County Durham and Roger Vincent travelled to Croft to witness the final sealing of deeds and exchange of contracts which completed a complex exchange of property between Richard Clervaux and John, Lord Scrope in Croft, Stapleton and Cleasby.[41] On 12 March 1476, Roger Aske, William Burgh and Thomas Mountford went down to York to witness the sealing of deeds which completed an exchange of property in Hipswell between Alan Fulthorpe and the abbey of St Mary's.[42] And on 12 June 1482, Sir James Strangways, jnr, Sir John Conyers, Thomas Mountford, Richard Clervaux and Roger Aske gathered at Brough Hall to witness the taking of a hundred-year lease of the mills of Richmond from Mount Grace Priory by William Burgh.[43]

These same gentry also helped out in the arbitration and settlement of disputes. The frequency with which this occurred suggests that as a group they found it speedier and less expensive to settle such differences amongst themselves rather than go through the due processes of the law. In 1463, for example, Richard Clervaux called upon his friends and neighbours to resolve a dispute with Thomas Fitton of Cawarden in Cheshire over a rent of £5 which Fitton claimed out of East Cowton from the time when his ancestor had sold the estate to the Clervaux family in the early fourteenth century. Sir James Strangways and John Nedeham, a justice of Common Pleas, agreed to arbitrate. Clervaux apparently accepted their recommendation that he should buy Fitton out for £53 13s. 8d. Accordingly, at Croft on 15 June, Fitton ceremoniously quit his claim to the rent in the presence of Strangways, Sir John Conyers, Thomas Mountford, John Catterick and John Killinghall. The party then travelled over to Strangways' residence of Harlsey castle where the agreement was finally sealed and contracts for the payment were exchanged.[44] In August 1477, the Archdeacon of Richmond turned as a matter of course to the local gentry to decide a dispute over the right of presentation to the living of Bedale and he commissioned Roger Aske, William Burgh, Thomas

Frank, Alan Fulthorpe, Thomas Mountford, John Wycliffe and John Thomson of Bedale to make enquiry and recommendation.[45] Two of these men, Burgh and Mountford, with the lawyers Sir Guy Fairfax and Richard Pigot, were at the same time engaged in settling a quarrel between the Abbeys of St Mary's York and St Agatha's Easby over their boundaries and the possession of moorland in Hudswell upon which they made judgement on 10 March 1478.[46] Burgh and Mountford were kept fairly busy at this time, for a month later they appear to have been at Middleham when they were appointed by Richard, duke of Gloucester, with Frank again and William Pudsay, the late Rector of Croft, to act as guarantors of an arbitration which Gloucester had given in a quarrel which had blown up over several issues between Richard Clervaux and Roland Place in the parish of Croft, where they both resided. In fact, two years later the guarantors had to deal with a fresh dispute between the parties.[47]

Through marriage, through the network of mutual co-operation with which they handled property, and through their other mutual interests, the landowning class of Richmondshire formed a community of their own. It was almost as introspective as it was close-knit. There seems to have been a low level of involvement with gentry from neighbouring districts. A certain amount of reciprocity existed with the gentry of south Durham, Cleveland and Allertonshire, stimulated by the property interests of the Conyers and Strangways families in particular. Conyers penetration of the area of Stokesley, for instance, seems to have flowed from their possession of the advowson of Rudby parish.[48] But there was very little reciprocity with the gentry of Craven and the Honour of Knaresbrough to the south. The Plumpton papers provide a useful correlation here. Plumpton marriages in their turn only exceptionally involved Richmondshire families. Trustees and witnesses in Plumpton deeds were drawn mostly from that circle of families – Babthorpes, Beckwiths, Gascoignes, Hamertons, Vavasours – associated with that part of the West Riding.[49] Some families, like the Inglebys and Pigots, had feet in both camps. And, as one would expect, lawyers like Robert Danby and Richard Pigot enjoyed the confidence of clients from both districts. One cannot, obviously, talk of these circles as county communities. Yorkshire was the county, but it was so large and administratively complex that it was almost impossible for there to have been a fully developed notion of the body of the whole shire. Moreover, it was only in the early fifteenth century itself that election of representatives to parliament became the responsibility of the gentry themselves.[50] Much of the feeling of belonging to a community of gentry thus seems to have been absorbed within these 'counties' within the county, whose boundaries were determined not administratively, but partly geographically, partly historically and partly politically.

The political element is of great importance. Throughout England, we need no reminding, any sense of community as gentry was overlain by the vertical bonds of lordship and bastard feudalism. It is no accident that the gentry communities of northern and western Yorkshire, especially those of Richmondshire and Knaresborough, coincided with the zones of influence of the Neville and Percy families. The Plumpton letters show quite vividly how Sir William Plumpton in the 1470s was bound to the Percy interest. When the earl of Northumberland took away the deputyship of Constable, Steward and Forester of Knaresborough and granted it to William Gascoigne, try as he might, Plumpton found no other lord who would help him. And when Northumberland also proved less than willing to promote his ambition of becoming a J.P. and turned to Lord Hastings, Hastings refused to intervene and accused Plumpton of trying to set up a conflict between the two lords. 'Sir, I took that as a watchword for medling betwixt lords' wrote Godfrey Green who had received the snub on his master's behalf.[51] Exactly the same went for the Neville interest in

Richmondshire. The gentry there came within the Middleham zone of influence. At the same time these ties of lordship also helped bind the community more closely together. Several of the gentry were mesne tenants of the lordship of Middleham. Many more were mesne tenants of the Honour of Richmond, whose local prestige and authority the lords of Middleham then possessed. The annual rendering of a peppercorn or rose in rent had more than a symbolic meaning. The employment they offered, the hospitality they made available and the patronage they commanded, especially when they were in favour at court, enabled the lords of Middleham to make themselves the focus of local landowning society. Lordship, therefore, was not just an alternative pattern of association; it provided itself another of the means by which the sense of community was reinforced.[52]

It does not follow that all the gentry of Richmondshire were ardent followers of Salisbury, then Warwick, then Gloucester. Before 1460, the Percys and their allies found some friends like Richard Clervaux in their rival's camp.[53] And some other families, the Lascelles and Nortons, for instance, seem to have stayed quietly in the background during these tumultuous years. But after 1461 until 1485, when Warwick and Gloucester were unassailable in the north, there were powerful inducements for the ambitous, the importunate or the needy to turn to the 'Godfather' at Middleham. The best placed of the Richmondshire gentry were those dozen or so who managed to become retainers or office-holders of the lords of Middleham, some of whom received exceptionally generous fees. Successive lords retained different men, but certain families seem to have had a special relationship with the lord of Middleham. One was the Metcalfe family, the number of whom receiving fees grew from just one under Salisbury to nine under Warwick.[54] But the Metcalfes in terms of the gentry community were a fairly insignificant family. Far more important were the Conyers. It seems to have been a tradition that the head of the family took the office of Steward of the lordship and of the rights of the Honour of Richmond possessed by the Nevilles and Gloucester.[55] It appears to be the case that they used this position to place as many of their (admittedly numerous) relations as possible on the payroll. Sir John, whose authority in the district under Warwick seems to have been all embracing, would appear to have been the man who smoothed the transition from the last of the Nevilles to his erstwhile enemy, even before Gloucester married his heiress. One of Gloucester's first acts on gaining possession of the lordship was to confirm Sir John's position with the inducement of an increase in his fee from £13 6s. 8d., to £20. Between 1471 and 1474, the following immediate relations of Sir John were retained:

> his brothers Richard and William, whose contracts were renewed in December 1471 and January 1472 respectively, and likewise his brother-in-law John Robinson (n.d.),
> his grandson and heir, John (n.d.),
> his second son Richard in December 1471,
> his brother Roger in September 1473,
> his brothers-in-law William Burgh (Oct, 1471), Roland Pudsay (Oct, 1471) and Robert Wycliffe (Oct, 1473),
> his son-in-law Thomas Markenfield (Dec, 1471),
> his nephew Lionel Claxton (n.d.),
> and his wife's half-brother, Thomas Tunstall, the younger brother of Sir Richard Tunstall, retained in November 1471 with the huge fee of £33 6s. 8d.[56]

One cannot help wondering whether Richard of Gloucester's early retainers at Middleham were chosen by Conyers rather than by him.

28. The damaged effigies of Sir Thomas Markenfield (d.1497) and his wife, from their tomb at Ripon Cathedral, Yorkshire.

29. Detail of effigy to Sir Richard Conyers (d. 1493), South Cowton, Yorkshire.

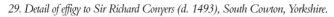

Others of the Richmondshire gentry who are not known to have been actually retained or given office were active in the service of the lord of Middleham or looked to him for assistance. William Burgh II, who died in 1465, was a prominent activist in the service of both the earl of Salisbury and the earl of Warwick, but he does not appear to have received any fee from either of them.[57] Thomas Mountford, on the other hand, had been retained by Warwick but was apparently dropped by Richard of Gloucester. He was, however, one of those Richmondshire men richly rewarded by Richard after 1483, which suggests that he gave his active support to the usurper.[58] Other Richmondshire men who are not known to have been retainers or office holders, James Strangways, jnr, Ralph FitzRandall, Randolph Pigot and William Ingleby, were knighted by Gloucester on his Scottish campaigns in 1481 and 1482.[59] But perhaps the most instructive example of an unretained follower and well-willer of the lords of Middleham is provided by Richard Clervaux. Clervaux in 1459-61 was one of the minority in the district who stayed loyal to Henry VI and benefited by it. But, after Edward's usurpation, he wasted little time in making up for his misjudgement. It would appear that over the winter of 1462-3 he was summoned to join the royal forces besieging the northern castles, for on 17 January 1463 he secured a royal licence exempting him from all royal service and allowing him to abide at his own place at his ease. The licence, given under the signet at Middleham, was granted because, as the king wrote,

> we been enformed by our ryght trusty entirely biloved cosyn of Warrewyke that ye
> be vexed with such infirmite and diseease that ye ne be of any power to laboure
> withoute grete jeopardies, we of our grace especial in concideracion of your sayde
> impotencie and at thinstance of our sayde cosyn have pardonned you... [60]

That a recent opponent, who just two years earlier had been enjoying the office of under-steward of his lordship and the revenues of one of his manors granted by his enemies, could thus success-fully approach Warwick for favours, shows clearly enough that the earl saw himself, and was accepted by others, as the natural leader of all the gentry of the district. It is no surprise to find that after the Readeption, Clervaux found it prudent to buy a general pardon, but he was soon drawn into Gloucester's net. It was Gloucester's constable of Barnard Castle and newcomer to the local scene, Richard Ratcliffe, whom he made the steward of his court at East Cowton in or before 1476. It was to Gloucester that he and his neighbour Roland Place turned to resolve their dispute in 1478.[61] And on 26 September 1483, in gratitude for certain recent but unspecified services rendered by both Richard and his son Marmaduke, Clervaux, who had already been granted by the king the offices of steward and receiver of the lordship of Manfield during the minority of John FitzHenry (his grandson), was additionally granted the whole revenue of the lordship without account. And almost a year later, Richard the king's servant, was granted a tun of wine from the customs at Hull.[62] Never a retainer, sometimes an opponent, Clervaux perhaps best represents the level-headed and calculating political relationship between the gentry of Richmondshire and the lords of Middleham. Loyalty was not unquestioning. They might look elsewhere if they could; they usually accepted quite pragmatically the local political situation as it was; and they were quick to take advantage of any opportunities that came their way.

The last is clearly demonstrated in their relationship with Richard of Gloucester. Many of the gentry were not averse to basking in the all too brief sunshine of Richard III's reign. This is not the place to go into the use made by Richard of gentry drawn from his Middleham connection in the usurpation and defence of the throne. But his rich gifts to some of these friends are worthy of note.

Sir John Conyers was made Knight of the Garter, was granted an annuity of 200 marks from the issues of Yorkshire and granted the manors of Aldbrough, St John and Catterick from the lordship of Middleham. His brother Richard perhaps received the similar grant of South Cowton at the same time, as well as an additional annuity of £26 13s. from Barnard Castle until he should have better provision. Thomas Markenfield, sheriff of Yorkshire in 1484, had his annuity from Middleham increased from £10 to 100 marks. Thomas Mountford was granted an annuity of £10 from the lordship of Rochester and appointed steward of Windsor Castle with a fee of £30.[63] And so one could continue. For the gentry of Richmondshire, loyalty to the lord of Middleham in his rebellions and treasons which went unpunished in 1469-71, paid handsome dividends after 1483. For a few, the sudden loss of all this in August 1485 did prove too great and they joined Lords Lovell and Scrope in raising rebellion against the new regime in 1486 and 1487.[64] These were Vergil's savages. But the majority were in fact civilized and quickly adjusted to the new circumstances. The Conyers family, for whom Sir Richard was in the party which assembled at Robin Hood's Stone to welcome Henry VII to York in April 1486, Markenfield, Mountford and Richard Clervaux, knighted in 1487, quickly adapted. Sir John Conyers' heir, William, who succeeded his grandfather in 1490, was raised to the peerage in 1509 and slipped into the role played over the last century by the Nevilles.[65] And the community of gentry of Richmondshire continued to arrange marriages, settle estates and exploit their property as they had always done, while the heady days of Warwick the Kingmaker and Richard III soon became but distant memories.

5

THE MIDDLEHAM
CONNECTION: RICHARD III
AND RICHMONDSHIRE,
1471–1485

Of all the places in the north of England with which Richard III was associated, and there were many, Middleham was the closest to him. The castle was his favourite residence, where he spent at least some of his childhood, and where he returned frequently after 1471. His son Edward was born there in 1476 and died there eight years later. He gained for the town the right to hold two fairs a year. He transformed the parish church into a collegiate establishment. And in 1480 he persuaded John Shirwood, the archdeacon of Richmond, to make the parish an ecclesiastical peculiar, independent of the archidiaconal jurisdiction. The collegiate church and town fairs long outlasted him. This personal association with town and parish is good reason itself to remember the king five hundred years later. But Middleham was more than a favoured community; it was a lordship and the largest and richest of the estates which he acquired in 1471 from the inheritance of Richard Neville, earl of Warwick. The estate contained some two dozen manors, parks and forests in Swaledale, Wensleydale, Coverdale and Wharfedale as well as on the moors between them. It included rich, arable lands in the lower dales, sheep runs and dairy farms on less fertile and higher ground, and mineral resources such as the lead mines of Kettlewell, all of which produced revenues of some £1,000 a year. This wealth enabled Richard to build up a substantial retinue in Richmondshire and neighbouring parts of north Yorkshire and south Durham; a following, with others based in Cumberland, Durham, the West Riding and elsewhere in Yorkshire, which provided him with the power to usurp and hold the throne of England between 1483 and 1485. This chapter looks at the relationship between Richard, both as duke of Gloucester and King, and those members of his northern following who were connected with the lordship of Middleham itself. The starting point is a group of people who entered into legal contracts of service with him between 1471 and 1473, and who were paid fees from the revenues of the lordship as listed in the one surviving financial account, that of the Receiver in 1473-4. These men, and others of the district who entered Richard's service then and later, formed the 'Middleham Connection' which came to play a prominent part in the events of 1483 and the following two years.

Richard of Gloucester's acquisition of Middleham was controversial and his title to the lordship uncertain. He was granted Middleham and all the Neville inheritance of Richard, earl of Warwick, the Kingmaker, on 14 July 1471, three months after Warwick's death at the battle of Barnet. The true heir was the six-year-old George Neville, duke of Bedford, the son of John, marquis Montagu

30 & 31. Seal of Richard Neville, earl of Warwick, obverse (left) and reverse.

and Warwick's nephew, for the lordship was held in tail male, the descent being fixed on the nearest male heir. Since neither Richard nor John was found guilty of treason there was no legal impediment to George inheriting the estate. That he did not was the result of purely political considerations, the most pressing of which was Edward IV's need in 1471 both to reward his youngest brother and to find a reliable adult to fill the vacuum in the north left by Warwick's treason.

The grant of the northern Neville estates to Richard of Gloucester did not please his elder brother, George, duke of Clarence who, as husband of Warwick's elder daughter, Isabel, had his eye on the whole of the vast inheritance, much of which anyway belonged to the widowed countess Anne. Richard's marriage to the younger daughter Anne in the spring of 1472, whether or not it was a love match (she was sixteen, he was eighteen), challenged Clarence and his duchess to an equal share of all these lands. It was for this reason that Clarence, although he came to accept the marriage, was unwilling to part with any property. Over the next two years therefore the brothers (and their wives) were locked in an unseemly tussle over the division of an inheritance which in large part belonged to none of them. At one time, in the autumn of 1473, they almost came to blows. However, by July 1474 Edward IV was able to impose a settlement on the warring parties which in effect partitioned the inheritance (in England) north and south of the river Trent. This agreement, enshrined in acts of Parliament in 1474 and 1475, disinherited the countess of Warwick and the duke of Bedford and settled the estates on Gloucester and Clarence. In the act of 1475, Gloucester's possession of the northern Neville estates was confirmed; by the terms of the partition he had also acquired the neighbouring Beauchamp lordship of Barnard Castle and Gainford in County Durham and the North Yorkshire manor of Deighton from the earldom of Salisbury.

The act of 1475 appears also to have defused a further issue of conflict in North Yorkshire between the brothers. Since 1444, the Neville lords of Middleham had occupied a considerable part of the honour of Richmond lands in the district, for in that year Richard, earl of Salisbury had been granted two-thirds of eight manors and various forests in Richmondshire (with reversion of the other third held in dower by Jacquetta, duchess of Bedford) in tail male. The creation of Edmund Tudor as earl of Richmond ten years later had threatened that grant, but Tudor's early death had left Salisbury and subsequently Warwick undisturbed during the minority of his son Henry. In 1471, Edward IV granted all the honour of Richmond to Clarence for life (including the Richmondshire lands) and in 1472 the third held until her death that year by the dowager duchess of Bedford. In 1474 these were converted to tail male. Thus there was an anomaly in the settlement of that year, for both Clarence and Gloucester were left with lands in Richmondshire once held by Warwick. It was a situation clearly unacceptable to Gloucester as well as being a contradiction of the regional partition of the rest of the property. Part of the purpose of the act of 1475 was to put this right, for by its terms Gloucester was vested in the

> manors of the honour and all the homages, rents called castleward, knights fees, rents and services of free tenants to the castle, honour and lordship of Richmond… and all other the premises that late were Richard Neville late earl of Warwick.[1]

Only the castle itself and the fee farm of the borough were left to Clarence – and these were granted to Gloucester immediately after Clarence's death three years later. Thus after much trial and tribulation Gloucester was able to acquire the entire estate which the earl of Warwick had enjoyed in Richmondshire as if he were his heir.

Nevertheless, as lord of Middleham and the honour of Richmond in Richmondshire by statute Richard of Gloucester did not have as secure a title as of inheritance; acts of parliament could always be repealed in changed political circumstances. It was important to Gloucester that potential rivals were muzzled. In 1478, he was helped by the removal of Clarence from the world. To protect himself further, in the same year, he negotiated a formal quittance of all claims from Ralph, lord Neville, heir to the earldom of Westmorland, whose line had been excluded from Middleham earlier in the century. In 1480 he acquired the wardship of George Neville (stripped of all his titles in 1478 and later known as plain master Neville). To make assurance doubly sure in the same year he secured the custody of George Neville's own heir – his twelve-year-old cousin, Richard Neville, Lord Latimer. When the unfortunate George died in May 1483, the wisdom of having Lord Latimer residing in his household became apparent. The one claimant to any of his Richmondshire lands on whom Gloucester was never able to lay his hands was the earl of Richmond – Henry Tudor.

The story of Richard of Gloucester's acquisition of Middleham, and the steps he took to protect his title, cannot be said to reflect well on him. It involved the dispossession of a defenceless widow and two orphans as well as connivance in the overthrow of his own brother. Needless to say, after 1485, Henry Tudor showed little more sensibility to natural justice. He recovered his rights in the honour of Richmond and confiscated Middleham. Lord Latimer's rights as male heir to the Neville estates were ignored. The countess of Warwick was restored, but only for life and only on condition that she made the new king her heir. For Richard of Gloucester and Henry Tudor alike, the pursuit of wealth and power overrode the niceties of the law.

Middleham Retainers and Other Servants 1471-83

It was as important to Richard of Gloucester in the early 1470s to win over local support as it was to exclude rival claimants to Middleham. The principal means available to him when he first entered the lordship was to employ its resources to retain the Richmondshire gentry in his service. The desirability of doing so was made the greater by the knowledge that the men of the district

32. The Swine Cross, Middleham. thought to commemorate the grant obtained by Richard in 1479 of the right to hold a fair and market twice a year.

had been particularly prominent in Warwick's repeated rebellions between 1469 and 1471. Of these the most significant was Sir John Conyers. Conyers had been retained by the lords of Middleham since 1450, had been attainted as a Yorkist in 1459, and had been Warwick's steward of the lordship since his father's death, c.1463. He may well have been the mastermind behind Robin of Redesdale's rising against Edward IV, which culminated in victory at the battle of Edgecote in July 1469. A chronicler with northern connections identified 'Robin' as William Conyers – probably Sir John's brother, lord of Marske in Swaledale. In the course of the battle, although on the winning side, Sir John's son and heir was killed. Nine months later Sir John helped to call out the men of Richmondshire again. The Chronicle of the Lincolnshire Rebellion tells how he and Lord Scrope of Bolton were responsible for the 'commotion in moving people in Richmondshire' on behalf of Warwick 'to have fought with the King's highness in plain field' but they were prevented by the Marquis Montagu and so 'left their gathering and sat still'.[2] A few days later, between 22 and 26 March, Conyers and other leaders were constrained to come to the king at York and submit. Nevertheless within five months two members of his family – his grandson John and his illegitimate brother Henry – were involved in rebellion again, this time under the leadership of Henry, Lord FitzHugh of Ravensworth. This rising achieved its purpose, for, while Edward IV was in the north suppressing it, Warwick landed from France in the south and forced Edward himself to flee the kingdom. Finally, The *Arrivall of Edward IV*, the official account of the king's triumphant recovery of the throne in the spring of 1471, reports that in May of that year, after Edward had crushed all his enemies, there was yet one more forlorn rising in the north which quickly collapsed on hearing of the king's threatened approach, and because they did not have 'any of Warwick's or Neville's blood unto whom they might have rested, as they had done afore'.[3] It is in fact by no means certain that Sir John or any of his family actually fought for Warwick in his last campaign, and unlikely that he countenanced this last futile gesture of defiance. Indeed, he may already have made his peace with the victorious Edward and agreed to throw his weight behind Gloucester as the new lord of Middleham. His reward was the confirmation of the stewardship of the lordship with a fee enhanced from £13 6s. 8d. to £20 and his appointment as the constable of the castle with its fee of £6 13s. 4d.

Conyers was thus in a position to ensure a smooth transition of power at Middleham from

33. Memorial brass inscription to Katherine Brackenbury, sister of Richard III's Constable of the Tower, who died in 1485 and was buried with her husband, William Pegg, in Gainford Church, County Durham.

Warwick to Gloucester. During the autumn and winter of 1471-2, a significant number of his relations, as well as former servants of Warwick, were retained by the duke. In the space of six months Sir John's grandson and heir John, his son Richard, his brother Richard, his brothers-in-law William Burgh (an old Warwick servant) and Rowland Pudsay, his son-in-law Sir Thomas Markenfield and his wife's half-brother Thomas Tunstall all joined the Middleham payroll. Tunstall who was granted a larger fee (£33 6s. 8d.) than Sir John was a particularly important recruit for he, with his brother Sir Richard of Thurland Castle, near Tunstall, Lancashire had been a prominent supporter of the readeption of Henry VI. He appears to have settled in Yorkshire and was in 1473 to father an illegitimate child, Cuthbert, later bishop of Durham, by one of Conyers' daughters. Members of the other family which traditionally served the lords of Middleham - the Metcalfes of Nappa - were also quickly retained. Thomas and Brian, sons of James, the founder of the family, were recruited in the autumn of 1471. The Metcalfes were of relatively modest means and specialised in estate management and service. Under Warwick, no fewer than nine of them had been retained, the majority as reeves, parkers and foresters. In time Gloucester was to find similar employment for an even larger number. It was also important for Gloucester to secure the best legal counsel that was available. Hence he retained Sir Robert Danby, seated at Thorp Perrow, Chief Justice of Common Pleas since 1462, who was no doubt engaged in the matter of the title to the estate. A last recruit in 1471 was Robert Clifford, youngest son of Thomas, Lord Clifford who was killed at the first battle of St Albans in 1455 and an uncle of the attainted Henry, the 'shepherd' lord who had taken to the Cumbrian fells rather than submit to Edward IV. Clifford, as it will be seen, proved to be a less than reliable servant to Richard of Gloucester. By bringing these men into his service, many of them old followers of Warwick, most of local stature, one or two old enemies of his family, the duke was able quickly to establish his position in Middleham and Richmondshire.

In 1473, Gloucester undertook a further round of retaining from Middleham which seems to have been more expansionist in aim. By the spring of that year he was competing with Henry Percy, earl of Northumberland for influence in Yorkshire, especially in the honour of Knaresborough to the south where Northumberland was the principal landowner and steward of the duchy of Lancaster. On 20 March Gloucester retained John Redman, youngest son of Sir Richard Redman of Harewood, himself an old retainer of Warwick (Warwick had been steward of Knaresborough) and on 27 April Richard Knaresbrough, a local tenant of the duchy. This may have brought the conflict to a head, for two weeks later in the presence of the king at Nottingham the duke and earl patched up their differences, the duke promising that he would no longer seek to acquire any royal offices in the earl's possession or to retain any of his

34. *Tomb and effigies of Sir Richard Herbert and his wife Margaret, Abergavenny Church, Monmouthshire. He was beheaded at Banbury after the Battle of Edgecote in 1469.*

servants. Ultimately, Gloucester and Northumberland were to agree to respect their different spheres of influence in the county. In 1473, Gloucester was also in the throes of his conflict with Clarence and this might explain some of the contracts he made later in the year. William Clerionet, retained on 3 July, was one of the leading townsmen of Richmond, the castle and fee-farm of which belonged to Clarence. The retaining of Durham men in September – Sir Roger Conyers (another brother of Sir John) of Wynyard near Stockton, his neighbour Thomas Blakeston, and perhaps at the same time Lionel Claxton of Horden (a brother-in-law of Sir John's second son, Richard) – might well reflect an attempt by Gloucester to win support in the Palatinate at a time when he was competing not only with Clarence, but also with the bishop for possession of Barnard Castle.

After 1474, until he became king in 1483, there is no further evidence from the lordship of Middleham concerning the growth of Gloucester's following formally retained there. But Middleham was not the only source of patronage available to him with which to recruit local men into his service. From 4 July 1471 he had been Chief Steward of the duchy of Lancaster in the north. Miles Metcalfe, who had been Warwick's attorney general, became his deputy – a position of considerable influence – which opened the way for him to become recorder of York and second justice of the duchy at Lancaster. Another one-time Middleham retainer of the earl of Warwick, Sir James Harrington of Hornby, Lancs, and Brierley, Yorks became Gloucester's deputy as master forester of Bowland as well as Steward of Pontefract, both duchy of Lancaster offices. As well as the duchy of Lancaster offices, after 1474 Gloucester had the revenues of Barnard Castle at his disposal. By 1476, his constable there was Richard Ratcliffe, the second son of Thomas Ratcliffe of Derwentwater who had settled in Richmondshire as the second husband of Agnes, widow of Christopher Boynton of Sedbury who was a sister of John, Lord Scrope of Bolton. Knighted in 1482, he quickly became one of Richard's closest confidantes as both duke and king. A second close adviser, Robert Brackenbury of Denton near Gainford in south Durham was another probable Barnard Castle retainer.

35. Ruins of Furness Abbey, Cumbria.

Gloucester's pre-eminence in Richmondshire after 1471 was such that he also attracted the local peerage into his service. John, Lord Scrope of Bolton, Richard Lord FitzHugh of Ravensworth, and Ralph, Lord Greystoke are known to have been councillors of the duke after 1475. More personal relationships were developed with Thomas, Lord Scrope of Masham and Francis, Lord Lovell. On 14 January 1476, Elizabeth, dowager Lady Scrope agreed with Gloucester, in a contract which foreshadowed later arrangements concerning Richard, Lord Latimer, that not only would her teenage son Thomas 'be retained with the said duke and wholly be at his rule and guiding', but that also,

> all her servants, tenants and inhabitants in and upon any of the lands late her husband's should belong to (serve) the duke and to him give faithful attendance.[4]

By such means, Gloucester was able to enhance his direct authority in the district. With Francis, Lord Lovell, on the other hand, there seem to have been bonds of personal affection. Lovell, who in 1474 inherited a share of the lordship of Bedale, had spent part of his upbringing with Richard at Middleham and was never to desert his cause.

There were many others of Richmondshire landed society who, by the end of the decade, turned to Gloucester's good lordship or responded to his call for service, but who are not known to have been formally retained at Middleham or elsewhere. In 1478, for example, Richard Clervaux of Croft and Rowland Place of Halnaby in the same parish turned to Gloucester and his council at Middleham to resolve their differences. Amongst those who advised the duke and agreed to act as guarantors of the arbitration was Thomas Mountford of Hackforth. In 1481 and 1482, several men with local connections were knighted while campaigning under Gloucester's command against the Scots. Two, Sir Richard Conyers and

Sir Thomas Talbot, were Middleham retainers; but others, Sir James Danby of Thorpe Perrow, (son of Robert), Sir William Ingleby of Ripley, Sir Piers Middleton of Stokeld, near Wetherby, Sir James Strangways of West Harsley and Sir Ralph FitzRandolph of Spennithorne across the Ure from Middleham, were not, as far as it is known, retainers from there or elsewhere at the time. By the end of Edward IV's reign there was scarcely a family of note in Richmondshire and its vicinity which had not, in one way or another, been attracted into the service of the royal duke at Midddleham (see Map 4).

Middleham and the King, 1483-1485

The Richmondshire followers and servants of Richard of Gloucester played an important, if shadowy, role in the usurpation of the throne. Some travelled to London with their lord in April; others answered the summons carried north in June by Sir Richard Ratcliffe,

> to aid and assist us against the queen, her blood adherents and
> affinity, which have intended and daily doeth intend, to murder
> and utterly destroy us… and the final destruction and
> disherison of you and all other inheritors and men of honour, as
> well as of the north parties as other countries… [5]

The army, which was subsequently raised, arrived only after the usurpation and destruction of one or two other 'inheritors and men of honour', but in time to protect the new king at his coronation on 6 July. The appropriate rewards followed quickly. Sir John Conyers, as well as Sir Richard Ratcliffe, were made knights of the garter. On the day after the coronation, Thomas Metcalfe became chancellor of the duchy of Lancaster. And a few weeks later, his brother James, already coroner of the marshalsea of the king's household, was granted the master forestership of Wensleydale 'for his great labours, charges and expenses, especially lately about the acceptance of the royal crowne of this kingdom'.[6] The king's largesse was spread bounteously when he returned triumphantly to Yorkshire in September. Richard Clervaux was rewarded for his 'labours, costs and charges in sundry wises done';[7] Thomas Wandesford of Kirklington successfully petitioned the king for an annuity of £3 'towards his relief and sustenance in his old and unwieldley age' in recognition of good service once done to the king's father;[18] the abbot and convent of Coverham were granted £20 from the revenues of Middleham for construction work at the abbey; and no doubt there were many other commoners like the 'wife besides Doncaster' to whom the king gave 3s. 4d. as he passed.[9]

The summer and autumn of 1483 were heady days for the new king's loyal subjects of Middleham and Richmondshire. But the accession of their lord as King Richard III brought important changes to their relationship. After April 1483, Richard only visited Middleham once – for a few days in May 1484. By December of that year, the lordship had been placed in the hands of feoffees. To some extent, especially after the death of Edward, prince of Wales in April 1484, Middleham was reduced to being merely a source of revenue and patronage for the king. Since 1474 there had been changes in the personnel of the retainers of the lordship. Blakeston, John Conyers the younger and Sir Robert Danby were all dead. In 1482 or earlier, Geoffrey Frank of Knayton had replaced Sir Richard Conyers as receiver. And Robert Clifford had joined the ranks of Richard's enemies. Now, during

1484, at least sixteen new annuities were charged to the lordship which added almost £300 to its costs. Sir John Conyers and Sir Thomas Markenfield alone were beneficiaries of grants worth £200 between them. Others rewarded were William Conyers the younger (Sir John's second grandson and heir), Sir Robert Middleton and Sir James Strangways. Furthermore, two manors and other property were granted for life to Sir John and the manor of Deighton to Strangways. It is hard not to believe that the particularly close relationship between Richard and Middleham was ended by his accession to the throne.

On the other hand, the accession of Richard III brought a new prominence and new opportunities for many of the king's northern followers, especially after the southern rebellions of October 1483 forced the king to rely more exclusively on them. From November 1483, there was a stream of grants of lands and offices forfeited from the rebels which created, in the opinion of one contemporary commentator, a veritable plantation of northerners in the south. Inevitably, there were Middleham retainers who shared in the spoils. Sir Thomas Markenfield was granted lands in Somerset to the value of £100, where he became a justice of the peace and commissioner of array. Thomas Metcalfe was granted the manor of Wemington, Bedfordshire worth over £50 a year. And Thomas Tunstall, appointed constable of Conway Castle and sheriff of Caernarvon, was also granted Goodrington near Totnes in Devon worth £40 a year. It is known too that John Redman, in the company of his elder brother, was active in the south-west in 1484. More substantial rewards were granted to Lords Scrope of Bolton and FitzHugh, Ratcliffe and Brackenbury. But for the most part the men of Richmondshire remained in their own region to help maintain the king's authority in the north. Eight of the retainers were named in a list of 'reliable' men of the North Riding, drawn up in 1485. And indeed, Sir Thomas Markenfield returned north in November 1484 to take up the appointment of sheriff of Yorkshire while Sir John Conyers would appear to have been a member of the newly established council of the north.

The final service which Richard's northern friends were called upon to give was to fight for his throne at Bosworth. In fact few of the Middleham retainers are known to have done so. Sir Thomas Markenfield and Sir Robert Middleton were later said to have been on the field, as was William Conyers. If the report that Conyers was killed is true, it would suggest that it was Sir John's youngest son, of whom little is known, rather than William of Marske, or William 'the younger' both of whom it is known survived the battle. Also killed was Ralph Danby, grandson to Sir Richard Conyers. But the casualties generally among northern men, prominent household men such as Ratcliffe and Brackenbury excepted, seem to have been low, perhaps because they were in the company led by the earl of Northumberland which failed to become engaged. Whether represented there or not, the king's fall on 22 August brought to an abrupt end an all too brief period of political prominence and material prosperity for the numerous noble and gentry families of north-west Yorkshire and elsewhere who had gathered round the dead king since 1471.

Aftermath

It should come as no suprise to us that most of the leading figures of Richmondshire (including Sir John Conyers) reconciled themselves to Henry VII. After all, they had been quick to adapt to the new situation after the death of the earl of Warwick in 1471. Some of Richard III's old retainers at Middleham were near the ends of their lives anyway; William Conyers of Marske died in 1487; Thomas Tunstall in 1489; Sir John Conyers in 1490; and William Burgh in 1492. Others lived longer in retirement – Markenfield until 1497, Sir Richard Conyers until 1502. William Conyers, the successor to Sir John, in time regained his grandfather's offices and annuities in Middleham and in 1509 was promoted to a peerage by the young Henry VIII. The Metcalfes too continued to prosper. Thomas, removed from his office of chancellor of the duchy of Lancaster by Henry VII, nevertheless remained much in demand locally for Leland wrote later of him that he 'was in those parts (Wensleydale) a great officer, steward, surveier, recevver of Richemont Lands, wherby he waxed riche'.[10]

Yet there were some who refused at first to submit to Tudor. Indeed Richmondshire was one of the few parts of England to offer any kind of resistance to the new regime. In the spring of 1486, 'the folk of the north, savage and more eager than others for upheaval' were, it was later said by Polydore Vergil, gathering 'a little beyond Middleham'.[11] The movement quickly collapsed, but at least three of Richard's retainers there, Geoffrey Frank, Thomas Otter and Sir Robert Middleton took to the Furness fells with other diehards before submitting in August 1486. A year later, when the earl of Lincoln and Viscount Lovell raised a second rebellion against Henry VII, they found support in north Yorkshire whence Lords Scrope of Bolton and Masham led an abortive attack on York. But this rebellion too was crushed at the battle of Stoke. After this setback, even the more recalcitrant of Richard's one-time servants seem to have accepted the irreversibility of Henry VII's victory. While in the end it was the more pragmatic behaviour of the majority of the Richmondshire families which was characteristic of the local reaction to Richard III's overthrow, it is perhaps indicative of the loyalty he inspired that a significant minority was prepared to risk all in a cause which appeared to most to be futile.

Richard III's relationship with Middleham and its district over fourteen years was undoubtedly tinged with mutual self-interest and ambition. Had he reigned longer the cares and preoccupations of kingship would probably have taken him further away from the close association of his years as duke of Gloucester. But there is no reason to doubt that his attachment to the lordship was genuine or that he revealed in those years an almost charismatic quality of leadership. His Middleham retainers and servants followed him not only for self-advantage. He was able, through his council, to bring a degree of harmony and unity to Yorkshire society which had been noticeably lacking in the preceding decades. Moreover, he led them in successful war against the Scots. It is no wonder that his memory lived on long after Middleham itself became a neglected backwater. It is a memory encapsulated by Sir George Buck (himself of Yorkshire descent) from a casualty of Bosworth, who wrote the first sustained panegyric of Richard III some 130 years later, stating:

> he was generally well beloved and honoured of all the northern people, his coun-trymen, because he was a valiant, wise, and a bountiful and liberal prince.[12]

Those retained at Middleham between 1471 and 1485, their neighbours, friends and relations would have cried 'amen' to that.

6

THE BURGHS OF
BROUGH HALL

This history of a typical gentry family of the late middle ages is made possible by the survival of some one hundred documents dating from the late thirteenth century.[1] The collection concerning the Burghs seems to have been put together first in a systematic way by Richard de Richmond, who married a Burgh heiress in the fourteenth century and whose descendants, having adopted their mother's name, held the estate in the male line until 1574. Its survival is probably the consequence of the great dispute over the possession of Brough between 1505 and 1510 and the subsequent care of first Roger Burgh (inherited 1546), and then Sir Ralph Lawson (inherited 1574), to make sure that they had evidences with which to defend any challenges to their titles. It is perhaps not as complete as it might have been because, for an unknown length of time after 1510, the family archive was deposited in the care of one of the neighbouring religious houses from which it might not all have returned.[2] As usual with family archives preserved to prove titles, practically all the documents are concerned with land, whether they be title deeds, marriage settlements, chantry endowments, royal grants or even pardons (which protected the lands from confiscation). Our history is, therefore, inevitably slanted towards the story of the Burghs and their property – what they acquired when and from whom, the extent and value of the estate, and disputes over its possession. But the Lawson MSS can be supplemented from other sources. Other private collections, in this case the Wandesford MSS and the Clervaux Cartulary, extend our knowledge of the family's connections with other local gentry families[3] – but again primarily in the management and care of their property. Public records provide another supplement – again concerned with property, for transfers of property could be registered with the Court of Common Pleas or Chancery to give greater security. But public records also provide useful information on political involvement, from royal letters and commands.[4] In the last resort, however, we are desperately short of personal material. The gentry of the late middle ages were literate and did write letters, but few families were concerned to preserve them.[5] As a result, we know little of the characters, personalities and motives of the men and women whose history we are reconstructing. As will be seen, these can only be inferred, hinted at and presumed. Regrettably, only the will of the last male head of the family has survived in the probate records of the diocese. Almost the only personal evidence concerning the Burghs in the fifteenth century is provided by the brasses in Catterick church and these are now hidden by the furniture, leaving us to work from nineteenth-century copies and rubbings.[6] But these tell us the dates of death of the heads of family and their wives and provide us with rudimentary and stylized portraits.

Appendix 1

The Family of Burgh, *c*.1270-1574

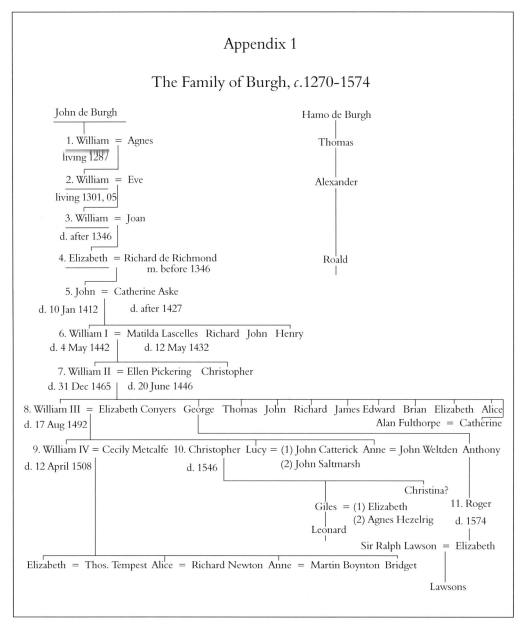

36. *The Burgh family tree, 1270 to 1574.*

From the portraits, all one can conclude is that the William Burghs, father and son, who died in 1442 and 1465 respectively, wore their hair short, in the 'pudding-basin' style made familiar to us by portraits of Henry V, and that the next generation, William Burgh who died in 1492, favoured the flowing locks of the Yorkist kings.

The Burghs are a confusing family to write about, because so many of them were named William – seven in all – and because they took their name from their principal estate. In the account that follows I have adopted the style 'de Burgh', of whom there were three Williams, for the heads of the first family which ended in the male line in the mid-fourteenth century and have adopted the modern form 'Burgh' for the descendants of Richard de Richmond, even though this was not actually used by the family until after 1412. There were four Williams who succeeded each other between 1412 and 1508, and I have numbered these I to IV. Finally, throughout this account, I have used the modern spelling of the place – Brough – even though it was usually spelt Burgh during our period. The family tree (*Illus. 36*), which I have adapted from Raine in his Catterick Church, shows as clearly as I can the relationships of the various members of the family over 10 generations. There is only one point of controversy and this is over the date of death of William II. Whitaker, Raine and McCall all give 31 December 1462, following the early sixteenth-century note endorsed on the contract for building St Anne's Catterick. This note, it is clear, is a reading of the memorial plates and brasses in the church. Whitaker's reproduction of the relevant brass shows the year as 1465, although in his text he repeats 1462. Spencer Perceval in his report on the documents in the late nineteenth century had the benefit of a new rubbing which confirmed 1465. In 1909, another rubbing of the inscription was taken for the Yorkshire Archaeological Society, which also confirmed the date of 1465. And this reading is reinforced by William II's last will which is dated 1 November 1465. Perceval's suggestion that the Roman numerals lxv were misread as lxii is entirely convincing and so, although I have not been able to see the brass myself, I have followed Perceval and the Yorkshire Archaeological Society in dating William II's death in 1465.[7]

As is clear from the above discussion, several antiquaries have made use of these documents. Both Raine and McCall were concerned with the church. Perceval himself admits that his remarks,

> at times amount to little more than a 'narrative pedigree' linking together transcripts of some of the documents concerning the Burgh family.

His account ends with the death of Roger Burgh and it must be admitted that its usefulness, and even more its readability, is hampered by his long digressions on the seals which so obviously fascinated him. In addition to the contract for the church, transcripts of which were published by both Raine and McCall and more recently by L.S. Salzman, and the transcripts published by Perceval, selections from the collections have been published without comment by the Yorkshire Archaeological Society and also in the *Archaeological Journal*.[8] I have endeavoured to supply references to all these transcripts where appropriate in the text.

The account which follows is presented in three parts. The first traces the early history of the family and the accumulation of its estate from the first recorded emergence of the de Burghs from the peasantry until the death of Richard de Richmond, at which point the

37. (above) Richard's signature from an indenture signed between him and William Burgh, October 1471.

38. Brass of William Burgh and his wife Elizabeth Conyers, 1492, Catterick church.

family was clearly established in the county gentry – that is from *c*.1270 to *c*.1385. The second part discusses the family during the period of its greatest importance from *c*.1485 to 1508. This encompasses an analysis of its social circle, a narrative of its involvement in national politics, with special emphasis on the period known as the Wars of the Roses, and comment on its religious foundations. The third and last part traces the decline of the Burghs in the sixteenth century.

The early history of both the township of Brough and the family of Burgh is obscure and confused. All one can do is offer a conjectural reconstruction of the descent of the manor and the rise of the family. According to the sheriff's return for Brough in Kirkby's Inquest of 1287, the inquiry into tenancies in chief ordered by Edward I, there were seven carucates of arable land (approximately 700 acres) of which one was held by the abbey of Jervaulx and six in divers fees held of Roald FitzRoald, hereditary constable of Richmond, who held himself of the earl of Richmond. Some of these undertenants can be identified. One was Avicia de Marmion who held approximately one carucate which descended to the Marmions of Tanfield. A second was the Hospital of St Giles. A third was a William, son of John de Burgh. A fourth was a Thomas, son of Hamo de Burgh. And a fifth was Stephen de Maunsel of Northallerton.[9] The Marmions would appear to have been the longest established under-tenants and they also seem to have been granted a part of the manorial rights. In the *Nomina Villarum* of 1316, John Marmion was stated to be one of the lords of the manor, and in 1343 the Marmions were described in a deed as holding, *inter alia*, the manor of Burgh. Indeed, when in 1372 the Burgh family acquired the Marmion interest in Brough, it included the suit of court of three free tenants.[10] But it does not seem that this was the principal share of the manorial rights. This was gained by the first William de Burgh, by all indications a relatively new undertenant of Roald FitzRoald, from Richard de Latun shortly before Kirkby's inquest. It amounted to the capital messuage, or manor house (perhaps even then on the site of the present Hall) three tofts, all the meadows, the advowson of half the Hospital of St Giles (the other half belonged to the Marmions), the suit of court of four free tenants and all Latun's villeinage rights and villeins.[11] This latter crucial item implies at least a share of the demesne and the manorial court through which villeinage rights were exercised. William de Burgh may thus have held a moiety of the manor in 1287 (some doubt remains since in 1316 this second moiety was said to be held by a certain Thomas of Richmond): on the other hand he had possession of only a small proportion of the land. Equal amounts seem to have been occupied by Thomas de Burgh, one presumes a kinsman, who was a free tenant of both William de Burgh and the Marmions, and by Stephen Maunsel who was also one of his free tenants. This situation was rectified in part in 1296, when William's son William purchased Maunsel's six tofts and six oxgangs (approximately seventy-two acres).[12] But even so, when in 1301 a subsidy of a fifteenth of the value of the movable goods of the inhabitants of Brough was levied, William was only one of the three richer of the eleven taxpayers in the township. William was assessed at 8s. 9d. out of Brough's contribution of fifty shillings. The master of the Hospital was assessed at 9s. 9¾d. and Alexander de Burgh, one takes it the son of Thomas the son of Hamo, at 6s. 5½d. Next in the list was Alan the Reeve, assessed at 1s. 8d. The master of the Hospital and the two Burghs were quite clearly the three wealthy inhabitants.[13] Thus it would appear that during the thirteenth century, two families bearing the name of their birthplace emerged from the peasantry. (The first reference in public records to Thomas son of Hamo of Burgh dates from 1268; the first reference to William son of John de Burgh from 1278).[14] By 1300, their sons were established as the leading laymen resident in the township. But already by acquiring a moiety of the manor, the line of William de Burgh had established a pre-eminence which was to become a dominance before the end of the fourteenth century.

The principal architect of the family's rise into the county gentry appears to have been Richard de Richmond. Richard was in reality the founder of a second family, for he was the husband of Elizabeth, the granddaughter of the taxpayer in 1301. In 1346 William de Burgh, the last male representative of the original line, settled the descent of 'the manor of Burgh and its appurtenances in Burgh and Thornburgh' on his daughter Elizabeth, Richard de Richmond her husband and the heirs of their bodies.[15] These heirs adopted their mother's name. When William de Burgh died we do not know, but Richard must have been in possession by 1370, when he became active in the land market consolidating the Burgh holding in Brough itself and extending his property elsewhere. Firstly, in 1372 he acquired, through part exchange and purchase, the old Marmion holding in Brough, including its manorial rights. Secondly, before 1378 he purchased all the property of Roald de Burgh in Scotton, Hipswell and Brough itself. He had already in 1362 taken possession of Roald's property in Cleasby. Roald would appear to have been the descendant of Alexander de Burgh and was named as a free tenant in the deed which settled Brough in 1346.[16] By these acquisitions, Richard brought the whole manor together, extended his arable lands in the township by some 150 acres, and removed the second Burgh line from the scene. Yet the family did not even now own the whole of Brough. Jervaulx and the Hospital of St Giles were permanent fixtures right up until the Dissolution. Richard's son John did manage to purchase a close called Furnaysgarth and half an acre of arable lying beside his orchard from the Abbey in 1390, but for the rest, the best he could do was to get a lease for his life. This lease was not renewed after his death.[17] On the other hand it did prove possible for the Burghs and the Hospital to rationalise their separate holdings in the open fields. In 1376, Richard exchanged just over nine acres with the Master for a period of 60 years. It was perhaps at the end of these sixty years that a second, undated, exchange took place involving almost 46 acres. After 1378 there seems to have been only one other substantial, independent, free tenant left in Brough. He was named in 1346 as John, son of Robert de Scotland. It was perhaps his descendant, John Thomasson de Burgh, who finally surrendered this holding to Richard's grandson in 1414 .[18]

Richard de Richmond was as interested in acquisitions beyond Brough as in consolidating his holdings within the township. What property he himself, as distinct from his wife, possessed we do not know. It would be reasonable to assume that he owned property in Richmond. He also acquired five houses or messuages in Richmond in 1351 and 1376. He may also have inherited property in Catterick and Tunstall, which he added to in 1351, for in 1373 he was granted free warren in all his demesne lands in Brough and Tunstall as well as all the lands he held jointly with Elizabeth his wife in the same townships.[19] The estate in Brough, Richmond and Tunstall brought together by Richard de Richmond remained the family's basic endowment until the early sixteenth century. But the family also held a fluctuating number of small parcels of land scattered further afield in Richmondshire. One of these was a messuage and two oxgangs in Ainderby Myers acquired by Richard de Richmond in 1375. At times, in the fifteenth century, they possessed properties in Leeming, Walburn, Eppleby, and Hornby.[20] We know of these because they were set aside for marriage settlements and chantry endowments. If other parcels did not remain perpetually in the estate, it is probably because they were used to provide for younger sons and daughters.

No exact or detailed valuation of the estate created by Richard de Richmond is possible. The only direct evidence we have is a statement made in 1427 that William II would eventually inherit lands to the value of 100 marks (£66 13s. 4d.) per annum.[21] The figure itself is suspiciously rounded, suggesting only an estimate. Even if accepted as a rough guide, it should be applied to any other date only with extreme caution. One reason is that we have no idea on what the valuation was based, or of what lands were included. Another reason is that we have to take account of the effects of possible economic decline. That the neighbourhood of Brough did not escape the general trend of late medieval economic decline is suggested by various pieces of evidence. When in 1390 John Burgh, the son of Richard de Richmond, took a lease for life of all the Jervaulx property in Brough, he did so on condition of maintaining all the buildings at his cost and restoring them in good repair at the end of the lease, unless they were destroyed by common war or pestilence. Common war presumably refers to the Scots (this was two years after Otterburn). Pestilence can only be a reference to depopulation and decay brought about by the ravages of the plague. The same thing was in the mind of the burgesses of Richmond when they applied in 1440 to the King for a reduction in their fee farm because, they claimed, the population had decreased as a result of epidemics and emigration and the market was held less frequently than of old.[22] Further, indirect, evidence of depopulation in Brough itself is provided, we shall see, by the enclosure of the township towards the end of the fifteenth century. Finally, the valuation of 1427 does not include income from other sources and, as we shall see, income from milling seems to have been of some importance in the later fifteenth century.

Of the actual economy and management of the family estate, even in Brough itself, the records reveal little. Calculating from Kirkby's inquest and the details contained in later deeds it would appear that the size of the Burgh estate in Brough in the fifteenth century was approximately 400 acres of arable land with meadow land and waste attached. Yet in 1546 the estate was extended at 1,000 acres of arable and 1,000 of meadow.[23] Again we have suspiciously round figures, but even so this is a wide gap. Part may have been filled by the lands of Jervaulx which the Burghs may have acquired after the Dissolution. (In 1546 the Hospital was still in existence.) Part may also have been filled by recent extensions of cultivated land. And part may be explained by a simple difference in the size of the acre – the customary acres used to measure carucates and oxgangs being different from the statute acre used in 1546. In 1300 this land, whatever its size, was farmed by villeins working in open fields. The number of tenants and size of village at Brough is not known. From the various deeds it would appear that there were at least twenty houses. But to judge by the tax assessment of 1301, when there were only eight villeins wealthy enough to be taxed, it was small compared with neighbouring villages. That it shrank over the next two centuries can be inferred from the process of enclosure that took place. In 1440 or thereabouts this was already under way for William I and the Master of St Giles had exchanged newly made closes, each of twenty acres. Fifty years later, in 1494, when William III leased the farm of a close called Clyntle Bank to John Carter of Richmond for twenty-one years, enclosure was probably almost complete.[24] Certainly, in 1510 the estate was finally divided into at least ten separate closes. Enclosure in the fifteenth century usually followed rather than preceded depopulation and one may reasonably guess that the village of Brough had already been half-deserted before 1500. The final enclosure of the open fields whenever it took place would have entailed the final abandonment of the old village, no trace of which survives today, and the dispersal of tenants into the scattered farmhouses which characterise the modern landscape.

In the middle of the fifteenth century, the Burghs maintained a home farm at Brough, as is revealed by the existence of a barn and a separate grange near to the buildings of St Giles.[25] This was retained after enclosure and was flourishing on Roger Burgh's death in 1574. In addition to rents from tenants and the profit of the produce of the home farm, later in the fifteenth century the Burghs enjoyed the profits of various mills. In 1546, the estate was said to have one water mill and three fulling mills. How long the fulling mills had been in existence it is impossible to tell, but it would be reasonable to assume that as the population of the township shrank in the fifteenth century and as arable lands became vacant, the Burghs expanded their sheep flocks and became involved more directly in the production of woollen cloth. But also in the early 1450s William II took up the lease of the castle mills in Richmond from the newly founded Eton College. In 1456 Burgh and William Colville, his partner, contracted to rebuild both mills, supplying all the timber and paying the wrights £13 6s. 8d. In 1482, shortly after Edward IV had granted the mills to the priory of Mountgrace, William renewed the lease for a further 100 years (with an option of another 100 years after that) for a rent of 13 marks a year.[26] This surely is an indication of William's confidence in the profitability of the mills.

39 & 40. Alnwick Castle (above) and the Keep Gatehouse of Dunstanburgh Castle, Northumberland. Both capitulated to the earl of Warwick and Lord Montague in 1464.

However intractable the evidence, it is abundantly clear that by the fifteenth century, perhaps following the death of Richard de Richmond in c.1385, the Burgh family was fully established in the ranks of the county gentry of north-west Yorkshire. An annual income of something over £50 a year drawn from all sources placed them in the same economic bracket as, for instance, the Clervaux of Croft. And despite any economic difficulties which afflicted them, they remained within the charmed circle of the local élite for at least a century. It is to the place of the Burghs in county society between 1385 and 1508 that we can now turn.

The most immediate evidence of the Burgh family's membership of the county community is provided by its marriage alliances. The eldest sons over five generations all married into established gentry families. John Burgh, the eldest son and heir of Richard de Richmond and Elizabeth Burgh married Catherine daughter of Roger Aske of Aske and Marrick. Their eldest son, William I, married Matilda Lascelles of Sowerby before 1408. William II married Ellen, daughter of John Pickering of Oswaldkirk and Ampleforth, in 1427. William III married Elizabeth, daughter of Christopher Conyers of Hornby – a marriage which related him to most of the gentry of Richmondshire. And William IV married Cecily, a daughter of the Metcalfes of Nappa. Burgh daughters were married off likewise. William II's daughter Catherine married her neighbour Alan Fulthorpe of Hipswell. William III's elder daughter Lucy married firstly John Catterick of Stanwick, who died in 1478, and secondly, another neighbour, John Saltmarsh of Colburn in 1483. His second daughter Anne married John Weltden, presumably the son of John Weltden, retainer of the earl of Warwick and Richard of Gloucester, in 1477. The marriage contract between William I and the widow of John Pickering for the marriage of their children in 1427 demonstrates quite clearly the nature of these alliances as business deals. The marriage was to take place at York, on 5 October. The bride's mother was to pay for the wedding feast – the cost of 'mete, drynk and array' and to provide a marriage portion of £133 13s. 4d. The groom's father contracted to make a settlement of lands to the value of £10 on the couple and guaranteed the full inheritance of his property to his son.[27]

Members of these families to which the Burghs allied themselves, most notably Aske and Conyers, were among witnesses to deeds or in other ways associated with land transactions over several generations. In 1408 both Roger Aske, John Burgh's father-in-law, and John Conyers, grandfather of William III's wife, were witnesses to a deed settling property on William I and his wife Matilda. In 1482 these witnesses' grandsons, Roger Aske and Sir John Conyers, witnessed William III's lease of Castle Mills in Richmond; and in 1510 a great-grandson, William Aske and a great-great-grandson, William Conyers, witnessed a settlement of lands in Brough on Christopher Burgh. Of course, the Burghs called upon others than known blood relations to witness their more important legal documents. In 1408 the witnesses included John Clervaux of Croft; in 1474 Thomas Frank of Kneeton was a witness to a deed; in 1482 they included John Clervaux's grandson Richard. In 1414 William I called upon Thomas Mountford of Hackforth to be one of the witnesses to the deed by which he secured John Thomasson's holding in Brough; Thomas's grandson Thomas was another who was present in 1482.[28]

Another frequent call upon neighbours and friends was to appoint them executors of wills. Only an abstract of the provisions of one of the last wills of these generations of Burghs has survived: that of William II, made in 1465. William's executors were his brother Richard and two prominent local lawyers, Sir Robert Danby of Thorpe Perrow, Chief Justice of Common Pleas since 1462, and Richard Pigot, serjeant-at-law, a member of a cadet branch of the Pigots of Clotherham near Ripon and a second cousin through his mother Elizabeth Aske.[29] It is not surprising that for this, the final settlement of his property, Burgh should turn to two of his most frequently employed men of law in the area.

So far we have seen examples of how members of the Burgh family, in the fifteenth century, called upon the services of their social equals to assist in various property settlements. This was not, of course, a one-way traffic; Burghs themselves were just as often assisting their neighbours. Evidence of members of the family acting as trustees or witnesses in conveyances of property is to be found in both public records and other collections of private documents. In 1427, William I was a witness to the enfeoffment of Sedbury in Gilling by Thomas Clare the younger. In 1432, he himself with Christopher Conyers was enfeoffed by Thomas Fulthorpe in the manor of Hipswell. A year later, this time with his cousin Roger Aske, he was enfeoffed by John Barton in his manor of Metton in Lincolnshire. And he was a feoffee for a third time with Robert Danby of Yafforth (father of the Chief Justice) and others of Thomas Lescrope, son of Lord Scrope of Bolton, in Great Burton on Ure in 1436. The witnesses to this deed, which included John Clervaux, Christopher Conyers and Roger Aske, read like a roll call of the Richmondshire gentry. William II was feoffee for some years for John Wandesford of Kirklington. In 1463, he and his fellow feoffees, including Sir James Strangways of West Harlsey and Christopher Conyers, handed over their responsibilities to a new, and perhaps younger group, which included Thomas Mountford and Richard Pigot. Thirteen years later, when Alan Fulthorpe exchanged property in Hipswell with the Abbot of St Mary's York, William III, Thomas Mountford and Roger Aske journeyed down to York to witness the signing of the deed on 12 March. And finally, in 1496 William IV was a witness of yet another enfeoffment of the manor of Kirklington.[30]

A less frequently recorded type of cooperation between prominent local gentry was in performing acts of public service. An example of this is provided by the contract to build a new bridge at Catterick in 1422, in which seven neighbouring undertakers – William I, Christopher Conyers, Roger Aske and William Frank included – together put up 260 marks (£173 6s. 8d.) for labour and found the materials for a stone structure modelled on the bridge at Barnard Castle.[31] A more interesting role played by the gentry was in helping to resolve disputes, again usually over property, which sprang up between their friends and neighbours. In September 1460, William II was called upon by John Stanowe of Richmond to help settle a dispute with John Gainford, also of Richmond. On 7 August 1477, William III and other members of a commission of enquiry which included Roger Aske, Thomas Frank, Alan Fulthorpe and Thomas Mountford as lay members, gave judgement on behalf of the Archdeacon of Richmond as to who had the right of presentment to the parish church of Bedale in favour of Francis, Lord Lovell. William II was again involved in the settlement of two quarrels within ten days of each other in the following March. On 10 March 1478, again with Mountford and also Richard Pigot and Sir Guy Fairfax, he arbitrated in a quarrel between the Abbot of St Mary's, York and the Abbot of St Agatha's, Easby over the boundaries of their lands in Hudswell. On 20 March he must have been present at Middleham Castle, yet again with Mountford and Frank and also William Pudsay, parson of Bolton in Bowland when Richard, duke of Gloucester gave his judgement in a quarrel between Richard Clervaux and Rowland Place over the boundary between their places of Croft and Halnaby, for the four of them were appointed guarantors of the settlement and arbitrators of future disputes – a responsibility they were

41. Engraving of Prudhoe Castle.

required to carry out two years later. In 1510, it was the Burghs themselves who had recourse to arbitrators to help divide the family inheritance. Christopher Fulthorpe, William Aske and John Place were among the friends who helped out. And finally, a few years later, in 1522, Christopher Burgh arbitrated in a dispute between Fulthorpe and the Abbot of St Agatha's.[32]

Our records thus show quite abundantly how totally part of and fully absorbed in the society of the local gentry of Richmondshire the Burghs were. Membership of the county community additionally brought political responsibilities and opportunities. In the polity of late medieval England, men of the standing of the Burghs were expected to be the local governors and administrators and their connections with men of higher rank offered for the talented and ambitious opportunities for dramatic political advancement. To judge by his continuous service as a Justice of the Peace for the North Riding from 3 April 1386 until his death, John Burgh was a powerful and highly respected local figure. In Richard II's reign the Commission of the Peace had reached its full development as a policing and judicial body, but the number of commissioners was still small. When John was reappointed to the Commission in November 1389, for instance, he was one of only eight. There can be no doubt therefore that he was kept busy, both during and between Quarter Sessions, as a general administrator and as a criminal judge in the North Riding. The only tangible royal reward John seems to have received was the office of bailiff of the Honour of Richmond granted to him by Queen Anne in 1392. But the most remarkable aspect of John's long service as a Justice of the Peace is that it was unin-terrupted by the Lancastrian Revolution of 1399. He continued to serve under Henry IV as he had under Richard II.[33] From this, one can perhaps surmise that John did not become involved in high politics and placed the day-to-day well-being and running of his own country above dynastic conflict. When John died in 1412, his son and heir did not take his place as a Justice;

indeed William I never did serve on the Commission of the Peace, a fact which suggests John's distinguished career in local government owed as much to his personal qualities as to his family's recent rise to prominence.

William I appears never to have exerted himself in politics. When eventually towards the end of his life William II emerged as a local politician, it was in a form in direct contrast to his grandfather. John appears to have been a man who maintained some independence from magnate influence and partisanship. William II, on the other hand, seems to have owed his political involvement almost entirely to his being of the Neville affinity based on Middleham. The development of Richmondshire as the distinctive power base of the Nevilles appears to have followed the promotion by Ralph Neville, first earl of Westmorland, of his second family by Joan Beaufort at the expense of the senior line. Ralph divided his inheritance so that Richard, earl of Salisbury, his eldest son by Joan Beaufort, and his line should enjoy his Yorkshire estates (based on Middleham and Sheriff Hutton), leaving his heir Ralph, the second earl of Westmorland, to be content with his Durham property (based on Raby and Brancepeth). It would appear that the Nevilles of Middleham first drew many of the gentry of Richmondshire into their service whilst successfully defending their claim against the earl of Westmorland in the 1420s and 1430s. The attachments were only strengthened in the early 1450s when the great feud between Neville and Percy in Yorkshire flared up, and were finally cemented in the wider conflagration of 1459-61 which saw the establishment of the Yorkist dynasty, carried, in the north at least, on the shoulders of its Neville allies.[34] It is not surprising, therefore, that William II, whose lands in Brough bounded onto Catterick, one of the manors of the lordship of Richmond in Neville hands, should find himself, along with many of his relations, friends and neighbours, deeply involved in his last years in the Yorkist cause. Indeed, the Middleham connection provides the key to the political affiliations of three generations of Burghs up to 1488. No evidence has survived of William II having a formal tie with Richard Neville, earl of Salisbury. We do not know of any office he held or of any fee or annuity he received. It is possible that he was not a retainer as such. But there is plentiful indirect evidence that he was at least a well-wisher. William's links with several of Salisbury's retainers are well documented. He married his son William III to a daughter of Christopher Conyers, who held the prestigious office of Steward of the Middleham lordship. One of his executors was to be Sir Robert Danby, who was one of Salisbury's closest and most trusted servants. And for an unknown number of years before 1468 he was a feoffee, with Christopher Conyers and Sir James Strangways, another of Salisbury's retainers, for John Wandesford who was yet another. Even stronger evidence for a close connection with Salisbury is provided by the fact that he and his son were amongst that small band of North Riding gentry, the majority of whom were known retainers of Salisbury, who bought royal pardons following their lord's attainder at the Coventry Parliament of December 1459. We do not know whether William II and III did in fact take part with Sir John Conyers in the rebellion which ended in confusion at the rout of Ludford, but the fact of their having recourse to pardons for treason which were issued on 22 March 1460 suggests a degree of involvement.[35]

William survived the vicissitudes of fortune which saw the triumphant return of the Yorkists in July 1460, Salisbury's death at Wakefield in December of the same year and the final victory of the new Yorkist King, Edward IV, at Towton in April 1461. He went on to play a prominent role in the service of the new lord of Middleham, Richard Neville, earl of Warwick – the

Kingmaker - in the pacification of the north. On 13 May, he was one of those commissioned under Warwick to arrest and imprison rebels in the North Riding – a commission to mop up lingering Lancastrian resistance. Fifteen days later he was appointed to the Commission of the Peace for the county. On 13 November he was made, under the nominal command of the royal dukes Clarence and Gloucester, but the real command of Warwick, one of the commissioners to array the men of Yorkshire for the defence of the north against the Scots, Henry VI, Margaret his wife and their adherents.[36] On this occasion, the threatened atttack did not materialise, but this commission possibly marks the beginning of a period of active service in the far north which was to last for almost the rest of the last four years of William's life.

It took Edward IV three years to gain complete and lasting control of Northumberland. Between 1461 and 1464 the Percy castle of Alnwick and the royal castles of Bamburgh and Dunstanburgh passed through a bewildering series of change of hands. The Yorkists gained and lost them twice, before finally reducing them in the summer of 1464.[37] At an early stage in this border skirmishing, on 10 February 1462, William Burgh was appointed constable of Prudhoe Castle on the Tyne by Edward IV.[38] Prudhoe was a Percy castle in royal hands by reason of forfeiture from the Lancastrian earl of Northumberland. It would appear that William did in fact take up residence with a garrison in person, for when in March 1463 the grant of the constableship was renewed (and the stewardship added) in the name of the young duke of Clarence, on whom Edward IV had recently settled Prudhoe, William undertook to keep the castle at his own cost. The wording of the indenture is as follows:

> The same William is to kepe the said Castell at his proper charges and costes at
> his owne perill to the use of the said Duke, onlesse that such casualte falls by
> infortune of werre that it shall pass his might and power so to doo, for the which
> in such case it is to be kepte at the costes and charges of the said Duke.

Perhaps it was to help defray these 'costes' that, on the same day, William was granted the lease of all the demesne of the lordship for a farm of £6 13s. 4d.[39]

'Infortune of werre' was no remote possibility. In October 1462, Margaret of Anjou and Henry VI landed at Bamburgh, and Northumberland declared for them; both Alnwick and Dunstanburgh opened their gates. William Burgh held Prudhoe safe. By the end of November, he and other Yorkist commanders controlling the Tyne were reinforced by Warwick and a large army. Presumably Burgh was in the army which rapidly recaptured all three castles by mid - January.[40] But despite this success, first Bamburgh and Dunstanburgh in March and then Alnwick in May 1463 turned yet again to the Lancastrians. This time there was no instant response. Indeed, for the following year Northumberland remained out of Yorkist control. The small garrisons in the three castles offered no immediate threat outside the county, but when at the end of November or in early December Henry VI slipped across the border from Scotland into Bamburgh, and loyal Lancastrians including the duke of Somerset rallied to him there, the situation became more serious. It is in this context that we should view the most remarkable document in the Burgh papers – a letter of protection from Henry VI sealed under the signet at Bamburgh on 8 December 1463. The letter declares: 'to alle oure true liegemen and sugetts within this oure Reaulme of England',

42. The Devil's Water, from the Linnels Bridge, site of the Battle of Hexham in 1484, where the duke of Somerset was surprised by Lord Montague, captured and later executed.

> We have now late taken under oure protection and savegarde William of Burgh and William his son, Cristofer of Burgh and vi persons with theyme or any of theyme joynctely or severally to doo theyme service... unto the feest of the Nativite of Seint John Baptiste next comyng... Provided allwey that the said William etc be of goode bering and also doe nothing nor procure to be doone that shalbe hurte or prejudicial unto us or any of oure true sugetts.[41]

At first sight this letter would appear to demonstrate that William had at this late stage turned his coat. The inclusion of his younger brother, Christopher, in his company gives possible credence to this interpretation, since there is evidence of Christopher having been in the service of the earl of Northumberland before 1461.[42] But on the whole, it is more probable that the letter represents a kind of truce between the Lancastrians in Bamburgh and one of the commanders holding the Yorkist front line. Henry VI's charge in the letter that no man should 'vexe, trouble nor hurt' William and his servants 'in there bodies, goods or catelles' could be a reflection of the fact that the Lancastrians were or had been making depredations as far south as the lordship of Prudhoe itself. That such a truce was undertaken with the approval of King Edward IV is unlikely, but with the garrison of Newcastle also full of treason in December it is hardly surprising that Burgh was treating with his enemies. Certainly the Burgh family did not lose favour with the Neville family as a result. Eighteen months later, in May 1465 John Neville, newly created earl of Northumberland, to whom Prudhoe was transferred by Edward IV in the autumn of 1464, granted to William Burgh the younger, esquire (William III) the orchard of Prudhoe rent free for life and appointed him to 'be of counsell of the letynge of my land and tenandries withyn the sayd lordschipe' during pleasure. Four months earlier, in January 1464, Warwick himself had appointed William's younger brother John steward of another forfeited Percy lordship, Topcliffe.[43] Nor is there any reason to suppose that the Burghs, father and son, did not take part on the Neville side in the battles of Hedgeley Moor and Hexham, which finally put an end to Lancastrian resistance in the north. In April, John Neville set out from Newcastle to provide an escort for Scots ambassadors coming to treat with Edward IV at York. On or about 25 April he was attacked by the main body of the Lancastrians on Hedgeley Moor, some nine miles from Alnwick, whom he beat off. The Scots were brought safely to York. Three weeks later the duke of Somerset led a raid in strength into the upper Tyne valley. John Neville set out immediately from Newcastle, with all the men he could muster. His route upstream took him through Prudhoe. On 15 May Neville's force fell on the Lancastrian camp near Hexham and routed them. All the Lancastrian leaders were captured. Before the end of the month thirty of them had been executed. After this it only remained for the three northern castles to be reduced for the last time. This was completed at the end of June and the Burghs, father and son, were then able to return to the North Riding.[44]

For the last year and a half of his life, William II enjoyed the fruits of victory. On 30 September 1465, no doubt as a consequence of age catching up on him, he received from the Archdeacon a licence to celebrate divine service in an oratory, or private chapel, in his own house for two years. A month later he drew up his last will. He left all the manor of Brough to his eldest son William, as he had it of his father, and amongst the various legacies left £40 to his son Thomas 'to fynd him at London in court'. Thomas, in the end, did not achieve a spectacular career in the law. All we know of him is that in the summer of 1464 he had received a safe conduct from Alexander, the first Lord Home, to travel to Home and back, perhaps on some matter concerned with the administration of the truce signed between England and Scotland on 1 June in that year.[45] William III immediately assumed his father's mantle. He took his place on the Commission of the Peace and was in January 1466 employed as a commissioner, with his brother-in-law Sir John Conyers amongst others, to arrest nine citizens of Newcastle and bring them before the king in Chancery to answer for certain riots.[46] As with his father, the dominant factor in his career was loyalty to the lords of Middleham. This at first took him, or his young son William IV, into conflict with Edward IV. From the end of 1466 Warwick, who had been so powerful and influential in Edward IV's first years, moved into overt opposition. He withdrew from court and spent much of his time at Middleham or Sheriff Hutton. From these places, as part of his plans to force himself back into favour, he began, covertly, to foment unrest. In early 1468 there were disturbances in Yorkshire, instigated by a captain who called himself Robin, by malcontents who were said to have offered their services to Warwick. Later in the same year, on 20 November, William Burgh, son of William Burgh of Burgh was constrained to acquire a royal pardon for all offences committed before 10 April last.[47] Had he been implicated in these disturbances? Between April and June 1469 there were no less than three risings in Yorkshire associated with various Robins, culminating in the Rising of Robin of Redesdale whose levies actually defeated an army raised by Edward IV's court at Edgecote on 26 July, which delivered Edward himself into Warwick's hands for a short while. Robin of Redesdale is widely supposed to have been none other than Sir John Conyers – in fact, Conyers' son John was amongst those on the victor's side killed in the battle.[48] It is possible, although there is no evidence to the effect, that William III or IV was also involved, Warwick's victory in 1469 proved short lasting and in the spring of 1470, following the failure of a second attempt to impose himself on the king, he fled to France. There now followed a remarkable *volte face*. Under Louis XI's skilled guiding, Warwick patched up his quarrel with Margaret of Anjou and agreed to help restore the Lancastrian dynasty. By July he was ready to invade England. Word was sent to Yorkshire to raise yet another rebellion. At the end of the month his brother-in-law Lord FitzHugh of Ravensworth raised the men of Richmondshire. Amongst their number was William Burgh. As intended, Edward IV marched to crush them. They quickly submitted, and on 10 September over 100 men were pardoned.[49] But while Edward was still in Yorkshire, Warwick and his army landed in the west country. On 2 October, Edward IV fled the kingdom and Henry VI was restored.

Although the evidence is slight, there cannot be much doubt that William III, either in person or through his son, lent his support to Warwick's machinations between 1468 and 1470. It is surprising, therefore, that he was removed from the Commission of the Peace when it was reorganised for the new regime on 20 November 1470.[50] Perhaps William was unacceptable to Warwick's Lancastrian allies, who would have remembered his and his father's activities in the early 1460s. Perhaps William himself had lost his appetite for dynastic politics and its attendant risks. Be that as it may, William III does not seem to have played any further role in national affairs. He would appear to have been one of the many who stood aside and awaited on events when Edward IV returned to reconquer his kingdom in March 1471. Warwick's overthrow at Barnet and the final elimination of the Lancastrians at Tewkesbury may well have appeared at first sight to be a disaster for the dissident gentry of Richmondshire, but in the event they presented new opportunities through the person of the king's brother, Richard, duke of Gloucester. On 29 June, the nineteen year old duke was granted Warwick's lordships of Middleham and Sheriff Hutton and the whole of the dead earl's paternal inheritance in the north.[51] Perhaps even then it was intended that he should marry Warwick's younger daughter and joint heiress Anne, although this did not actually take place until early 1472. Gloucester paid his first visit to his new estates in the autumn of 1471 and immediately set about recruiting a retinue of prominent local men. The core of this following was provided by the men who had served the Neville lords.

A crucial appointment was the confirmation of Sir John Conyers in his office of Steward of Richmondshire, with a fee prudently increased from the £13 6s. 8d. paid by Warwick, to £20. With Conyers' services secured, many others of the gentry followed. One of the first was Conyer's brother-in-law William Burgh, who was formally retained for life by Gloucester at Middleham on 4 October. The indenture of retainer is set out in standard form. Burgh contracted, 'wele and covenably horsed and harnessed' to

> be redie to ride come and goo with toward and for the said Duk as wel in tyme
> of peas as of werr, at all tymes and into alle places uppon resoonable warnyng to
> be yoven unto him on behalf of the said Duc, at his costes or reasonable reward.

He was paid a fee of £6 13s. 6d. which was provided from the vaccary, or dairy farm, at Sleightholm in Stainmore. Also retained in October 1471, or later, were two other brothers-in-law of Sir John Conyers: Rowland Pudsay who was married to his sister Isabel and Robert

Wycliffe married to his sister Marjory. Alan Fulthorpe, to whom William Burgh's sister was married, also had connections with the duke, and later in the decade William arranged for his daughter to marry John Weltden, the son of the Feodary of Middleham lordship.[52]

Despite his early recruitment and manifold connections, William does not appear to have been prominent in Gloucester's service. Gloucester's influence was not exercised to put him back on the Commission of the Peace. The only occasion of which we have evidence of him being employed by the duke is as a guarantor of the settlement made in 1478 of the dispute between Richard Clervaux and Rowland Place. The terms of William's indenture would lead us to expect that William took part in Gloucester's company in the Scottish campaigns of 1480-82, which culminated in the occupation of Edinburgh for a brief while in 1482. But we have no evidence concerning this. Nor do we know whether he was called upon by Gloucester in June 1483 to march south with other Yorkshiremen to ensure a peaceful coronation after the usurpation of the throne. And, although the now Richard III came to rely heavily on his northern adherents like William, and although some of them were lavishly rewarded, William himself seems not to have profited. His only employment during Richard's reign was to be twice a commissioner of array in the North Riding.[53] Finally, we have no knowledge as to whether he responded to his lord's last call for assistance by riding 'wele and covenably horsed and harnassed' to the field of Bosworth. After Richard's fall in 1485, William III lived out his last remaining years quietly in Brough to die in 1492. With all his advantages and opportunities after 1471, he seems to have been a man of somewhat less forceful personality than his father. His own son, William IV, appears also to have eschewed a public life and died in 1508 without legitimate male issue. After his death, as we shall see below, the family slipped into decline.

It would seem that only John Burgh and William II made any lasting impact on their contemporaries as political figures. For the most part, the lords of Brough appear to have been content to lead the lives of unaspiring country squires. But there was one distinctive feature shared by William I, III and IV which may provide a clue to their lack of political ambition – this lies in their religious foundations. Between them these men turned the church of St Anne, Catterick into a veritable shrine for their family. This was begun by the building of a new church in 1412-15. The contract for the building of this church is the best known of the Burgh papers. In it, William I and his mother Katherine hired Richard of Cracall (Crakehall) to pull down the existing church and to build a new one on a new site nearby. Cracall was to work to an agreed plan and hire all the labour. William and Katherine were to provide materials and to pay 160 marks (£106 13s. 4d.). The contract provides for what was clearly to be the first stage encompassing quire, nave and two aisles, for bonding stones were to be left for the future building of a vestry and a tower. The contract is remarkable for the fact that William I and his mother were the sole founders. The parishioners of Catterick were not involved, nor was the abbot and convent of St Mary's, York to whom, as impropriators of the rectory, the chancel belonged. Whitaker suggested, and McCall in his 'Richmondshire Churches' endorsed the idea, that the Burghs were the lessees of the Great Tithes and therefore responsible for maintaining the fabric of the church. And it is indeed the case that John Burgh had been since 1392 the lessee of tithes from the abbey of Jervaulx for life. John died on 10 January, and the contract was drawn up on 18 April following, a circumstance which suggests that his widow and son were acting on instructions from his last will.[54] It may well be that income that John had received from the tithes was set aside for the purpose of rebuilding the church. The extent to which the family was merely carrying out a duty, or was motivated by piety or pride is not possible to tell. It may, however, be of significance that John Burgh's neighbour, John Conyers of Hornby, had in January 1410 employed the same mason to add a south aisle and chapel at its eastern end to the church of St Mary's, Hornby at a cost of £34 6s. 8d. Were the Burghs ostentatiously getting one up on their neighbours? Whatever the motive, and genuine piety should not be ruled out, it was exceptional for a family of this rank to build a complete church entirely on its own. Members of the nobility undertook this sort of venture – for instance in 1434 Richard, duke of York paid £300 for the building of an eighty-foot long nave and eighty-foot high tower as an extension to the family's collegiate church at Fotheringay – but members of the gentry usually contented themselves with chantry chapels. The Burghs continued to add to the fabric of the church during the fifteenth century; the vestry and tower were built as planned and a stone font, engraved with the initials 'W.B.' and bearing the family's coat of arms, was presented. The proprietary attitude of the gentry of Yorkshire and elsewhere to the places in which they were buried is frequently observable, but St Anne's, Catterick would seem to be the only church in Yorkshire which in its entirety was converted into a 'private mausoleum for the most prominent local family'.[55]

The late-fifteenth-century heads of the family were more conventional in their foundations than their early century forbears. William III's first endowment in November 1474 was of property to the value of 26s. 8d. to the Friars Minor of Richmond for mass to be celebrated on Wednesday and Saturday in every week in the chapel of St Anne on Catterick Bridge. Near the end of his life, in November 1491, in association with Richard Swaldale he founded a perpetual chantry in the parish church dedicated to St James, which he endowed with property in Catterick and Tunstall to the value of £2 14s. The chantry chapel was created out of the east end of the north aisle built by his grandfather. Under its floor were buried his great-grandfather, grandfather, and father. Memorial brasses were laid down for them, the one jointly commemorating William I and William II, portrayed in elaborate armour, was presumably commissioned by William himself. William IV continued in his father's footsteps. In 1500 or 1501, he added to the endowment of the chantry of St James two burgages in Frenchgate, Richmond. In May 1505, he went one better and founded a new chantry dedicated to the B.V. Mary with one priest to say mass daily for the soul of the founder. For its endowment he transferred the two burgages in Richmond (previously granted to the chantry of St James), a tenement in Eppleby and a property in Herlaywall (Healaugh?) in Swaledale which he had recently acquired. Its total value was £3 18s. 4d. In the chapel, newly built as an extension to the south aisle, he interred the remains of his parents and set a memorial brass in the floor.[56] The foundation of two perpetual chantries by the same family in the space of fourteen years is exceptional even for a county which, despite the contrary trend elsewhere, witnessed a spate of new foundations after 1480. Here again one would seem to have evidence of a more than conventional piety. Can one infer from this record that the last two representatives of the direct male line from Richard de Richmond turned increasingly from the cares of this world to their hopes in the world to come?

William IV died on 12 April 1508. He left four daughters, three of whom were under age, and confusion over his inheritance. According to a deposition made by the ninety-two year old Christopher Geffreyson in 1546, William had settled Brough on his brother Christopher some two years before he died. Geffreyson testified that he himself had been present when William enfeoffed Christopher Fulthorpe and William Conyers in the manor of Brough and all its lands in Brough and Thornburgh so that they, the feoffees, could convey it back to him in tail male, namely with remainder to his brother Christopher and his heirs male and after them to his cousin Anthony Burgh of London and his heirs male. This 'final' settlement may well have been made at the same time as William made a grant of lands to his illegitimate son, which was on 20 January 1506. On the strength of this conveyance, Christopher Burgh took possession after his brother's death, as Geffreyson later stated. Thomas Tempest, the husband of William IV's eldest daughter Elizabeth, complained to the king's council that Christopher had entered without right. At approximately the same time, whether it was before or after Tempest challenged his father-in-law's settlement we do not know, the king granted the wardship and marriage of the three other daughters (Anne, Alice and Bridget) together with the custody of one-third of the estate to Cuthbert Place and John Bulmer. And acting on Tempest's complaint, he sent orders down to Yorkshire, carried by servants of Empson and Dudley, commanding Christopher to present himself at council with an answer. Christopher sent Geffreyson, who presented the appropriate title deeds to the council sitting at Bridewell. But Christopher was still required in person and so he went up to town in the following term. In the end judgement was given for him.[57] This was probably in the early months of 1509, shortly before Henry VII's death (21 April). The subsequent disgrace of Empson and Dudley and the young Henry VIII's willingness to reverse many of these unpopular ministers' decisions may have given the heiresses an opportunity to revive their claims. What actually happened we do not know, but on 1 January 1510 an agreement was reached between all the parties, 'by gret labor and especyall mediation of fryndes', including among others William Aske and Christopher Fulthorpe, which settled the dispute once and for all on slightly different terms. The agreement was that Aske and the other friends were to act as trustees to hold the disputed manor of Brough and its lands to the use of Christopher Burgh and the heirs male of his body lawfully begotten for ever, and in default of such issue to the heirs of the body of William IV, that is to his daughters. The trustees were also to make settlements on Christopher and Agnes his wife and on their son Giles and his wife, presumably to provide for dower in the event of reversion to the daughters. Elizabeth Burgh, Christopher's aunt, was to make a quitclaim before Christmas, which she did on 1 March. And finally, no doubt to prevent deliberate destruction or alteration, all the family deeds were to be put into sealed chests in the custody of either the Prior of Durham, or the Abbot of Jervaulx, or the Abbot of St Agatha's.[58] The settlement was in substance a victory for Christopher; the daughters and their husbands had to wait on the unlikely event of the failure of Christopher's male line if they were to gain possession of the manor. But they were not left empty-handed. Only the manor itself had been in dispute. In effect, the Burgh inheritance had been partitioned; the central property had remained in the male line, whilst the peripheral possessions in Tunstall, Hornby, Ainderby and elsewhere were divided amongst William IV's heiresses. The new lord of Brough was left a much poorer man than his predecessor.

Christopher Burgh made the settlements on his wife and son provided for in the agreement of 1510. But in 1516, these arrangements were changed as a result of Giles' second marriage. On 20 August Giles entered into a contract of marriage with Agnes, widow of Robert Hesilrig. Property to the value of 20 marks was settled on the couple and Christopher also undertook to provide Giles and Agnes with a manservant, a womanservant, a chamber and meat and drink in his house as long as they lived, rent free for the first year and for £5 a year thereafter. Giles subsequently quit his claim to the lands settled on him and his first wife.[59] The marriage contract is unusual and the provision of board and lodging for a grown man and his wife suggests that Giles was in some way disabled and incapable of maintaining his own household. Christopher himself lived to a ripe old age; he must have been of an age of his and his brother's servant Christopher Geffreyson. At the end of his life, in 1546, he took it upon himself to break the entail of 1510, to disinherit his grandson Leonard (it is not clear whether Giles was still alive) and to settle the estate on the next male heir, Roger, the son of Anthony Burgh of London named by William IV in 1506. By common recovery and exemplification, the manor and estate were transferred to Roger Burgh in tail male. This remarkable act was achieved with the apparent agreement of Leonard Burgh, who was himself a witness to one of the attendant deeds. Leonard appears to have been content to become a mere tenant on the estate, for, a year before Christopher's death, he had taken a lease from his grandfather and father jointly of the 'great house or tenement called the Inn of Catterick Bridge' for a period of twenty-one years at a rent of 46s. 8d. After this, apart from a small legacy in Roger Burgh's will, Leonard disappears into obscurity. Roger who succeeded peacably towards the end of 1546 faced only one other counter claim – from Christopher, bastard son of Christopher, who was satisfied by the grant of an annuity of £6 13s. 4d.[60] Curiously, nobody appears to have revived the claim of the heirs of the body of William IV which had been made so forcefully in 1508. Roger Burgh had only the one daughter, Elizabeth, who married Sir Ralph Lawson. In 1560, he broke the entail of 1546 by a second recovery and exemplification, so that his estate could descend to his daughter and her issue. So it was that when Roger died in 1574 the estate of Brough passed to the Lawsons, even though, as his will amply demonstrates, there were many collateral male heirs and, as the deeds reveal, several potential counter claimants.[61]

Under old Christopher Burgh the wealth and prestige of the family suffered a decline. Having inherited a truncated and disputed estate neither Christopher nor his son were a force to be reckoned with in Richmondshire. They kept their heads down during the Pilgrimage of Grace – although this may have been because Christopher was all of eighty and Giles seems to have been incapacitated. Only the young Leonard seems to have taken part. He was, according to the abbot of Jervaulx, one of the leaders of the commons of Mashamshire who 'persuaded' the abbot and his monks to join the Pilgrimage on 15 October 1536 and took them off to the great rendezvous of North Riding Pilgrims at Oxneyfield, south of Darlington on the following day. It is revealing, however, that the Abbot did not recognise him as a gentleman. Under Roger, after 1546, the wealth and prestige seem to have recovered. When he died he left a farm with over 60 acres of standing cereals, a herd of 129 cattle and a flock of 413 sheep and total assets of just under £1,000. Little of Roger's career is known. Family tradition would suggest that he stayed loyal to the old religion. If he did, he did so politiquely, not fanatically. He did not throw in his lot with the Northern Earls in 1569 – a rebellion which drew its inspiration from a shared loyalty to Rome. In November 1569 he rallied to the crown. Sir George Bowes informed Cecil on the nineteenth that:

> I have drawen away, according to their bounden duty, the whole gentlemen of Richmondshire…which, with me, remaineth here at the Quencs Majesties Castle, at Barnard Castle.

Does the tone of this remark indicate that he did not trust them? The following day he wrote to a Captain William Drury, 'I am here, of mine own friends, two hundred horsemen and four hundred footmen. All gentlemen of Richmondshire of any effect be with me'. And one of the gentlemen of effect was Roger Burgh who supplied, according to a muster of 23 November, three of the horsemen, himself included. Barnard Castle was beseiged by the rebels and fell to them in December. The defendants were allowed to march out with all their arms and armour and join the Lord Lieutenant of the North, the earl of Sussex in Yorkshire.[63] Before the end of the year the rebel earls fled and the rebellion collapsed. Roger died five years later. In his will dated 10 October 1574, he studiously avoided any expression of particular religious faith. Starkly, he stated:

> Firste I bequeath my soule unto Almightie God and my bodie to be buried in
> the porche of Sanct James within the parishe church of Catterigg.

The 'porche of Sanct James' was the old Chantry Chapel, still being used as a family burial place. That he was not a committed protestant can be safely inferred from the absence of any expression of theological conviction: that his sympathies lay with Rome we can only surmise. If so, he was certainly more circumspect than Reginald Hyndmersh, parson of Wensley, who six months earlier originally bequeathed his soul to the Blessed Virgin Mary and all the saints in heaven, as well as God Almighty. Later, he had second thoughts because all but Almighty God were erased.[64] Elizabeth I had already been excommunicated but it was still possible for a country squire quietly to go his own way. Jesuits and persecution arrived after his death.

The story of the Burghs between 1270 and 1274 is the story of the rise of one family and the prosperity and decline of a second. The first rose from the peasantry in circumstances and by means no doubt deliberately forgotten, and by prudent management and assiduous accumulation of land they pushed themselves into the ranks of the gentry. The second established themselves firmly in the county community of Richmondshire. That they never rose further, as for instance did their neighbours, the Conyers of Hornby, was probably the result of the limitation of their material resources and a lack of ambition. The years of greatest prominence, the decade of the 1460s, were as much a consequence of the power of Warwick the Kingmaker, to whose interest they were attached, as the creation of their independent political ambition. The decline of the family fortunes in the sixteenth century was in part the consequence of the failure of the direct male line; in part self-inflicted by deliberate disinheritance; in part the consequence of personal inadequacies. On two occasions, failure in the male line made way for new wealth and a new family. On the second, it made way for a new name as well. After 1574, the family name was preserved only by junior branches, which themselves disappeared during the seventeenth century. But in one respect the name of Burgh still lives on. It is enshrined in the church at Catterick, the private mausoleum which survives virtually unchanged to this day as a memorial to a pre-reformation family distinguished by its more than conventional piety.

Plate 1. Bolton Castle, family home of the Scropes in Wensleydale, Yorkshire.

Plate 2. Garter stall plate of John, Lord Scrope of Bolton, 1461-1498, St Georges Chapel, Windsor.

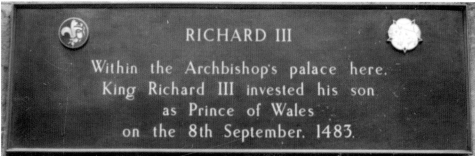

RICHARD III

Within the Archbishop's palace here,
King Richard III invested his son
as Prince of Wales
on the 8th September. 1483.

Plate 3. View of York Minster.
Plate 4. Plaque on Old Minster Library, York, recording the Investiture of Richard III's son,
Edward, as Prince of Wales in 1483.

Plate 5. Ruins of St Mary's Abbey, York.

Plate 6. Boar Badge of Richard III,
fifteenth century glass, St Martin-cum-
Gregory church, Micklegate, York. Richard
was patron of the church in 1476.

Plate 7. (top) Wall crest of Medieval York, showing the king and clergy. St Mary's Heritage Centre, York.

Plate 8. Wall crest symbolising the Church, the King, the Guilds and commoners. St Mary's Heritage Centre, York.

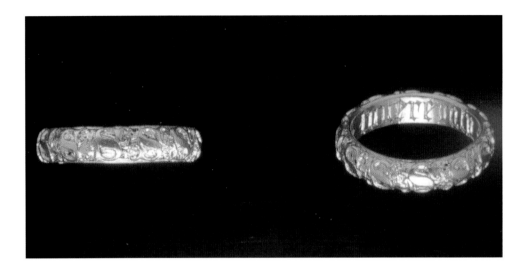

Plate 9. The Middleham Ring, discovered in 1990 carries the repeated letters 'SS' on the outside which form the livery collar of the Lancastrian dukes and kings, with the motto 'Sovereynly' inside. Plate 10. The Middleham Jewel, excavated in 1985. The front has an engraving of The Trinity with a large sapphire and inscription suggesting it was worn as a protection against illness. The reverse has a Nativity scene and figures of fifteen saints.

Plate 11. Micklegate Bar, York, guarding the southern entrance to the city.

Plate 12. The Chapel, Middleham Castle.

Plate 13. Effigy of Sir John Saville (d. 1482) and his wife, Thornhill, Yorkshire.
Plate 14. Fifteenth-century glass showing kneeling donor figures of the Saville family. Thornhill church, Yorkshire.

Plate 15. Barnard Castle, County Durham.
Plate 16. Fifteenth-century carving of Richard's boar badge on the sossit of the oriel window (in the centre of the photo above), Barnard Castle, County Durham.

Plate 17. Effigy of Edward Redman (d. 1510) and his wife, Harewood, Yorkshire.
Plate 18. Middleham Castle from the south, a favourite residence of Richard III
and birthplace of his son, Edward.

Ad Dei gloriam et in piam memoriam
Collegium fieri fecit Anno domini

icardi tertii Regis Anglie qui hanc

Plate 19 & 20. King Richard III, Queen Anne Neville (bottom) and Prince Edward at prayer.
Details from the memorial window (1934) in the Parish church of St Alkelda, Middleham.

Plate 21. Victorian glass of Isabel Neville, Cardiff Castle.

Plate 22. Garter stall plate of Richard, duke of Gloucester. St George's Chapel, Windsor.

Plate 23. Garter stall plate of George, duke of Clarence, St George's Chapel, Windsor.

Plate 24. Richard III, from Rous Roll. The king stands on the White Boar with the crested helms of St Edward, France, Gascony & Guienne, England, Ireland and Wales. Painting by Linda Miller.

Plate 25. Tomb said to be of Prince Edward, Sheriff Hutton Church, Yorkshire.
Plate 26. Reconstruction of the tomb of Edward Prince of Wales, son of Richard III, from
Dodsworth's original in the Bodleian Library, Oxford. S. Saxon Barton.

Plate 27. Detail from the effigy said to be of Prince Edward, Sheriff Hutton Church, Yorkshire.

7

RICHARD CLERVAUX OF CROFT

The history of the fifteenth century is written largely from the point of view of the ruling dynasties and of the great magnates of the realm. This is because they were the principal participants, and because most of the evidence concerns them. The history of the greater part of the political nation – the county gentry – has, with a few notable exceptions, been hidden from us by the dearth of evidence. Yet, as our awareness of the importance of the lesser landowning class in the political and social structure of later medieval England grows, this becomes more apparently a distorting gap in our knowledge.[1] Any documentation concerning the life of a county squire is thus of great interest for the light it can throw, however dimly, on the attitudes, interests and behaviour of his class. Richard Clervaux of Croft is one of this select band, because early on entering into his inheritance, he decided to have a cartulary compiled, and because his descendants have treasured this book ever since.[2]

The Clervaux Cartulary is one of the comparatively few medieval lay cartularies to have survived the ravages of time. It was used by Longstaffe for his note on the Clervaux family which he appended to his history of Darlington. And early in this century it was the subject of a preliminary study by A.H. Thompson, which amply demonstrated its shortcomings, but did rather less than justice to its merits, the greatest of which is the collection in its later folios of materials concerning the life and career of its compiler.[3] The Cartulary is in fact two separate compositions: the first, and larger, is the work commissioned by Richard Clervaux, which is a register of the deeds of all the property inherited by him in 1443, brought neatly to a close by a manuscript of his father's will (folio 43). The second part is a continuation put together by several hands at different dates, and is in effect an on-going register of deeds and miscellaneous documents concerning Richard Clervaux. The original cartulary appears to have been compiled in 1450 by the scribe called Cressi who recorded his authorship in the following couplet at the foot of folio 148d:

> Cressi cognomen scriptor det deus sibi omen
> scripsit temporamen clerveis que honoris amen.

As A.H. Thompson commented, these are singularly clumsy hexameters. Translated liberally they are: 'the writer of the record of the temporal goods and honour of Clervaux was called Cressi; God bring him luck'.[4] This is written on the last leaf of the nineteen quires which made up the original book (folio 148d); five and a half leaves being left empty between the last entry and the signature. The date when this was done can be fixed fairly certainly from internal evidence. Although the cartulary was designed to show the property inherited by Richard

43. Tomb of Sir Richard Clervaux (d. 1490), showing part of the Latin epitaph and the impaled arms of his family and wife on the shield, Croft Church, Yorkshire.

Clervaux, Cressi was not averse to including transcripts of deeds relating to property acquired in the recent past by his master. Six of these were even collected separately under the heading 'carte de nova querita Ricardi Clervaux' on folios 33-34d. Of the dates transcribed in this section, the latest is St George's Day, 1450. All of these deeds relating to the years 1443-50 are transcribed again in the continuation. The earliest deed in the continuation not also transcribed by Cressi is dated 2 January 1451. From this, one can deduce that Cressi composed his epigram and laid down his pen before the beginning of 1451, and that he was working on the greater part of the book after 23 April 1450. The leaves left empty by Cressi at the beginning of 1451 were soon being used for supplementary entries by possibly as many as eight later scribes. The first recorded royal and private grants to Richard Clervaux between 1443 and 1447 (folios 143-44d). The second noted a royal grant of 1457; the third a royal grant of 1460 (folio 144d). A fourth scribe added transcripts of collected deeds for 1443-1451, including the repetition of all those previously included by Cressi (folios 145-46). A fifth hand was responsible for three more deeds of 1453-5 (folios 146-46d). A sixth entered documents relating to the year 1465 (folios 146d-47d). A seventh noted a further deed from 1450 (folio 148), and an eighth hand filled in the remaining space with material relating to the Scrope family's interest in Croft dating from the early fourteenth century (folios 148-48d).

One of these scribes, the sixth, to judge by the similarity of the hand and the continuity of subject matter, was responsible for the extensive continuation of twelve leaves which was started on a new quire. This appendix starts with further documents relating to 1465, but goes on to become a comprehensive collection of deeds from 1446 to 1489 (folios 151-162d). This repeats for a third time deeds from before 1450. Between the two quires, the last of the original sheets and the first of the additional, is a supplementary sheet (folios 149-150d) which is a later intrusion containing ancillary information relating to the deeds of 1465 and, in later hands, documents relating to 1483-9. At the very end is a series of miscellaneous documents not relating directly to Richard Clervaux containing, *inter alia*, examples of court rolls concerning East Cowton, information on free tenants in Cowton, and a draft of a will of Richard's son Marmaduke (folios 163-67d). The final binding of the book, made in part of used parchment acquired from the estate office of the lordship of Middleham, and the placing of it between the wooden boards which survive to this day, appear not to have been carried out until after the end of Richard's life. It is impossible to determine in which order the entries in the continuation were made, except to say that it was not one after another. There seems to have been very little method or care taken until the addition of a new quire. The impression one receives from the text is that from time to time someone decided to up-date the cartulary, making use of any available space until the original was filled. In this haphazard and repetitive way the supplement of some 115 entries which forms the basis of this study was completed.

The content of this supplement is not comprehensive. The most serious drawback is the absence of personal material; the family correspondence such as illumines the lives of the Plumptons further to the south in the county. The greater part of the documentation in the continuations, as one would expect, concerns the management of the Clervaux inheritance; the acquisition of new property, the economy of the estate and the tenantry. But in addition it includes useful information on Clervaux's social circle and material relevant to his political career. From this, augmented by public and other private records, one can recreate at least some aspects of its owner's life.

It is appropriate to consider first the most fully documented aspect of Clervaux's life: the management of his inheritance. Most of the Clervaux estate lay in or bounding onto the parish of Croft on the south bank of the river Tees in the far north of the county, in the district of Richmondshire. The principal holdings lay in the township of Croft, where also was Clervaux's residence, or *manerius* as it was styled in one deed;[5] in the townships of Jolby, Walmire and Stapleton (also in the parish of Croft in the fifteenth century); and in East Cowton, of which Clervaux was lord of the manor, in the neighbouring parish to the south (see Map 5). The family also held extensive property in York, where they had a second dwelling house, and in Darlington. There were a few other scattered properties in Yorkshire, some as far south as Doncaster. But the heart of the estate and that which took pride of place in the Cartulary was the holding in Croft first acquired in 1240. The dominant feature of Richard Clervaux's tenure of his inheritance was the consolidation of this principal holding.

Croft was in the fifteenth century a large parish which contained within it no less than six separate townships – Croft, Jolby and Walmire, Halnaby in the possession of the Place family, Dalton in the possession of the Dean and Chapter of St Peter's, York, and Stapleton, divided principally between the Clervaux and Methams.[6] The Clervaux held all the land of Walmire, parts of Jolby and parts of Croft. The township of Croft contained approximately 700 acres of arable land with the customary meadowland, pasture, woods and moorland. There was just one very large open field, broken up naturally by the streams, or sikes as they were called locally, which flowed into two becks – Clowbeck and Sunbeck (now Spabeck). This field was farmed in common; as is shown by its many strips, by the scattering of holdings throughout the field, and by the apportioning of pasture to arable holdings.[7] There was at least one area of common moorland lying between Croft, Dalton and Walmire. This moorland was partitioned in 1476, so as the tenants of Dalton shall now have their common in parte assigned to them in the same more also severelly as thei have her arabyll londe.[8]

Even though Dalton was held in severalty, Jolby and Walmire were, like Croft, one large field farmed communally. In 1443, Richard Clervaux inherited only just over half of the land of Croft. There were 20 oxgangs and 3 acres of what were apparently old bondage holdings, which in the thirteenth century had been attached to thirteen homesteads.[9] He also held the mills of Croft and their appurtenances and a further five homesteads and land totalling 184 acres which were freehold. In 1465, two of the houses and half the land were occupied by relations, his uncle Thomas Clervaux and a Richard Clervaux junior. But the capital messuage, eight other houses and a total of 253 acres, including the demesne of 173 acres were held by Lord Scrope of Bolton. All of this was tenanted. Finally there were at least eight other properties of 40 acres and more, including five homesteads which were held in freehold of Lord Scrope.[10] The record suggests a thriving farming community in which Clervaux was the principal but by no means exclusive landowner.

In the later 1440s, not long after entering the estate, Richard Clervaux set about acquiring the other half of Croft, an ambition which was to take him 26 years to achieve in two periods of intense activity. He began with the smaller parcels of land. On 25 March 1447, William Frank of Kneeton in Middleton Tyas agreed to lease his messuage and approximately 30 acres of arable in Croft 'for evermore', for an annual rent of 22s. 10d. Clervaux was probably anxious to buy this property outright from an unwilling Frank. The best that he could get out of a renewal of the lease negotiated with Frank's son Thomas in 1467 was an option on the property.[11] Clervaux was more successful in 1449 when he acquired a messuage and arable lands from his 'yhoman' William Cabery. Cabery, an old family retainer, was at the same time granted board and livery in the Clervaux household for the rest of his life. A year later, he added the lands of John Sharpe of Darlington. And in 1458 Clervaux acquired yet another messuage in Croft, with its garden and half acre of land from the heiresses of John Makadoo.[12] The gathering crisis facing the house of Lancaster may now have taken Clervaux's attention for there were no more transactions until after the Yorkist dynasty was well established.

The consolidation of the estate came to a climax on 11 January 1465 when Clervaux and John, Lord Scrope sealed an agreement exchanging all Clervaux's lands in Jolby and Stapleton and a plot in York for all Scrope's 253 acres and property in Croft. Included, it would seem, in the lands handed over to Scrope were two messuages and 15 acres in Stapleton acquired from one Robert Spawde in 1446 and 1447; and properties in Jolby acquired in 1451 from the trustees of Thomas Horston, clerk; in 1452 from Thomas Wylkynson of Sherburn in Elmet, West Riding, and in 1455 from one Robert Alan.[13] In addition to these, the indenture of agreement specified ten properties in Stapleton and Cleasby with a total of 150 acres, of which sixty-four belonged to the 'chief mese' of Stapleton being farmed by Robert Bellamy. In Jolby, Clervaux surrendered the whole holding of 90 acres being farmed by Thomas Hipper, two tofts also held by Hipper and a cottage held by Richard Blacman, all the land specified in the agreement totalling 109 acres. The income from the rents of all these lands was £12 3s. 0d. and the capital value fixed at £226 13s. 4d. In exchange, Scrope surrendered his nine homesteads and 253 acres in Croft including the chief mese and 173 acres of demesne land in the farm of William Hobson. The total rent income was £7 15s. 2d. and the capital value fixed at £133 6s. 8d. The deal was completed and fines levied in April 1468, by which time Scrope had presumably paid over the balance of £93 6s. 8d. on the value of the properties exchanged.[14] Thus Clervaux not only gained possession of the largest single block of lands in Croft, but also raised a handsome capital sum as well.

A spate of further purchases and exchanges of property in Croft followed in the next eight years. Part of the capital raised in 1465 may well have been invested in this land. In August 1466, Clervaux purchased a messuage and its appurtenances from Thomas Shorte of Long Newton. In January 1468, he acquired a half-acre strip in Croft field from John Bellamy, husbandman of Stapleton in exchange for three small plots in Stapleton and Jolby. He completed two exchanges with neighbouring gentlemen on the same day in January 1470. He took a messuage and its appurtenances from Ralph Rokeby of Mortham in exchange for property in Hutton Magna, which he had acquired way back in 1451 from John Barklay and Alice, his wife.[15] And he took possession of a second messuage and other parcels in Dalton and Jolby from Sir Thomas Markenfield, lord of nearby Eryholme, in exchange for a tenement and 21 acres in Eryholme which he had acquired, also in 1451, from Sybil Hodding. And in October 1471 he secured possession of all the property in Croft which Richard Stertforth of Dalton had inherited from both his father, Robert and his mother, Alice Laton.[16] In these very active years in the land market Clervaux also began to acquire new property in Jolby. He purchased a messuage and $5\frac{1}{2}$ acres in Jolby field from William Manners, who was also one of his tenants in Croft, in October 1465, and another messuage and a waste cottage with the attached lands from Sir William Pudsay of Selaby for a house in Darlington and £5 in 1470. But these, with the exception of a parcel on Brakynbere Hill, were then exchanged for a toft and lands in Croft belonging to Rowland Place of Halnaby. This deal of April 1473 brought to an end Clervaux's consolidation of Croft. One may suppose that there was then nothing remaining in other hands, and that he at last owned all that he could of the township of Croft. After 1473 he was the sole and unchallenged master of Croft and Walmire.

The time-consuming and no doubt expensive process by which Richard Clervaux concentrated his property within the township of Croft stands out clearly from the record. His motivation on the other hand is shrouded in mystery. It did not make him lord of the manor. Both before and after the exchange he styled himself, or was styled, Lord of Croft on several occasions: in the grant of an oratory in 1453; in deeds of 1467, 1468 and 1476; and in the epitaph he caused to be inscribed on his tomb ('Crofte quondam dominus'[17]). It is abundantly clear from the agreement between Clervaux and Scrope, however, that Scrope retained all the rights and privileges of the lordship of the manor. He specifically reserved for himself all fealty, rents and suits Richard owed for the land he held of him by knights service, the free tenements; for the land he held in socage, the original family holding; and of all 'other tenantes that haldeth ioyntly or severally of the same John Lord Scrope as of the same manor and seynorye of Croft' – a clause which would encompass Clervaux's other acquisitions.[18] According to a later memorandum, Scrope conceded his right to relief and wardship on the lands involved in the exchange.[19] But this did not give Clervaux the right to call himself lord of the manor: that privilege remained firmly with Scrope who was the residual legatee of the honour of Richmond in Croft. The only manor of which Clervaux was lord was that of East Cowton and it is only in East Cowton that he held courts.

44. *Medieval silver spoons of the type inherited by Richard Clervaux from his father.*
45. *Carved stone representations of Sir Ralph Pudsay of Bolton-by-Bowland, and the twenty-eight members of his family, on his tomb.*

Nor does the concentration of ownership into Clervaux's hands seem to have led to any striking reorganisation in the economy of the estate at Croft. The creation of one consolidated estate might well have been the prelude to direct exploitation on a large scale, or to enclosure. Neither of these seems to have taken place. The small, unified, easily manageable estate of the country squire, such as that created by Richard Clervaux was, it has been suggested, more suitable for direct exploitation and potentially more profitable than the large, widely scattered estates of the magnates in the fifteenth century. Some of the country gentry were experimenting in such direct management, as has been demonstrated in the case of John Brome of Baddesley Clinton, Warwickshire, who in the decade 1442-52 turned over his consolidated estate of some 300 acres to pastoral farming.[20] However, nothing like this seems to have happened at Croft. That there was some direct exploitation of the estate when Richard inherited it is shown by his father's will. In it John Clervaux disposed of a herd of at least 45 cattle, most of it to Richard himself, and of an acre of standing wheat, presumably only a part of his arable crop that year. Richard continued to operate this home farm.[21] There was still a herd of cattle in 1478, for straying beasts were a cause of friction between Clervaux and his neighbour, Rowland Place. Richard also had land under the plough. The acquisition in 1468 of 'a rig of land called half one acre lying upon long longlands in Crofte soile', which was bounded on both sides by land he already farmed, would appear to have been made to consolidate some of this. Additionally, Richard had a much larger section of Croft field in severalty in 1467. This was the area west of the village known as Stokmire, bounded by the 'dyke that departys Crofte soile and Joylby soile unto Sonbeke and fro the dyke in Stutfath sieke unto the sieke that is called Edyndalessieke', upon which it was agreed Thomas Frank could distrain animals or standing crops for arrears of rent (should they arise) for the land which Clervaux rented from him.[22]

But it is impossible to see how Clervaux could have undertaken direct exploitation throughout the estate. All the land acquired from Scrope was tenanted, including all of the demesne land. That tenants also occupied some of the original Clervaux holdings is revealed by descriptions of some of the purchased land as lying between the holdings of named tenants. There is no evidence that these tenants were evicted. For the same reason immediate enclosure of the estate seems to have been out of the question. Stokmire was enclosed before the end of the century, for in the draft will drawn up by Clervaux's son Marmaduke it is described as Stolkmire Park and is one of the closes where a flock of at least 300 sheep was kept.[23] But this was only enclosure of land already held in severalty. It was not in fact until the 1540s that the whole estate was eventually reorganised and enclosed, with completely new farms being created.[24] This, it is true, could not have been done without Richard's consolidation, but one could hardly argue from the available evidence that it was Richard's intention to create the conditions for eventual enclosure. If then Richard Clervaux had had any ambitions for immediate agrarian reorganisation, or agricultural experiment when he undertook the consolidation of his estate in Croft, he found them impossible to fulfil.

It may just be possible that Clervaux was moved more by a love of hunting than by any hard-headed materialistic calculation. It could be more than coincidence that he acquired the right to free warreny in Croft, Walmire and East Cowton in 1478, only after he had completed the consolidation. That he was a keen huntsman is suggested by the agreement reached with Rowland Place, also in 1478, that neither himself nor his hounds would trespass on Place's land while following game.[25] A desire to extend the land over which he could hunt without dispute may have been a contributory factor, but it could hardly have been the sole reason why he spent so much time and energy on consolidating his estate. Without there being any obvious and immediate material benefits, the consolidation remains an enigma. Did Clervaux have entirely personal reasons about which he has left no record? It may be that he was moved only by a desire to have complete control of his native township – a pride in ownership reflected also in his unwarranted description of himself as Lord of Croft.

Croft, it has become abundantly clear, was predominantly a rentier estate. After consolidation in 1465, it was held by some two dozen tenants yielding rents of some £18-£20 per annum. Any income which Richard Clervaux received from the direct management of his home farm on Stokmire and other lands was only a supplement to this. There is evidence in the Cartulary to suggest that the income he received from these rents had declined over the 160 years preceding the exchange with Scrope. In 1305, Henry, Lord Scrope had leased all of his lands in Croft for a term of eighteen years to Richard Clervaux's ancestor, William, for a rent of £12 per annum. A century later, in 1404, Scrope's lands were held by several tenants, not including a Clervaux, for a total rental of £9 10s. 8d. In 1465, at the time of the exchange, there were nine tenants owing a total of £7 15s. 2d. in rent.[26] It is likely, given the economy of open field farming, that rents throughout the estate had suffered an equivalent decline. And indeed at least two tenancies were vacant in the 1460s, one, at Jolby, described as waste. It is worth noting, therefore, that Clervaux and Scrope at Croft seem to have shared the experience of most rentier landlords during the later middle ages. Thus, in as much as Clervaux remained primarily a rentier landlord, the evidence suggests, and by its nature it can do no more, that he at least was not one of the gentry able to stand out against the prevailing economic trend.

A suggestion that the income from rents on one estate had fallen by some 35% in the century and a half following 1300 does not imply that Richard Clervaux was impoverished. In addition to the lands at Croft, Richard inherited extensive property in York, and the lordship of East Cowton which in the early fourteenth century had been valued at a minimum of £15 per annum.[27] In 1442, to judge by Richard's marriage settlement, the net revenue from all the Clervaux possessions seems to have been assessed at £50 per annum, for the jointure (presumably the customary one-third) was set at 25 marks or £16. 13s. 4d. per annum.[28] Nor did Richard depend exclusively on his landed income. For one, he engaged in overseas trade. On 14 February 1444, he received a royal licence to trade with two ships to Iceland, exporting any merchandise except raw wool and importing stockfish, for a term of seven years. Whether he continued to trade after 1451 is not known for certain, but it is likely that he did.[29] For another, Richard was in receipt of handsome fees for life from two local magnates. On 20 April 1445, Robert Neville, bishop of Durham, granted him an annual fee of £5 from the episcopal revenues in Darlington and on 20 January 1448 Ralph Neville, earl of Westmorland, granted him a fee of 10 marks (£16 13s. 4d.) out of the manor of Oxenhall, which lay in Durham just across the river Tees from Croft.[30] And finally, he received from time to time royal grants and commissions all of which must have brought some profit.[31] It is impossible to give any exact estimate of Richard's annual income, but a man who was receiving from all sources something in the region of £50 or more was undoubtedly one of the 'most sufficient' gentry of Richmondshire.

Certainly Richard Clervaux seems to have maintained an impressive standard of living. His father had added a new chamber to Croft Hall and Richard himself set up a private chapel there in 1453, and may well have undertaken further rebuilding.[32] The most valued family possessions passed on to Richard by his father were three covered cups, two uncovered cups and twelve spoons, presumably of silver, a large number of vessels of brass and pewter, a hanging and canopy of arras for the dais in the hall, a master bed with curtains and a tester and five other plain beds.[33] Richard appears to have been served by a household of two or more yeomen and at least two chaplains at any one time. The yeomen, like William Cabery who retired in 1449 with a generous pension after a lifetime of service to both son and father, received free board, lodging and their master's livery.[34] The chaplains were no doubt principally for the servicing of the chapel. The names and, in the case of the chaplains, the status of these members of his household are recorded in the appointments of attorneys for receiving possession of Clervaux's acquisitions. Laurence Wederherd, an attorney three times between 1446 and 1452, and William Clerk, once in 1470, who were given no designated status in the letters of appointment, may well have been yeomen of the household. Named chaplains acting as attorneys were: John Smith and William Bell on occasions in 1451-2; John Smith and John Mason on occasions in 1465-6; John Johnson and William Smethon on occasions in 1470-1.[35] Smith and Wederherd were present in the household at Croft on 22 January 1450, when they witnessed the taking of the homage of William Thuglisth for his free tenement in East Cowton. John Smith also acted as a feoffee in the transfer of the Makadoo property to Clervaux from February 1452, when he received the messuage, to December 1458, when he surrendered it to its new owner. This was possibly the same as the John Smith of South Cowton who was, with Richard Clervaux himself amongst others, a witness to a deed settling lands in East Cowton on yet another chaplain, William Smethon in 1453, and who was commissioned on 4 January 1454 to administer the goods of Nicholas Paintour, late rector of Croft who had died intestate.[36] None of these chaplains seems to have received preferment in the church, not even in the parish of Croft. But they were, one may guess, the men responsible for the continuations to the Cartulary after 1450.

Several of Clervaux's household servants were also his tenants: Cabery, Clerk and Smethon were all freeholders in Croft and East Cowton. In 1465, Clervaux had eight free tenants in Croft. Two of these, with two of the largest holdings, were his relations who held only a life interest in lands granted to them by Richard's grandfather. One of these holdings was still known as Marshallsland after the family from whom it had been acquired between 1340 and 1420. The other six were villagers. John de Croft had a holding of 60 acres, but the rest had only smallholdings. John Dernlove, chaplain held 12 acres; William Shipyard and William Cabery shared 10 acres; Thomas Bell had 2 acres and William Clerk but one rood.[37] In Croft, as elsewhere in England, freehold was strictly a legal tenurial distinction: economically and socially freeholders fitted into the same spectrum as unfree tenants.[38] The names and sizes of holdings of nineteen who either became or ceased to be Clervaux's tenants in Croft, Jolby and Stapleton as a consequence of the exchange of 1465, are listed in the Cartulary. Of these, three (William Hobson in Croft, Thomas Hipper in Jolby and Robert Bellamy in Stapleton) were farming demesne lands of 64 acres or more and were clearly the type of men of independent means, as was John de Croft, to whom the word yeoman was increasingly being applied. Indeed, Robert Bellamy, who had the smallest of these farms, was so styled in a deed of 1471.[39] The next discernable group is that of five husbandmen who had holdings of 28 to 30 acres, large enough to provide an independent living from the land. They were William Lessy and Harry Butcher in Stapleton, and William Manners, John Alan and John Appleby in Croft. The remaining eleven holdings for which we have evidence were in the hands of men with 10 acres or less – men, who if they did not hold land elsewhere would need, like the greater part of Clervaux's freeholders in Croft, to work as labourers or in household service to make ends meet. In fact several of Clervaux's tenants did hold land elsewhere, some of it freehold. A case in point is John Bellamy, husbandman of Stapleton, and presumably a kinsman of the farmer in Stapleton, who held a paltry quarter acre of freehold in Croft field until his exchange with Clervaux in 1468, but also had land in Jolby and Stapleton. His modest wealth is indicated not only by his title of husbandman, but also by the fact that in 1450 he was sued for damages to the tune of £10, after his cattle had strayed onto the land in Jolby of William Pudsay of Selaby.[40] Again, William Manners, who held 18 acres in Croft also had 5 and a half acres of freehold land in no less than fifteen separate strips scattered throughout Jolby field, which he sold to Clervaux in 1465.

Some of these men were also rising in the world. William Manners, son of William Manners above, had migrated to Bishop Auckland in 1465 and so was willing to surrender his claim to his father's freehold land. William Thuglisth of East Cowton, who inherited one messuage and one oxgang of freeholdland in 1450, left four messuages and three oxgangs to his son Richard when he died in 1476, which were estimated for the purpose of relief to have an annual value of 40s beyond charge. This put Richard into the enfranchised élite, although his holding was not much larger than those of husbandmen such as Manners and John Bellamy and was distinctly smaller than those of any of the four yeomen living in the parish. Incomplete and fragmentary as this evidence is, it suggests that amongst Richard Clervaux's tenants in Croft and the neighbouring townships, there was a small group of prosperous men on the threshold of gentility and on the fringe of the society in which Clervaux himself moved.[41]

Richard Clervaux was undoubtedly a leading member of the gentry community of Richmondshire. From the marriage alliances negotiated by his grandfather and himself, and from the lists of the more important witnesses to his charters over the years 1443-1478, one can reconstruct a clear picture of his social circle. The marriages of the eldest Clervaux son in the fifteenth century tended to be made with the leading gentry families of Yorkshire and beyond. Richard's mother was Margaret, daughter of Sir Ralph Lumley of Lumley, County Durham, a niece of Ralph Neville, first earl of Westmorland, through whom he claimed sanguinity with the Yorkist kings. He himself was married in 1442 to Elizabeth, daughter of Sir Henry Vavasour of Hazlewood in the West Riding.[42] His eldest son John was married to Jane, daughter of John Hussey of Sleaford, Lincs., and sister of William Hussey, Chief Justice of King's Bench, 1481-1495. And their daughter and heiress, Margery, was married to John Fitzwilliam of Sprotburgh in the West Riding. Younger children were married into the more local gentry, although some of these were impressive matches. The marriages of Richard's uncles and aunts related him to many of his neighbours. His uncle Thomas (still living 1465) married Isabel, daughter of Robert Conyers of Sockburn. His five aunts were married as follows: Margaret to William Vincent of Great Smeaton (still living in 1450) on whom her father had settled all the Clervaux property in Smeaton; Joan to Henry Tailboys of Hurworth (died 1444), a younger son of Sir Walter Tailboys of Kyme, Lincolnshire who was lord of the manor, on whom her father had settled his lands in Hurworth; Beatrix to John Killinghall of Middleton St George (died 1442); Agnes to John Headlam of Stainton in the Carrs, County Durham and Nunthorpe, North Riding (died in 1461), of whose will Clervaux was an executor; and Elizabeth to William de Levesham, citizen of York, on whom her father had settled lands in Monkgate.[43] Richard himself had only one younger brother who was married, but to whom is not known. Richard's own children were married as follows: his second son Marmaduke, who eventually inherited the estate, to Elizabeth, daughter of Sir James Strangways of West Harlsey; his eldest daughter, Elizabeth, first to William FitzHenry of Manfield and second to William Clerionet of Richmond (c.1483); Margaret to Thomas Laton, eldest son of Robert Laton of Sexhow, Melsonby and Barton in 1458; Joan to Christopher Aske of Dalton in Kirby Ravensworth; and Isabel to William Conyers of Wynyard, County Durham, son and heir to Roger Conyers, fourth son of Christopher Conyers of Hornby. A son, Robert, seems to have remained unmarried; another, Henry, died young; and a daughter, Beatrix, became a nun. Of the marriages of his younger children those that brought him into the circle of prominent servants of the Nevilles of Middleham were most significant. Sir James Strangways (c.1410-80) was a life-long confidante of Richard, earl of Salisbury and his son, Richard, earl of Warwick. Strangways was the brother-in-law of Sir John Conyers of Hornby, a man equally committed to the Nevilles, who was an uncle of Clervaux's son-in-law, William Conyers.[44]

Many of Richard's uncles, cousins and sons-in-law acted from time to time as witnesses to his many land transactions. But the man who acted most frequently for him and who seems to have been his closest associate in his earlier years, Sir Ralph Pudsay of Bolton-in-Bowland and Barforth in Richmondshire, was not apparently related to him. Pudsay (c.1390-1468) was a witness to deeds seven times between 1443 and 1452 and once again in 1465. A man of his father's generation, Pudsay may have been Richard's principal adviser and mentor in his formative years. Richard's first recorded public appearance was when he witnessed, in 1440, a grant of lands in Barforth to Pudsay's kinsman William Pudsay of Selaby. In April 1461, another William Pudsay, one of Ralph's many sons (he had twenty-five children by three marriages) was presented by St Mary's Abbey, York, to the living of Croft, no doubt on Clervaux's recommendation.[45] William's sister Isabel was married to Clervaux's neighbour Robert Place who acted as a witness almost as frequently as Pudsay, six times between 1443 and 1458.[46] Of Richard's relations, his uncle Henry Tailboys acted once as a witness in 1443 and uncle William Vincent three times in the 1440s. Of his cousins, John Killinghall witnessed six deeds (1444-67), Christopher Conyers (of Sockburn) five (1451-66), Thomas Tailboys three (1458-66) and Roger Vincent two (1463-5). Of those with whom Richard himself forged marriage alliances, Sir James Strangways was a witness four times between 1444 and 1465, Robert Laton four times between 1452 and 1467 and Christopher Aske just once in 1471.[47] There were other members of the local gentry in addition to Pudsay and Place who had no blood relationship with Clervaux, who were called upon to witness deeds. Most prominent among them were William Frank of Kneeton, five times between 1447 and 1453; John and William Catterick of Stanwick, four times between 1457 and 1463; and Thomas Surtees of Dinsdale, Sir James Strangway's nephew, three times in 1465-6. And finally there were the following on the odd occasion: Sir John Conyers of Hornby in 1444 and 1463; Thomas Metham of Stapleton in 1451; John Wycliff of Wycliffe in 1451; Thomas Mountford of Hackforth in 1463 and Christopher Boynton of Sedbury in 1465.[48]

These representatives of nineteen gentry families, many of whom were relatives, all of whom were resident within twelve miles of Croft, witnessed those agreements reached by Clervaux not only with members of their own class, but also with men of much lower status, husbandmen such as William Manners or William Hodding. On one occasion only, on 18 November 1471 when Richard Stertforth of Dalton granted all his lands in Croft to Clervaux, were the witnesses themselves predominantly of lower status. On this unique occasion they were his son-in-law Christopher Aske, his chaplain William Smethon and the two local yeomen, Robert Bellamy and William Hobson. Not all of the deeds transcribed in the Cartulary concern Clervaux's land transactions. From time to time one can observe Richard and his circle active in other directions. In 1450 William Vincent enfeoffed Richard Neville, earl of Salisbury, Henry Percy, earl of Northumberland, three of his sons, Clervaux and John Vincent in his lands in Smeaton and elsewhere so that he could make provision for his younger son, Roger. The witnesses were Strangways, Ralph Pudsay, Christopher Conyers and Robert Place. Thirteen years later Richard called upon his friends to help resolve a dispute which had been rumbling for several years with Thomas Fitton of Cawerden, in the County of Chester, over a rent of £5 which Fitton claimed out of Croft and East Cowton. The Fittons had been lords of East Cowton before they sold it to the Clervaux in the early fourteenth century. James Strangways and John Nedeham, a justice of Common Pleas, were called in to arbitrate and in an indentured agreement made at Harlsey Castle on 15 June 1463, Clervaux bought out Fitton's claim for £53 13s. 8d. to be paid in four instalments ending on 24 June 1465. Strangways, Roger Vincent and Thomas Tailboys agreed to act as Clervaux's guarantors. Three days earlier, at Croft, Fitton had ceremoniously quit his claim to the rent in the presence of Strangways, Sir John Conyers, Thomas Mountford, John Catterick and John Killinghall.[49]

The impression given by these deeds is of a peaceful and harmonious society of gentry. So it seems to have been until in the 1470s a quarrel blew up between Clervaux and Rowland, the son of Robert Place, who succeeded his father at Halnaby at the end of the 1460s. This quarrel was only settled by the intervention of Richard, duke of Gloucester. On 20 March 1478, Clervaux and Place agreed to accept the arbitration of Gloucester and bound themselves over until such time as Gloucester should make his award. At Middleham Castle on 12 April, Gloucester,

> tendirring the peas and welle of the contre where the said parties inhabite and also gladly willyng gode concorde reste frendly suite to be had frohensfurth between the sayde parties,

duly made known his decision. The terms laid down were as follows: the parties should construct a fence between their properties before Easter next, so that cattle belonging to them or their tenants do not stray on each other's land, and if it should so happen that cattle should stray then they should not pound them nor take amends for the hurt, but 'esely' drive them back; both parties should remain content with exchange of lands made between them (in 1474); both parties and their wives should be content to occupy the pews in the parish church which their ancestors had always used, Clervaux on the south side of the chancel, Place on the north; neither party should retain or take to service the other's servant or tenant; neither should hunt, hawk or fish each other's game, and if any hounds chase game into the other's land the hunter is not to follow them but to call them back, whilst the other whose land has been trespassed upon should 'rebuke' them and do no other hurt. Having thus dealt with these five matters of dispute between the neighbours, Gloucester appointed Thomas Mountford, William Burgh of Brough Hall, near Catterick, William Pudsay, parson of Bolton-in-Bowland (late of Croft) and Thomas Frank to act as guarantors of the agreement and arbitrators in any future dispute. And indeed two years later the arbitrators were called upon to settle a dispute about the possession of part of the dike which lay between their lands and the responsibility for its maintenance. An agreement over this reached at Croft on 22 May 1480 seems to have been the last of their quarrels. It has been suggested that a lasting reconciliation between the neighbours was marked by their jointly building a new porch to the parish church, for the arms of Clervaux and Place with the initials R.C. and R.P. now set in the tower, which were before the rebuilding of the church in 1878 placed over the doorway.[50]

A man of Clervaux's means and standing in the county community carried political weight. His father, Sir John Clervaux, had been a justice of the peace in the North Riding and sheriff of the county in 1430. As a young man Richard appeared to be on the threshold of a more brilliant career at court. He was approximately the same age as the young King Henry VI and was already a member of the élite group of esquires of the body in February 1444, a few months after his father's death, when a flow of patronage in his direction began. He was in attendance during the destruction of

Humphrey, duke of Gloucester at Bury St Edmunds in February 1447, during which, like many others, he felt it prudent to purchase a general pardon. And at the end of this year he was appointed escheator in Yorkshire, which would have appeared to many to have been the first of many such royal offices. His rising star was clearly recognised by his more prominent neighbours. One assumes that it was because of his potential value at court that he was retained first by Robert Neville, bishop of Durham, on 20 April 1445 and secondly by Ralph Neville, earl of Westmorland, on 20 January 1448.[51] But after this his promising career comes to a sudden end and the flow of patronage dries up. Why this happened we do not know. He withdrew from Court before the fall of Suffolk and so could not have been implicated in his disgrace. It is just possible that he was implicated with Sir William Tailboys, his kinsman and absentee neighbour at Hurworth, in his reign of terror in Lincolnshire for which Tailboys received a scandalous pardon.[52] Some form of involvement in Lincolnshire society is suggested by the marriage of his eldest son into the Hussey family of Sleaford. But, if this was the case, it would seem to be an unlikely reason for his eclipse whilst Tailboys still enjoyed protection. More probable is that he was already beginning to suffer from that debilitating ill-health which appears to have left him an invalid by 1463. For in January 1463, Edward IV exempted him from all public service in person because, 'as the king was reliably informed, ye be vexed with such infirmite and disease that ye ne bee of any power to labure without great jeopardie'. Whatever the disease was, it was not terminal, for Richard had another 28 years left to him.[53] It is possible then that ill-health was responsible for ending Richard's career at court when he was still only a young man. Certainly there was a dramatic change in direction in Richard's interests around 1448. It was at this time that the first surge in the consolidation of the estate at Croft began and shortly afterwards the cartulary, the up-to-date record of all his property, was compiled.

Clervaux's poor health, if such it was, did not leave him completely without political significance. His wealth, his servants, his tenants and his social connections still gave him local weight. But after 1450, his political interest was only that of a member of the Richmondshire gentry. He was now of the county rather than of the court. Politics in Richmondshire between 1450 and 1490 were dominated by one force – the wealth, prestige and power of the lords of Middleham. Richard Neville, earl of Salisbury until 1460, his son Richard Neville, earl of Warwick from 1460 to 1471, and above all Warwick's son-in-law Richard, duke of Gloucester, later Richard III, from 1471-85 were the unchallenged rulers of northwest Yorkshire. Clervaux always had his friends within the Middleham connection. He made marriage alliances with Sir James Strangways of Harlsey, and the Conyers of Hornby, both prominent retainers of the earl of Salisbury. Moreover his uncle, Sir Thomas Lumley, his mother's brother, was also a prominent supporter of the Nevilles of Middleham.[54] And, by no means least of all, he himself had been retained by Salisbury's brother the bishop of Durham since 1445. But Clervaux also had associations outside the Middleham connecton which were to come into conflict with it during the 1450s. Sir Ralph Pudsay of Bolton was a staunch supporter of the Percy family and Ralph, earl of Westmorland, Clervaux's other patron, was a deadly enemy of Salisbury. These matters were of little consequence in 1450. Thus it was possible for Salisbury, Henry Percy, earl of Northumberland, his three sons, Strangways and Pudsay to meet together at Great Smeaton on 6 May in that year to take part in the settlement of old William Vincent's inheritance.[55] Within three years all was changed: Neville and Strangways were ranged against Percy and Pudsay. Clervaux, however, was not involved directly in any of the conflicts which disturbed Yorkshire between 1453 and 1455.

46. Humphrey, duke of Gloucester, from a drawing in the 'Recueil d'Arras'.

But as the local feud became inextricably bound up with the dynastic conflict between Lancaster and York, he was obliged eventually to declare himself. He chose with Pudsay and Westmorland against the Middleham connection for Percy and Lancaster. The death of Robert Neville, bishop of Durham in 1457, may have smoothed his path in this direction. Clervaux's general sympathies towards the court and his acceptability there may be indicated by his being appointed on 16 August with Sir Thomas Neville of Brancepeth and Bywell (the Earl of Westmorland's nephew) to collect the temporalities of the see during the vacancy. But it was only during the outright civil war of 1459-61, that Richard showed his hand. He was still an esquire of the body and a basic loyalty to the crown, perhaps even a personal attachment to the king, ensured his open opposition to the Yorkists after the rout of Ludford and the attainders of York, Salisbury, Sir John Conyers and others of their principal lieutenants at the Coventry Parliament of November 1459. He was rewarded, and his loyalty encouraged, by the grant of the office of understeward and bailiff of Richmond Castle on 13 January 1460. A month earlier John, Lord Neville, the Earl of Westmorland's brother, had been granted the offices of constable and steward. On 13 May following, Clervaux was additionally granted the custody of the manor of Deighton near Northallerton, one of the Earl of Salisbury's forfeited possessions, for a farm of £14 3s. 4d. per annum (hardly a knock-down price). At least one other of Richard's friends and neighbours also rallied to the court. John Catterick of Stanwick was appointed on 7 March to the Commission of the Peace and a week later to a commission to enquire into the goods and chattels of the Yorkist lords in the county. It may only have been Richard's uncertain health which kept him off these important commissions. The revolution of 1460-1461, which led eventually to Edward IV's seizure of the throne, reversed all this. On 8 October his grants of earlier in the year were revoked by Act of Parliament, but for the time being, Salisbury could not reimpose his authority as the whole of Yorkshire was firmly in Lancastrian hands.[56] Clervaux himself presumably was not fit enough to join Margaret of Anjou's army mustering in the county for the final test of strength with the Yorkists, although he may have sent a detachment of servants and tenants. Richard had to sit at Croft during the early months of 1461, awaiting events until news reached him, quite possibly brought by fleeing troops, of the Lancastrians' shattering defeat at Towton on 29 March. With the establishment of the new regime in which the new Neville Lord of Middleham, the Earl of Warwick, was all powerful, Clervaux and all the loyal Lancastrian gentry of Richmondshire had to start picking up the pieces again. For Richard Clervaux, his old lines of communication with the Middleham connection were still open. Sir James Strangways was now retained by Warwick, with enhanced fees, and was Speaker of the House of Commons in 1461 and Richard's uncle Thomas was now Lord Lumley, restored to his family title and serving with Warwick in the pacification of the Scottish Marches. It was perhaps through one of these two that Warwick was persuaded to press Richard's suit with the new king while he was staying at Middleham in January 1463. For it was 'at thinstance' of Warwick that Edward IV issued his warrant authorising Clervaux 'to abide at youre awne place or any other to your ease' on account of his infirmity. Clervaux's exemption from all public service may have been sought because at that time pressure was being put on him to join the forces besieging the Northumberland castles. A proviso in the letter carefully spelled out that Clervaux was always to be prepared to send his servants and tenants arrayed for the defence of the land,

> in competent nombre to the same entent accordyng with your degree as other
> gentylmen of the cuntre about you of like reputacon shall doo.[57]

But it is nevertheless a testimony not only to the Yorkist's need for support in the area, but also to Clervaux's capacity for survival, that he was already being granted favours within two years of the establishment of the Yorkist dynasty. There was obviously no question of his going to the wall for Henry VI.

During Edward IV's reign, Clervaux drew closer to the Middleham connection, although he does not appear to have become a feed member of it. He was, as contemporaries put it, a well-wisher to Warwick and then Gloucester. Several of his friends were retained by both men. In addition to Strangways and Conyers, William Frank of Kneeton and Thomas Mountford of Hackforth were both receiving Warwick's fee in 1465. Clervaux played no recorded part in the upheavals of 1469-71, but it is no surprise that he found it necessary to purchase a royal pardon on 5 November 1472. One may reasonably guess that he publicly declared himself for the Readeption of Henry VI. Richard of Gloucester's succession to Warwick's position in the north through his marriage to his daughter Anne caused no apparent tremors amongst the gentry of Richmondshire and the king's brother easily donned the mantle of his erstwhile enemy. New men were retained by the new lord of Middleham: Rowland, a younger son of Sir Ralph Pudsay and brother of William, rector of Croft, was retained by Gloucester on 26 October 1471, with a fee of £5; another was Clervaux's neighbour at Eryholme, Sir Thomas Markenfield, retained in December with a fee of £10; and a third was Sir Roger Conyers of Wynyard retained in September 1473 with a fee of £6 13s. 4d.[58] Clervaux's closer association with Gloucester's all powerful circle is perhaps indicated by the appointment of Richard Ratcliffe, one of Gloucester's most trusted servants, to the stewardship of the free court of East Cowton. Such stewardships were often employed in political patronage; at a higher level William, Lord Hastings, the trusted confidant of King Edward IV, had collected a string of stewardships from anxious or ambitious noblemen and women. Ratcliffe, who was then constable of Gloucester's fortress at Barnard Castle, was steward of East Cowton by the middle of 1476. Moreover, Clervaux's path to favour with the duke may well have been smoothed by the presence of his wife's nephew, John Vavasour, in Gloucester's council.[59] Later, one of Clervaux's daughters, Elizabeth, was to marry another of Gloucester's retainers, William Clerionet, as her second husband. It was thus apparently the normal course of action for Clervaux and Rowland Place to turn eventually to Gloucester in 1478 to settle their differences.[60] The full extent to which Richard had become involved in Gloucester's affinity was revealed during the usurpation of the throne; for on 26 September 1483, in gratitude for the recent unspecified services of both Richard and his son Marmaduke, Clervaux, who already held by King Richard's grant the offices of steward and receiver of the lordship of Manfield during the minority of John FitzHenry (his grandson, be it remembered), was additionally granted the whole revenue of the lordship without account. What the service was we do not know, but it may possibly have been that Marmaduke Clervaux had taken a 'competent nombre' of servants and tenants, defensively arrayed, to London in the company of Ralph, Lord Neville of Raby at the end of June. That Richard remained close to the new king is confirmed by the grant to 'the King's servant', Richard Clervaux esquire, of a tun of wine from the customs at Hull on 10 August 1484.[61] What part he or his men played in 1485 we do not know, but Richard III's defeat and death at Bosworth was potentially more disastrous to Clervaux than the failure of the House of Lancaster in 1461, for he and the men of Richmondshire had put all their eggs in King Richard's basket.

In some ways, the last five years of Richard Clervaux's life are the most remarkable in his long political career. The destruction of Richard III meant also the destruction of the Middleham connection which had been a steadily growing force in English politics since 1450. In the last eighteen months it had even been the instrument by which Richard III had ruled the antagonistic south.[62] In the aftermath of Bosworth it was thrown into disarray. It is not surprising that several of the gentry and lesser inhabitants of Richmondshire found it difficult to accept Henry Tudor and provided the only sustained resistance to the new king. In the spring of April 1486, while Henry VII was making his first visit to York, these 'ingrates from the north', as the Crowland Continuator called them, were reported to be gathering under Lord Lovell 'beyond Middleham'. In the following year the Earl of Lincoln, after landing with Lambert Simnel in Lancashire, made straight to north Yorkshire where he believed, 'he hath frendes enough upon the land'. And while Lincoln marched south into Nottinghamshire to take on the King's army at Stoke, John, Lord Scrope of Bolton led a contingent of Richmondshire men in a vain attempt to seize York. Even as late as 1489, there were treasonable disturbances in Wensleydale and Swaledale and it has reasonably been suggested that one of the causes of the murder of Henry Percy, earl of Northumberland, in the same year was lingering resentment against his desertion of King Richard at Bosworth.[63] Henry Tudor found it difficult to win friends in Richmondshire in the first five years of his reign.

But Henry VII found one in old Richard Clervaux. Clervaux probably helped rally Richmondshire to the crown in the summer of 1487, for on 10 August, at Durham, Henry was pleased to renew the grant of a tun of wine from Hull to the newly dubbed Sir Richard Clervaux. Two years later his son was escheator for Yorkshire. But Richard himself was still unable to take up any royal or public office and was obliged to renew his letters of exemption on 20 June 1489.[64] But now, age was creeping up on him as well, and in the following year he died. In these last years, as befitted the new régime, Richard made the most of his old Lancastrian connections. His epitaph, inscribed on his vast table tomb in Croft church, reads (in translation):

> Here buried beneath this marble lies Richard Clervaux,
> One time lord of Croft, God have mercy on him;
> He was esquire to the body of King Henry the sixth,
> Whom God brought to the stars of high heaven;
> Next he was of the blood of both Edward the fourth,
> And of Richard the third in the third degree;
> Who died in the year of our Lord fourteen hundred and ninety.[65]

It is Richard's politically remembered service to Henry VI which is given prominence here, not his whole-hearted support for the late King Richard. And it is expressed in terms which clearly reflect Henry Tudor's campaign to have the last Lancastrian canonized. The epitaph thus reflects not only a Lancastrian attachment, but also a newly found commitment to the Tudors. To make the point clear, the northern and southern sides of the tomb were decorated with the arms of Vavasour (for his wife) and Clervaux (sable, a saltire or) each surrounded by a collar of Lancastrian SS. Thus Clervaux ended where he began; a loyal servant of the House of Lancaster.

In his Ford Lectures delivered over fifty years ago, C.L. Kingsford made the following comment:

> the Stonor Letters afford us no evidence to suggest that either social disorder or civil war necessarily affected the lives of those who through their prudence or good fortune were not entangled in either. What we do get is a picture of the country gentleman busy with the management of his estates, taking his share in the work of local administration, living in friendly intercourse with neighbours in like circumstances to himself...[66]

This could stand as well for Richard Clervaux as it does for Thomas Stonor. Clervaux was typical of the county gentry of his age. With great circumspection he avoided entanglement in the civil wars. As Longstaffe put it, 'like his own willows in the holmes of Croft, Clervaux prudently bent to every storm and was always a loyal subject to whatever king was uppermost at that day'.[67] One cannot be sure whether this was entirely of his own volition. There is reason to suppose that Clervaux was forced to withdraw from the centre of national politics by his own infirmity: not many men abandoned willingly a promising career at the court of Henry VI. But whether or not it was engendered by his physical condition, Clervaux's political dexterity is apparent: he not only survived, but also prospered from his troubled and uncertain times. Like so many of his contemporaries, he began a loyal Lancastrian, became a Yorkist and accepted Tudor. No doubt in his closing years he found it easy to sweep under the carpet his one-time attachment to the last Yorkist and convinced himself that he had always been a Lancastrian at heart, but his pragmatism, even cynicism, is typical of the established country squire in fifteenth-century England.

For it is the case that in the later fifteenth century, men like Clervaux had come to be wary of dynastic politics and their attendant risks.[68] Far more important to them was the possession and enjoyment of their inheritances and the maintenance of their 'reputation' within their own local communities. It was Clervaux's standing with his tenants and with his neighbours in Richmondshire that mattered most to him. This played a crucial role in shaping his political career, but it was also reflected in his fierce pride in his blood and place. Clervaux prided himself as being of the ancient landed gentry of Richmondshire. The monolithic tomb, the assumption of the title of lord of the manor, the time-consuming concentration of his hold on the township of Croft, and above all the compilation of the cartulary itself which records the process, all suggest a man determined to let no one forget that he was master of Croft-on-Tees. It is arguable that Clervaux's career after his withdrawal from court was guided by his determination that nothing should disrupt his assumed role as lord of Croft: kings could come and kings could go, but his blood would be lords of Croft for ever.[69]

Appendix 1: Land Measurement

The land granted to William Clervaux by Roald son of Roald came to 20 oxgangs and 31 acres. It is impossible to give a conversion of this into statute acres. This is because the measurements of neither oxgangs nor acres was uniform in the middle ages. An oxgang, customarily an eighth of a carucate, is generally taken to be 12 acres. But within the neighbourhood of Croft there was wide variation. At Stapleton in 1465, an oxgang was said to contain 8 acres. At Hurworth the 12 acres granted to Henry Tailboys and Joan his wife in the early fifteenth century were said to be an oxgang. But in Bondgate, Darlington in 1506, the bishop's demesne was measured in oxgangs of 15 acres each.[70] I have not been able to find any specification of the size of an oxgang in Croft. In 1410, John Clervaux exchanged one and a half oxgangs, 3 acres and one cottage in Croft for two messuages and two oxgangs in Walmire, which suggests that an oxgang was taken to be 8 acres in those two places.[71] But even if this is correct, one is still left with the problem of exactly what an acre was. There were three kinds of acre; measured, customary and fiscal. There is no way of telling which was used at Croft; indeed all three could have been. That customary acres were used is indicated by the usage in several deeds of the division of 1 acre into 4 selions (or strips) rather than roods.[72] The exact size of a selion and therefore an acre of selions must have varied according to the topography. It is worth recalling Maitland's remark that

> to tell a man that one of these acre strips was not an acre because it was too small would at one time have been like telling him that his foot was not a foot because it fell short of twelve inches.[73]

Thus an oxgang of 8 acres could well have included more than 8 statute acres. Because of this, I have not tried to make concise comparisons, or offered exact totals of land: I have everywhere cited the actual measurements given in the cartulary.

Appendix 2: Richard Clervaux's Epitaph[74]

The translation of the epitaph enscribed on Clervaux's tomb has posed problems for historians. The text is as follows:

> Clervaux Ricardus jacet hic sub marmorie[75] clausus:
> Crofte quondam dominus huic miserere deus:
> armiger Henrici regis et pro corpore sexti:
> quem deus exelsi duxit ad astra poli:
> sanguinis Edwardi quarti ternique Ricardi:
> gradibus in ternis alter utrique fuit:
> qui obiit anno domini mcccclxxxx.

It is the fifth and sixth lines, the third of the elegiac couplets, especially the words *alter utrique,* which have caused the difficulty. Longstaffe was satisfied with '(he was) of the blood of Edward IV and Richard III in the third degree the one to the other',[76] a translation which makes little sense and effectively avoids the problem. Thompson argued that Longstaffe missed the point of *alter,* which he suggested referred to *armiger pro corpore* in the third line. Thus he offered a translation of the second and third couplets as follows:

> Esquire of the body to King Henry VI, whom God brought to the stars of high heaven, he was of the blood of both Edward IV and the third Richard in the third degree *and was also esquire to both.*[77]

This is both historically and grammatically unsatisfactory. Historically there is no evidence at all to corroborate the suggestion that Clervaux was esquire to the two Yorkists. That he was esquire to Edward IV is entirely implausible. That he was an esquire to Richard III is more conceivable, but here all we have is the evidence that he was the King's servant, a very loose designation, applied to well-wishers as much as to men actually retained by the King and distinct from the formal and honoured position of Esquire to the Body. In view of what we know of Clervaux's ill health it is unlikely that he was ever more than a well-wisher. Grammatically we are faced with the awkward latin of the whole piece. *Alter* should refer to the subject of the epitaph, *Clervaux Ricardus,* and not to *armiger* as Thompson suggested. In addition to meaning 'the other of two', 'one of two' (the sense adopted by Longstaffe), it is regularly used in latin of all periods as an ordinal numerical adjective with the sense of 'second' or 'next'. This could well be the sense here, following an implied 'first' in the second couplet. Thompson's translation of *uterque* as 'both' raises no problem. Thus an alternative translation of the third couplet could be: '*next* he was of the blood of *both* Edward the fourth and of Richard the third in the third degree'. This makes complete sense historically, for Richard Clervaux was just this. All three had a common great-grandfather in John, Lord Neville (d. 1388). Clervaux's maternal grandmother was John's daughter Eleanor, the sister of Ralph Neville, earl of Westmorland, the Yorkist kings' maternal grandfather.[78] They were, in short, second cousins.

Thompson was undoubtedly right when he wrote, 'it must be owned that the author was hampered in clearness of expression by the exigencies of latin verse', and we may never be certain of his exact intention; but the translation given above is suggested as more satisfactory than those offered by either Thompson or Longstaffe.

8

RICHARD III, HENRY VII AND RICHMOND

On 3 September 1485, Henry VII entered the city of London in triumph after his victory over Richard III at Bosworth. He made straight for St Paul's Cathedral, where he laid up his banners of St George, the Red Dragon and the Dun Cow at the Rood inside the north door. The banners of St George and Cadwallader are familiar enough; the banner of the Dun Cow was almost certainly, as Henry VIII later explained, 'apertaining of antiquity unto his Earldom of Richmond'.[1] In other words, Henry VII perceived his cause as not only rescuing the kingdom, but also as recovering his earldom from the man who had usurped them both.

Richard III, as duke of Gloucester, had occupied the lordship of Richmond, the head of the widespread Honour of Richmond, since 1471; he had held the town and castle of Richmond itself since 1478. The estates of the earldom of Richmond were scattered through several counties, principally Cambridgeshire, Hertfordshire, Lincolnshire and Westmorland in addition to Yorkshire. These, which had been granted by Edward IV to his brother, George, duke of Clarence, had been in the hands of the Crown since the duke's execution in 1478.[2] But possession of the lordship of Richmond itself had followed a different course from the rest of the Honour for most of the fifteenth century.

The story of who was lord of Richmond in the fifteenth century is complex. The appropriate starting point for an understanding of the events and circumstances of 1485 is the death fifty years earlier of John, duke of Bedford. Following Bedford's death without heirs, the lordship, one-third of which was charged with his widow's dower, reverted to the Crown. It remained in royal hands until 1444, when Henry VI granted his two-thirds to Richard Neville, earl of Salisbury, at first for life, but in a new grant five years later in tail male. Salisbury, who was the lord of nearby Middleham, had held the office of steward and chief forester of Richmond certainly since 1439, and in all likelihood during Bedford's life. He had probably had his eye on the lordship itself since the duke's death, as his father, Ralph, earl of Westmorland (d. 1425) had held it for life after 1399.[3] He now had the opportunity to go one step further than his father and to consolidate the two lordships into one hereditary fiefdom controlling Richmondshire.

The earl of Salisbury's ambitions were somewhat blighted, however, when in 1452 Henry VI created Edmund Tudor earl of Richmond and granted him the lordship as part of his hereditary endowment. The title and the endowment were inherited by his posthumously-born son, Henry (the future Henry VII) in 1456. Thus, in these characteristically contradictory grants by Henry VI, was created the conflict for possession of Richmond between the Tudor earl and the Nevilles which was not resolved until 1485. In the circumstances of the 1450s, '60s and '70s Henry Tudor stood little chance of making a reality of his claim. At first a child, latterly an exile, he could do nothing against the might of the Nevilles. Indeed the evidence from the administration of the lordship of Middleham demonstrates that first the earl of Salisbury, then, after his death in 1460, his son Warwick the Kingmaker, and finally after 1471 the Kingmaker's political heir, Richard of Gloucester, kept a tight grip on Richmond whatever alternative dispositions were made. In 1462, for instance, Edward IV granted it, along with the rest of the Honour to his brother George of Clarence. The part relating to Richmond was never enforced, for in 1465-6 Warwick received the revenues from the constituent manors, continued to employ, as his father had done, a joint steward for both the lordships of Middleham and Richmond, and had even used Richmond Castle as a place for meetings of his council to settle leases of parts of the Richmond estate.[4] Whatever settlement either Henry VI or Edward IV made in law, the Nevilles ignored in practice.

The freedom with which the lords of Middleham could disregard royal letters concerning Richmond is revealed in the manner in which Richard of Gloucester took control after 1471. A grateful Edward IV granted to him all the hereditary estates of Warwick the Kingmaker, including Middleham and, by implication, Richmond under the terms of the grant of 1449. At the same time, he confirmed Clarence in his possession of the Honour. Matters were further confused in 1472 when the dowager duchess of Bedford finally died, and Edward IV granted to Clarence all the parts of the earldom of Richmond that she had been holding in dower since 1435. But again the Middleham estate accounts show that Edward IV's grants to Clarence were not worth the parchment they were written on. In 1473, Gloucester not only received the same revenues from two-thirds of Richmond as Warwick had enjoyed, but also collected those due from the dower portion and paid additional fees to his administrators for handling them. In the following year Edward IV enforced a compromise on his brothers, who had almost come to blows over this and other disputes, in which Gloucester kept the full income of the estates of Richmond, with the exception of the fee farm of the town and possession of the castle. But when four years later Clarence fell from favour, Gloucester picked up these as well.[5] It looked then as though the ambition of Richard Nevillee senior to create a unified hereditary lordship for his heirs in Richmondshire would be fulfilled. However, by becoming king in 1483, Gloucester brought this lordship into the crown estate, and took full possession of the rest of the earldom of Richmond, previously occupied by Clarence. What dispositions he might subsequently have made cannot be known; for the two years of his reign he kept all these lands in hand, using the northern estates to support and finance his new Council of the North. Tudor's claim for possession of his earldom now lay against the Crown in the person of Richard.

What was the lordship of Richmond for the possession of which Richard III and Henry Tudor fought at Bosworth? First it was the castle with its feudal income of relief and wards, worth approximately £45 p.a. in 1485. Secondly it was the town of Richmond, which paid a fee farm of £12 p.a. to its lord. Thirdly it was the manors of Aldbrough St John, Bowes, Catterick, Danby, Forcett, Gilling and Moulton together worth approximately £230 p.a. Fourthly, there was the income generated by the vaccaries (dairy farms) maintained in Arkengarthdale and on the moors between the Greta and Swale at the Hopes, Helwith, Holgate and Kexwith. These and small-scale exploitation of lead mines were worth some £55 p.a. Fifthly, there was the income from the tolls levied on the passage of goods through the lordship on the roads at Leeming, Dishforth, Great Smeaton and on Stainmore worth a further £40. Of these, the tollgate on Stainmore was the most profitable, being leased in 1485 to the appropriately-named Thomas Cook for £20. The total annual income, including further miscellaneous rents such as those of tenements and the dye-

47. *The 'Dun Cow' of Warwick, an example of the beasts at the feet of the lords of Warwick in John Rous's Roll. (English version, British Library)*

works in Richmond itself, Earl's Orchard and the profits of the local courts was something in excess of £400.[6] And, if one bears in mind that Richmondshire was a great Liberty, in which the earl exercised the powers of sheriff and held the right to petty criminal jurisdiction in the five wapentakes of Hallikeld, Hang East and West and Gilling East and West, one can appreciate that the lordship was a prize worth fighting for.

However, the value of Richmond to its lord in 1485 had been significantly reduced over the preceding fifty years. In 1436-7 the manors of Aldbrough, Catterick and Gilling, for instance, generated a net income of £124; three years later this was reduced to £96; and by the 1460s it had fallen further to some £75, from which it had barely recovered by the beginning of Henry VII's reign. The principal cause of this catastrophic collapse in the rent produced by prime arable manors of the lordship was the agrarian crisis of 1438-40, which had significantly reduced rental incomes everywhere in the north-east of England. The detailed effects on these manors are revealed in some of the surviving accounts for Aldbrough. By 1465, the annual rent per acre of the bovates which made up the arable land was permanently reduced from 14s. to 8s., leading to a reduction of £6 12s. The rents of nine cottages fell from £1 8s. 9d. to just 12s. 11d. The two forges and the common oven could no longer attract tenants. And by 1473 the upper mill, nominally worth a rent of £2 3s. 4d., was also out of operation.[7] Only in the pastoral economy of the upper dales and moors, where the demand for beef and dairy products held up, was revenue in 1485 comparable to that enjoyed half a century earlier.

The effect of this local economic decline was bound to be felt in Richmond itself. In 1440 the burgesses appealed to the King, then retaining the earldom in his hands, for a reduction in their fee farm from £40. They explained how, in recent years, the prosperity of their market, which had relied on their position at the point of exchange between the grain producing lowlands of the upper vale of York and the pastoral produce of the dales in Yorkshire and beyond, had been undermined not only by the competition of other, newer markets, such as those at Middleham and Barnard Castle, but also by pestilence and epidemics. The petition did not recite the collapse of

48. George, duke of Clarence. A sixteenth-century portrait from a set of the 'Constables of Queenborough Castle', Brocket Hall.

the local agrarian economy in the immediate past, but the timing of the petition strongly suggests that the inhabitants of the town, depending as they did on the well-being of local farmers, were suffering as greatly as their rural neighbours. Notwithstanding their pleas of poverty, the townsmen had been able to scrape together just over £30 towards the payment of the fee farm in 1439-40. But the general plight of the town is confirmed by the dilapidated state of its principal corn mills. The town mill (at Whitcliffe) should have been rented for £5 in 1439-40, but it was in the hands of the King for want of tenants and described as totally in decay. The Castle Mills, which in 1442 were similarly valued at no more than £5, had virtually to be rebuilt by new tenants in 1456. The petition of 1440, sponsored by the steward of the lordship, the earl of Salisbury himself, was successful and, in the following year, the fee farm was reduced as requested to £19 13s. 8d. Trade could not have significantly improved thereafter, and indeed would appear to have contracted further, for by 1483 the fee farm had been cut once more to £12.[8]

A contributory factor to the economic decline of Richmond in the fifteenth century was the collapse of the cloth manufacturing industry of Richmondshire, which at the end of the fourteenth century had been more prosperous than the West Riding, and second only to the City of York in the yield of taxation in Yorkshire. After 1450, many of the fulling mills of the district went out of operation as the demand for Richmondshire cloth shrank and the West Riding towns prospered. The Richmond dye-works remained in business at a rent of £4 in 1485, but the level of production had been permanently reduced. As yet the mining of lead in Swaledale and Arkengarthdale offered little compensation. The earl of Warwick had sanctioned expenditure on mines in Arkengarthdale in 1466, but the profits from lead mined there remained small (£3 18s. in 1488-9) until the very end of the century. Richmond in 1485 was a town deep in recession.[9]

Of the people of Richmond little is known. The names of some tenants of the earl are recorded, usually after they had ceased to pay rent and their tenements had remained unlet. Thus in 1486, a

49. The keep, Richmond Castle, Yorkshire.

financial review of the lordship for Henry VII revealed that John Rose, William Smith, Gilbert Dereham, Edward Copeland, Robert Hobson, William Plummer and Elizabeth Burdon had ceased to be tenants. It was also reported that £2 10s. had been spent on repairs to several tenements over the past three years and that various burgage holdings, legally distinct from the earl's private estate in the town, in Frenchgate, Millgate, Aldbiggin, Finkle Street and Gallowgate were vacant. John Eston was the tenant of the dye-works; John Cock of Earl's Orchard; and William Burgh esquire, of nearby Brough Hall, the tenant of the Castle Mills. Burgh was also the landlord of several tenements in the town which he had inherited from his ancestor, a prominent and successful townsman in the fourteenth century.[10] Perhaps the wealthiest townsman in 1485 was William Clerionet, who in 1483 married, as his second wife, one of the daughters of Richard Clervaux of Croft, had been retained jointly with his first wife by the earl of Warwick with a fee of £6 13s. 4d. in 1466 and in 1483-6 was one of the four collectors of the fee farm.[11]

The other collectors of the fee farm were local gentlemen. The society of a small, impoverished market town was inevitably dominated by the local gentry, many of whom like William Burgh or Roger Aske, of Aske Hall, resided nearby and held property in the town. Of these by far and away the most important was Sir John Conyers of Hornby. It was he, his father, or their deputies, as constable of the castle, steward of the lordship under successive lords since 1450 and, since the 1430s, bailiff of the wapentake courts, who had provided a continuity and stability in local government that for the people of Richmond was more tangible than the changes in lordship and conflicts over title which preoccupied the Crown and rival magnates. And Sir John Conyers was a master of political survivorship. He had served the earl of Salisbury, the earl of Warwick and the duke of Gloucester with distinction. In 1483, his reward for his assistance in the usurpation of the throne by Richard III was promotion to the Order of the Garter, followed soon afterwards by the grant of revenues from the estates of Middleham and Richmond to the value of £133 13s. 4d. p.a. And, while Henry VII on his accession at first removed him from his offices, he was restored in February 1486 and his annuity retained. Although, because of his suspect loyalty, he was relieved of his duties again in 1487, in 1493, three years after his death, his heir and grandson, Sir William Conyers was regranted the same local offices. As far as the exercise of local rule was concerned, there was in fact for the people of Richmond very little change throughout the fifteenth century.[12]

Most of the peerage and gentry of Richmondshire followed the lead of Sir John Conyers in 1485. Although they may have benefited briefly from the support they gave to Richard III, few of them were committed personally to him. Their loyalty lay to the Crown, not to the individual who wore it. What was true for the local landed élite, was unavoidable for the townspeople of Richmond. Richard III, for all his northern association, was a more remote figure than Sir John Conyers; an occasional visitor no doubt (although never recorded), but one in a line of great lords of Richmond in recent years. Henry Tudor, when he recovered the title and the property in 1485, may well have appeared to local inhabitants to be yet another distant and transient earl. And they would have been right, although in an unanticipated way, for the new earl (and king) showed little interest in the town and lordship from which he took his title except as a source of revenue. Later in his reign he thought nothing of renaming his palace of Sheen on the Thames, and the insignificant town outside its gates, in honour of his earldom of Richmond. The Dun Cow came finally to graze in the luxuriant pastures of Surrey rather than on the rugged banks of the Swale.

9

St Cuthbert and the Hog: Richard III and the County Palatine of Durham, 1471-85

In the first year of the reign of King Richard III, Richard Redman, bishop of St Asaph, wrote to Robert Ebbchester, prior of the convent of St Cuthbert at Durham, asking for the presentation of Master William Brown to the vicarage of Merrington at its next vacancy. Ebbchester regretted that he could not, on this occasion, oblige the bishop. The reason, he explained, was that Sir Richard Ratcliffe had shown him a grant by his predecessor of the nomination to the same vicarage. He and his brethren had decided that they had no choice but to ratify this grant 'considering the grett rewll that he [Ratcliffe] berith under the kynges grace in oure cuntrey'.[1] It was customary for the priory to respect the wishes of prominent local laymen in the presentation to livings in its gift; to show such favour to an outsider and newcomer such as Ratcliffe was unusual. But these were evidently exceptional times. Ebbchester and his brethren recognised that it was then a fact of contemporary political life that within the patrimony of St Cuthbert, as well as in all England, the Rat ruled under the Hog.

Richard III's influence within the county palatine of Durham, ostensibly governed as a quasi-independent regality by its bishop, has not passed unnoticed since Ebbchester's time.[2] But the subject still awaits detailed examination. This chapter makes a first step in that direction. Drawing principally upon episcopal and priory records, it tells the story of how Gloucester gained control of the palatinate and explores his relationships with successive bishops and the county's political élite. The completeness with which Richard, first as duke and then as king, dominated Durham's affairs clearly emerges. The importance of the county palatine in Gloucester's northern dominion before 1483 is confirmed. Moreover, Richard's approach to palatine affairs after 1483 suggests that as king he was unwilling to surrender this personal supremacy to others. More light is thus thrown on the character of Richard III's kingship, especially his policy towards the north.

The story begins at Barnard Castle, the lordship north of the Tees acquired by Gloucester in the early 1470s. He gained possession of this estate only with the grudging acceptance of Bishop Laurence Booth, against the outright opposition of George, duke of Clarence, and at the expense of Anne, dowager countess of Warwick whom many considered to be the rightful owner. The protracted struggle for possession between these parties, resolved by October 1474 at the latest, remains, as William Hutchinson wrote two centuries ago, 'an obscure part of our provincial history'.[3] The occupant in April 1471 at the restoration of Edward IV would

50. Barnard Castle, County Durham. The Great Chamber and Hall, with oriel window (centre), Round tower and Postern tower.

seem to have been Bishop Booth, by virtue of a grant of 6 June 1470 by the king, following the seizure of the exiled earl of Warwick's estates.[4] This represented a signal, if short-lived, triumph for Booth, for successive bishops had endeavoured since the early-fourteenth century to recover the lordship for the palatinate from the heirs of Guy Beauchamp, earl of Warwick. The grant of June 1470 was a recognition by Edward IV that Barnard Castle had been wrongly forfeited to the crown by Edward I and that a reversal of this in the name of Edward III (though never subsequently implemented) was valid.[5] Booth had tried earlier to recover the lordship. In 1459, following the rebellion of Richard Neville, earl of Warwick, it had been granted to him. In April 1461, taking advantage of the presence of the victorious Edward IV at Durham, he had vainly attempted to persuade the king not to restore it to Warwick. He even produced a suitably contrite Robert Rodes to confess that in 1439, at an inquisition postmortem on Richard Beauchamp, he had wrongly given evidence to the harm of 'the libertei and title of the chirche of St Cuthbert' that Barnard Castle lay in Northumberland.[6] In 1470, when the tables were turned once more, Edward conceded Booth's request, not only depriving Warwick of the enjoyment of the revenues of his estate, but also denying his countess her right and title therein.

However, 1470 had been an exceptional year. Edward had then desperately needed Booth's support, just as he also had needed the support of Henry Percy, who was restored in the same year to the earldom of Northumberland. His political judgement had been rewarded, for Booth proved to be one of the few clerics to abstain from the acts of readeption. Yet by the summer of 1471, the king was overtaken by another, even more pressing, political debt to pay to his brother George, duke of Clarence, whose timely change of coat had done so much to ensure his restoration. Thus, Clarence was granted all the lands to which the heirs general of Warwick had hereditary expectation, including those belonging to and claimed by the dowager countess.[7] He was no more likely than his mother-in-law to accept the exclusion of Barnard Castle. At this stage Richard of Gloucester had no interest in it. He was occupied in establishing himself in the tail male Neville lands of Middleham, Sheriff Hutton and Penrith. By February 1472, however, he had become aware of the opportunity of gaining a greater share in the fallen earl's inheritance by championing the cause of his younger daughter Anne, who had been shut out by Clarence and her elder sister Isabel. In the agreement reached at Sheen that spring, Clarence was forced to concede that in principle the expectations of the sisters should be shared.[8] Thus, within a year of the Kingmaker's death, four parties came to press claims to Barnard Castle: Bishop Booth, the Dowager Countess Anne, Clarence and Gloucester, although there is no evidence that as yet Booth, the possessor, was willing to give way to any of his rivals.

Developments in 1473 required Edward IV to unravel this confusion of his own making. 1473 was a year of renewed crisis. Not only had the king to cope with worsening relationships between Clarence and Gloucester, but he also had to settle an incipient clash between Gloucester and Northumberland as well as to fend off raids by dissident Lancastrians in the south-west, East Anglia and even the north-east.[9] There was considerable pressure on him to put his own house in order. It is conceivable that the council meeting held at Nottingham in May which sought to resolve the differences between Northumberland and Gloucester, also agreed a strategy to settle Barnard Castle. Was it only coincidence that the Countess Anne was released from close guard in sanctuary and that she travelled north under Gloucester's protection shortly afterwards? If it were true, as was rumoured, that she was restored so as to settle her inheritance on Gloucester, a journey north can only mean that Barnard Castle was the part of her inheritance at issue.[10] Certainly, any agreement between Booth and Gloucester which denied Clarence would have been greatly strengthened by her being a party to it. The bishop's presence at Sheriff Hutton on at least one occasion in 1473 shows that Booth and Gloucester were at this time in consultation.[11] Moreover, Booth's promotion to the chancery on 27 July could be interpreted as a reward and consolation for his cooperation.[12] That Booth later contributed to the settlement of the dispute between the royal dukes is evident since he presided over the session of parliament which passed legislation to partition the Warwick inheritance. It seems plausible, therefore, that Booth was a party to the final settlement and that he agreed, if grudgingly, to surrender Barnard Castle once more. There is, however, no surviving grant to Richard of Gloucester recorded on either the royal or the episcopal patent roll. Perhaps Booth refused formally to abandon his claim and the king tactfully declined to reassert his own overlordship. Thus, Gloucester ran out the winner, but his title remained vulnerable to episcopal challenge.

For lack of a surviving grant, it is not known when Gloucester entered Barnard Castle. The earliest surviving evidence of his occupation is the record of a payment made on 31 October 1474 to Matthew Metcalfe, 'instaurer of Middleham, for cattle and sheep supplied for victualling the duke's household there.'[13] The evidence that in the autumn of 1473 Gloucester was retaining men within the bishopric with the resources of Middleham suggests that he was then not yet in possession of Barnard Castle.[14] On the other hand, the first of the duke's recorded visits to the priory of Durham in April 1474, on which occasion he was received into its fraternity, suggests that he had acquired an interest north of the Tees six months later.[15] The spring of 1474, which accords with the timing of other transfers of land involved in the final settlement of the Warwick inheritance, seems a likely date.[16] Approximately three years after the Kingmaker's death, Gloucester was installed in Barnard Castle. Although his title was weak, his possession, achieved after what were complex, and obscure, machinations, was thereafter to remain unchallenged.

51. Richard III's Boar Badge once on a house in Newgate, Barnard Castle, County Durham. Now removed to the Bowes Museum.

The castle of Barnard and barony of Gainford, to give it its ancient name, occupied an extensive tract of land along the north bank of the River Tees, running for twenty miles from its source to Whorlton below Barnard Castle itself (excluding Eggleston), through Gainford and Piercebridge, to the outlying manors of Longnewton and Newsham-on-Tees between Stockton and Darlington.[17] It dominated the extreme south-west of the later county of Durham (see Map 6). Gainford was the original, Anglo-Saxon, capital of the lordship, which explains why Barnard Castle itself was ecclesiastically but a chapelry in its parish. But the Norman castle, built by Bernard at the end of the eleventh century, with the town outside its walls, was the fifteenth-century centre.[18] From such a large estate, the lords of Barnard Castle drew a surprisingly modest revenue. The net revenue charged to the receiver in 1390-91 totalled £362. By 1420-21, it had fallen to £279. The earl of Warwick's receiver-general took delivery of £267 in 1390-91, but in 1417-18, the yield to him had fallen to just over £173.[19] A view of account for the year 1488-89 reveals that, after allowance of decays and wastes, the estate was expected to yield just under £325. Of this net revenue, some £25 was consumed by the fees and wages of bailiffs, reeves, foresters and parkers who were paid at source. Actual deliveries of cash to the receiver by officials only totalled approximately £230, leaving substantial new arrears.[20] No such documentation survives for the tenure of Richard III either as duke or as king. However, warrants for expenditure on works and fees as well as for delivery of cash in 1483-85 show that the receiver was committed by the king to find at least £244 in 1483-84 and £335 in 1484-85 beyond the normal fees of estate officials.[21] It is unlikely that the net revenue available to Richard III was significantly different from that available four or five years later. It seems, therefore, especially in his second year as king, that he was spending up to and beyond the estate's means.

Yet Barnard Castle possessed attractions other than financial. It occupied a strategic point in the geographical distribution of Gloucester's estates, linking his Richmondshire lordship of Middleham with Penrith in Cumberland.[22] This was probably one of the reasons why the duke, unlike any of the later Beauchamp lords, chose to make the castle one of his residences. He is known to have been there in the autumn of 1474, in August 1480 and May 1484.[23] Both archaeological and documentary evidence of his building programme in the castle has survived. In the later decades of the fifteenth century, the Mortham Tower was rebuilt and, probably, a suite of residential rooms opened between it and the Round Tower to the north. In this range is set the oriel window looking out over the Tees in which today is set a badge of the white boar. It seems likely that these are the works for which financial provision was made in 1483-85. As pertinent is the archaeological evidence of a lavish feast held at the castle before new works blocked the old kitchen drain.[24] The castle was not the only building to receive attention. As king, Richard set aside £40 for repairs to the church of St Mary in the town.[25] One can reasonably suppose that the badge of the white boar set high on the exterior stonework of the east window of the south transept identifies the work carried out. But perhaps the most significant indication of Gloucester's personal identification with the lordship lies in his plan, never executed, to transform the chapel within the castle into a college consisting of a dean, twelve priests, ten chaplains and six choristers, supported by an endowment of 400 marks per annum – a scheme grander in conception than that actually established at Middleham.[26]

Richard of Gloucester, literally, left his mark more visibly on Barnard Castle than on any other of his lordships.[27] It is not surprising to find, therefore, that he drew several of his household and personal servants from its tenants.[28] Thomas Merley, his valet in 1477 and sergeant-at-arms in 1483-85, may have been a member of the Gainford family of free tenants; Thomas Fenton, yeoman of the crown, and Thomas Thursby yeoman of the king's chamber after 1483, came from Barnard Castle itself.[29] Miles Forest, infamous smotherer of princes, was reputedly a resident of the town and was groom of the wardrobe at the castle until his death in 1484.[30] And above all, there is Robert Brackenbury. Second son of Ralph Brackenbury of Denton in the parish of Gainford, Brackenbury acquired the manor and parcels of nearby Selaby in 1481 and 1482. Although he played no recorded role in the affairs of the lordship or the county palatine either before or after his master's accession to the throne, he rose to great prominence in the king's service.[31]

Barnard Castle's other and arguably greatest attraction to Richard of Gloucester was as a base for the extension of his influence north of the Tees. At first, however, his ambition was thwarted by Bishop Booth, who may have surrendered the lordship but certainly had no intention of conceding the leadership of his palatinate. Booth had only recently emerged victorious from a bitter feud with the Middleham Nevilles. He is an enigmatic figure. Neither persistent Lancastrian partisan, nor merely a polished courtier,[32] he became a zealous and often tactless defender of the liberties of his diocese. This zeal led him into bitter conflict with the monks of his own cathedral priory over issues such as its claim to archidiaconal jurisdiction.[33] And it led him to pursue the claim to Barnard Castle with obstinacy. He had alienated the Middleham Nevilles at the very start of his pontificate by, understandably, cancelling the over-generous fees granted to them by Bishop Robert Neville.[34] This was not simply a factional act, for Booth, throughout his pontificate, and unlike his predecessor and successor, refrained from using episcopal resources to pay fees for political services.[35] But it was hardly tactful and was compounded by the occupation of Barnard Castle in 1459 and the promotion of Raby Nevilles.[36] Warwick and his brothers had gained their revenge, and Booth had been humiliated, when they persuaded the king in December 1462 to seize the temporalities of the diocese and place its administration in their hands.[37] Booth therefore had cause to rejoice at Warwick's final destruction in 1471, although he soon had new reason to distrust his political heir.

There seems also to have been a fundamental difference of opinion between bishop and duke on Scottish policy. Booth as lord of Norham[38] and Gloucester as warden of the west march had a direct interest in Anglo-Scottish relations. Booth emerged after 1471 as a leading executive of peace negotiations which culminated in the Treaty of Edinburgh in November 1474.[39] Gloucester disassociated himself from this diplomacy (or was not to be trusted in it) and showed himself to be unhappy with the policy. Not only was he unwilling to hold march days as required, or, as admiral, to settle naval disputes; he also threatened, independently, to raid Scotland at the height of negotiations in 1474.[40] Even after the treaty was signed his reluctance to implement its terms in his march, and his own blatant act of piracy against a Scottish ship, clearly exasperated his brother, the king.[41]

It is not surprising, therefore, that Booth kept his new neighbour at arm's length. No employment was found in the bishopric for the duke or his servants; no fees or favours were offered. Only in the last months of the pontificate does there seem to have been a slight thaw. In May 1476 Booth agreed, in response to Gloucester's request, to the appropriation of the living of Seaham to the abbey of Coverham,[42] while on 13 June, John Redman, Gloucester's retainer and farmer of the priory's tithes at Little Chilton since 1469, was appointed bailiff of Bishop Auckland and a week later Sir Ralph Ashton became master forester of Crayke.[43] This late rapprochement may have been encouraged by knowledge that he was soon to be translated. Until then, the only contact that duke and bishop seem regularly to have maintained was through the legal counsel they shared.[44] On the other hand, Booth assiduously began again to cultivate the Nevilles of Raby, especially in the person of the young Ralph, Lord Neville, nephew and heir of the earl of Westmorland, who was restored in 1472 to his father's estates and title. Neville, who was active on the commissions of the peace and gaol delivery from 1471, in 1472 married Booth's niece, Isabel.[45] And shortly before Booth's translation to York, on 4 June 1476, he was appointed steward of the palatinate for life. The appointment was clearly a sinecure, for Neville was required to find from his fee of £40 and the profits of office the fee of the sitting steward, Thomas Middleton, who was retained as his deputy with his existing fee of £20.[46]

Booth's translation to York and the elevation of William Dudley to Durham in September 1476 was thus a relief to Gloucester; and indeed it proved a watershed in the duke's relationship with the palatinate.[47] Booth's powerful presence had effectively excluded him; Dudley's arrival allowed him quickly to assume the leadership of local society. Dudley, dean of the chapel royal and of St George's chapel, Windsor, had been one of the first to rally to Edward IV and Gloucester on their return from exile in 1471. He was one of the king's most trusted confidants.[48] Although well-born, he fitted precisely the category of king's servant so often preferred for Durham.[49] He proved to be a pliant and unambitious figurehead, willing to accede to the wishes of the king and his brother in most matters. In the first year of his pontificate, for instance, much royal concern was shown for the security of Norham castle, through which payments of Princess Cecily's dower to the king of Scots regularly passed. One of the new bishop's first acts (perhaps on royal prompting) was to appoint a commission to survey and repair all his castles.[50] The episcopal commission having achieved little, in the following September the king himself sent down two commissioners (Alexander Lee, royal chaplain and ambassador to Scotland, and Sir Richard Tunstall, knight of the body) to supervise the repairs. Dudley seems happily to have accepted this royal intervention and to have cooperated fully with the king's servants.[51] His backing seems also to have been given to the trial of the duke of Clarence in February 1478. Although the bishopric was unrepresented in the commons, a place was found as a member for Gatton, Surrey, for Roland Ludworth of Northallerton, who later in the year became Dudley's attorney-general.[52] Dudley was helpful too in finding a reward for Sir John Pilkington, one of the members for Yorkshire, to whom on 8 March 1478 he granted an annuity from the revenues of Howden.[53] Pilkington was both a knight of the body and a councillor of the duke of Gloucester, so that the duke's prompting as well as the king's request may have lain behind this grant.

It is likely that the king encouraged Dudley to work closely with his brother. At first the delicate matter of Barnard Castle, which Dudley could hardly be seen to abandon, needed to be resolved. This seems to have been handled with tact. Care was taken in royal letters to give nominal recognition to the lordship's inclusion within the palatinate both by Edward IV and later Richard III. In 1478, although it was the king and not the bishop who issued the licence to Gloucester to found his college there, both the letters patent and the act of parliament allowing the alienation of property refer specifically to Barnard Castle as being in 'the Bishopricke of Duresme'. Indeed, in the act a clause was inserted saving to William, bishop of Durham and his successors their 'right, jurisdiction, liberties and title' in the advowson of the church of Middleton-in-Teesdale.[54] By this means offence to the bishop was avoided. In return, in 1480, Dudley publicly recognised the support which, he declared, the duke had always given to the rights, liberties and regality of his cathedral church.[55] With the issue of Barnard Castle safely defused, the way was open for Gloucester to be brought into the government of the palatinate. Immediately after Dudley's elevation, the duke had been appointed to the commission of the peace, in the work of which he became actively engaged. In August 1477, for instance, the bailiff of Bishop Middleham was sent up to London '*ad certificandam domino de bono disposisione ducis glosestri tempore sessionum apud Dunelmensem*'. And later in the same month the bailiff of Stockton appeared before the duke himself at these same sessions.[56] Gloucester was also retained by the bishop in May 1479, and in an act reminiscent of the favour shown by Bishop Neville to his brother, the earl of Salisbury, Dudley granted him for life the park of Stanhope and the forest of Weardale, which together were worth £100 (see Map 6).[57] The duke took full advantage of this extension of his territorial interest north of the Tees to retain several of the forest tenants in his own service.[58] A year later Dudley enthusiastically extended to the palatinate the king's appointment of his brother as his lieutenant with powers to call out the king's subjects in the marches and the adjoining counties.[59] Armed with this military commission, Gloucester's dominance of the bishopric was assured.

Where the duke led, his servants followed. Richard Pigot, the second justice of the bishopric, and Miles Metcalfe, both of whom were councillors of the duke, had been retained of the bishop's legal counsel since 1461 and 1467 respectively. As successful lawyers in their own right, counting among their clients many of the leading landowners and corporations of the region, they did not owe their palatine positions to the duke.[60] Nevertheless, their presence on episcopal council could only have benefited Gloucester. They were joined in 1476 by Miles's brother, Thomas, auditor and supervisor of Gloucester's Middleham estate and his future chancellor of the duchy of Lancaster, who became bishop's auditor rewarded with fees totalling £13 6s. 8d.[61] Metcalfe at once became active in the bishop's affairs. In February 1477, he came down from London to evaluate the episcopal estates. In March (on Lady Day) he sat with the whole council to grant the annual leases. For ten days in May he was at Norham evaluating the bishop's estate there and surveying the castle. In September, he attended the royal commissioners sent down to supervise the repair of episcopal castles. And finally, in November, he undertook the audit itself.[62] As a councillor he was employed on various commissions within the bishropic, including gaol delivery and array.[63] The presence of these councillors, Pigot and the Metcalfes, who were servants of the duke, perhaps eased the flow of offices and fees toward other of the duke's retainers – Edward Gower, William Tunstall, Sir Roger Conyers, Sir Richard Strangways, John Kendal, and John, Lord Scrope. By 1483 the resources of the bishopric were once again being diverted to benefit the affinity of a powerful lay magnate.[64]

There can be no doubting the rapid establishment of Gloucester's influence within Bishop Dudley's administration between 1476 and 1483. It extended elsewhere. Across Palace Green it was already strong within the cloister of the cathedral priory before 1476. Here the duke did not have to wait for Booth's departure to York, for Prior Bell and his brethren themselves had need of an *dominus specialissimus* who was willing to support the causes of St Cuthbert, even in dispute with their own bishop. Until 1478, when Bell was elevated with Gloucester's assistance to the see of Carlisle, priory and duke were as one. Both Gloucester and his duchess were received into the fraternity. The duke was entertained on what seem to have been annual visits to the shrine of St Cuthbert. In 1477, the vicarage of Bossall was made available for one of the duchess's chaplains at the expense of an earlier nominee. Gloucester even, and in the event ill-advisedly, threw his weight behind Bell's attempt to continue to hold the priory *in commendam* after his promotion to Carlisle. In this he was defeated by the monks who, with the support of Bishop Dudley, preserved their right to elect their own prior.[65] Not surprisingly, this affair soured the atmosphere in the convent. Just three months after his election, Robert Ebbchester, the new prior, received a request from the duchess of Gloucester for the nomination to the vicarage of Frampton (Lincs.), which she understood would shortly be vacant as the incumbent was 'aged and impotent'. Ebbchester, however, firmly informed her grace that not only was the incumbent a young man under thirty, but also that it was against the rule of his order to grant a benefice during his life.[66] Bell had never been restrained by this prohibition.[67] Moreover, a month later, when none other than the king wrote asking for the next prebend to be vacant in the college at Howden for his 'wellbeloved chaplain', Alexander Lee, the prior made it clear that, the prohibition notwithstanding, 'whenever the case shall require, I and my brethren will be of such disposicion that your highness shall be pleased herein'.[68] Furthermore, in a 'copy' to the bishop written the same day, Ebbchester confided that he had 'purposed' the prebend to Lee.[69] And indeed, three weeks later on 15 October Lee was presented to the prebend of Barnby-in-Howden, following the (clearly anticipated) death of Thomas Babthorpe.[70] The snub to the Gloucesters could not have been more plain.

Yet it did not take long for Gloucester to recover favour. Ebbchester and his brethren decided in 1478 to abandon their long running suit at the *curia* for the recovery of Coldingham in southeastern Scotland. In his letter instructing John Shirwood, the priory's proctor at Rome, Ebbchester explained that the cell was unlikely to be recovered unless the king of Scotland agree,

> or else that the town of Berwick were in Ynglisshemen's hands, like as it were afore
> we were spolyd and put forth be force and violence.

Where legal process and negotiation had failed, Ebbchester seemed to be hinting, force of arms might prevail.[71] Gloucester came forward as the champion of this alternative strategy. He was a visitor to the shrine again in 1479.[72] When war with Scotland was renewed, the priory quickly

52. Memorial brass to Bishop Richard Bell (d. 1496),
Carlise Cathedral..

lent support. In mid-September 1480, the duke was at Durham mustering troops to repulse the Scots, who 'in grete multitude entende this Saturday night in three hosts to entre into the marches of the north partyes'. The priory, as well as the city of York, responded to a request for soldiers by providing a company of its tenants to join him on what was to be the first of a series of raids into Scotland.[73] And in July 1482, the banner of St Cuthbert itself was unfurled to bless the campaign which successfully recaptured Berwick.[74] Unfortunately for prior and bretheren, the recovery of Berwick proved no more effectual than the suit at the *curia* as a means by which Coldingham could be restored to St Cuthbert. Gloucester, however, had proved by his deeds the mettle of his veneration of the saint. It was only fitting that he should be lavishly received in May 1484 when he came as king to make offering at the high altar and to present his 'parlement robe of blew vellet' at the shrine.[75]

Friendship with the monks of Durham paved the way for closer relationships with the third great landowner of the bishopric, the earl of Westmorland. Lord Neville having been much favoured by Booth, Dudley's arrival in 1476 did not auger well for his family. Neville was promptly dismissed from the stewardship, although he was compensated with a fee of £20 in November.[76] It may have been this slight to his 'worship' which was still rankling in the following March when Prior Bell raised with Dudley the question of 'cherisshyng' the Nevilles and 'such as belongyth them'. What precisely lay behind Bell's much quoted advice, 'and your lordship and thei stand as one ye may reule and guyde all other that inhabite the cuntrie', remains an enigma because, as he wrote, 'what I ment in my mocion… I dare not utterly disclose, unto tyme I may common with your lordship'.[77] It may be, however, that Bell was lobbying not on behalf of a member of the Neville family itself, but on behalf of one of those belonging to them, namely, his own lay steward, William Claxton; for coincidentally Claxton was granted an annuity by the bishop shortly after Bell 'commoned' with him.[78] Claxton, a member of the Old Park branch of a prolific local family, was constable of Brancepeth. He had been steward of the priory since 1467 and stood in a long line of senior Neville servants who held the post during the fifteenth century.[79] He was a man of considerable influence in the county palatine in his own right, and having been sheriff from 1466-69, was currently a commissioner of the peace.[80] A favour granted to Claxton was a favour granted both to the priory and to the earl.

Yet, at the very time that Prior Bell was lecturing his new bishop on the political niceties of the palatinate (inaccurately as it transpired), the Nevilles and Gloucester were coming to terms. For at Easter 1477 Lord Neville, as heir to the earldom, quit his claim to the family estates in Yorkshire which his uncle had lost in 1443 and which were now held by Gloucester.[81] Moreover, at an unspecified date between July 1477 and January 1479, the earl himself vested his lordship of Raby and a group of manors in south-east Durham (see Map 6) in his infant great-nephew (Lord Neville's son) and a panel of feoffees, the majority of whom were Gloucester's councillors.[82] Apart from Archbishop Booth of York, Robert Booth, dean of York, Ralph Booth, archdeacon of York (all three kinsmen of the child's mother) and William Claxton, the remaining seven were Gloucester's men. Six of them, his feoffees in Middleham, had also received Lord Neville's quitclaim on their lord's behalf.[83] Why so many of Gloucester's men were employed remains unknown, but it proclaims a substantial involvement in the earl's affairs, which was borne out by Gloucester's frequent visits to Raby and Lord Neville's subsequent service to the duke. Gloucester was at Raby in November 1478, used it as a meeting place for his learned counsel in the summer of 1480, and took counsel there twice with Bishop Dudley in the winter of 1480-81.[84] Neville campaigned with Gloucester in Scotland and in June 1483 was called upon by his 'lovyng cousyn and master… to do me gode service, as ye have always before done'.[85]

In truth, by the summer of 1480, it was the duke of Gloucester, not Bishop Dudley, who had the rule and guided all other that inhabited the country. He was the bishop's lieutenant; he was the *dominus specialissimus* of the priory; and he had convinced the earl of Westmorland and his family that he was the man best able to further their interests.[86] No wonder other prominent landowners of the bishopric, such as George Lumley, William Hilton and Ralph Bowes, followed into his service.[87] But Gloucester's pre-eminence is perhaps demonstrated most amply by two demands on his good lordship which assumed that it was he and not the bishop who was the real fount of justice in the palatinate: a perception which in one case at least the duke seems to have encouraged. In an undated draft of a begging letter addressed to the duke, his 'lowly orator' Gerard Salvin of Croxdale Hall, near Durham, petitioned him to intervene against Thomas Fishburn and others, who (he asserted) had assaulted him in his manor house. Claiming to be 'a pore gentilman at my liberte, stou[n]ding to take a maister', declaring that he loved 'none so well as yow under God and the king', Salvin offered himself as a feed retainer. Moreover (and this was the purpose of the letter), he pleaded with the duke to order the sheriff of the bishopric to arrest and arraign Fishburn.[88] Unfortunately, we do not know the outcome, but a second instance suggests that Salvin's extraordinary assumption that Gloucester was the man to command the bishop's sheriff may have been well-founded. In 1480, John Randson of Burntoft in the south-east of the bishopric appealed to Gloucester against his powerful neighbour, Sir Robert Claxton of Horden and Claxton, who, he claimed, was preventing him from working his land. Gloucester, moved by his 'pitueuse complaint', took Randson's part and, having in vain summoned Claxton to appear before his council at Raby, on 12 August 'advised' him to appear before his learned counsel at the next sessions at Durham, where justice would be administered. 'And so demeane you', warned the duke, 'that we have no cause to provide his lawful remedy in this behalve.'[89] The tone of the letter makes it clear that Gloucester was already convinced that right lay on Randson's side. Sir Robert was himself an aged and respected leader of local society, the father of one of Gloucester's retainers and the father-in-law of another.[90] Yet the duke appears not to have hesitated to act against him in what he believed to be a just cause, nor to have had any reservation about using his own learned counsel, even during a session of the peace, to supply his own alternative justice. Randson's case gives substance to the claim that Gloucester offered justice to the weak against the strong; it also confirms that in doing so he had no qualms about bypassing the usual channels.[91] In the context of local politics, however, it leaves little doubt that in the last years of Edward IV he was the unchallenged lord of the county palatine.

Thus, when Gloucester became king, he was already poised to take full control of the affairs of the county palatine. It was fortuitous that Bishop Dudley, who had supported him wholeheartedly in the early months of the reign, should die at a comparatively early age in November 1483.[92] The king's and the pope's independent choice as his successor was John Shirwood, archdeacon of Richmond, the king's proctor at the *curia* and a humanist scholar. Duly elected by the prior and chapter on 30 January, Shirwood was formally provided by Pope Sixtus IV on 29 March. Shirwood, however, had spent most of his recent career at Rome, only returning briefly for Richard III's coronation. He had been appointed the king's envoy to tender his master's obedience to the Holy See and was still there when he was promoted. Indeed, he did not return to England or visit his diocese until 1490.[93] Perhaps because he was an absentee bishop, perhaps also because he and the king tried to negotiate a reduction of first fruits,[94] the temporalities were retained in royal hands until 6 August 1485. Thus, for all but a few months at the beginning of the reign, secular authority in the bishopric lay directly in the king's hands.

There were obvious advantages to be gained by Durham men from the new régime. William Claxton, now a king's servant, was rewarded handsomely for his assistance in putting down the rebellion of October 1483. John Hoton of Hunwick, an esquire of the body, and Richard Hansard of Walworth likewise benefited from the king's largesse in the south.[95] But for some, the new régime proved to be a mixed blessing. Unfortunately, our knowledge of Richard III's administration of the county palatine is severely restricted by the loss of the early membranes of the patent roll for Shirwood's pontificate and the lack of either of the receiver-general's accounts for the eighteen months when the temporalities were in royal hands. Nevertheless, the direction it took is indicated by the changes which the king made in key offices, and by his disinclination to call on the service of powerful local families, which reveal a royal reluctance to trust other than his own servants. He had given warning of this tendency in his administration of Weardale, where the master forester of the bishopric, Sir George Lumley, whose family had exercised the office for generations, found himself excluded in February 1483 by a new chief forester there, John, Lord Scrope, and by his deputies.[96] The removal of Thomas Middleton, steward of the palatinate since 1476, and the appointment of Richard Danby exemplifies the king's desire to place his own men in important offices. Middleton, a lawyer, had been retained as counsel by Bishop Booth in 1467. He was the second son of William Middleton of Stockeld near Wetherby (Yorks.) and was himself seated at nearby Kirkby Overblow. In 1468 he had married Joan, daughter of Sir William Plumpton, and, like his father-in-law, his political affiliation leant towards the earl of Northumberland, whose feoffee he became on the eve of the expedition to France in 1475; he was also steward of the earl's courts in 1478. He enjoyed a modestly successful practice, being retained from 1470 by the city of York, and from 1478 by the priory of Durham. He served from time to time on Yorkshire commissions, including the west riding bench.[97] He is not to be confused with Thomas Middleton of Middleton Hall in Lonsdale, Westmorland, who had been master forester of Wensleydale for the earl of Warwick and was a prominent councillor of Richard III as duke of Gloucester until his death in 1480-81.[98] Richard Danby, also *legis peritus*, was the second son of Sir Robert Danby, C.J.C.P., and Elizabeth Aislaby, a Durham heiress. Chief Justice Danby had been prominent in episcopal affairs, having risen to be first justice of the county palatine, and he had been retained by Gloucester before his death in 1474-75.[99] Richard's brother, Sir James, had been knighted by Gloucester in 1481 and became a knight of the body and master of the king's harriers.[100] Richard himself joined the north riding bench on 30 November 1480. On 13 November 1483, he was one of the commissioners appointed by the king to arrest rebels and seize their property in the counties of Somerset and Devon, and he was made steward of the temporalities of the bishopric of Ely on 1 December following. He was an ideal candidate for the stewardship of Durham, to which he had succeeded before July 1484.[101] Middleton's dismissal may not have pleased Northumberland, but Danby's appointment ensured that the administration of the palatinate was conducted according to the wishes of the king and none other.

Similar consideration may well have lain behind the king's treatment of Lord Neville, who succeeded to the earldom of Westmorland in November 1484. Neville had reason to expect advancement. After all, in June 1483 the king had promised that his support 'shal be the makyng of you and yours'.[102] He assisted the king again in October 1483, in recognition of which he was granted lands in Somerset and Berkshire as well as a reversionary interest in two manors of the countess of Richmond (in lieu of which he received for the time being an annuity of £80 from the issues of Barnard Castle). The total value of these grants was approximately £200 per annum.[103] On the surface this seems generous enough. Yet Neville had reason to hope for more. As the male heir to his maternal uncle, Henry, duke of Exeter, his rights had been denied by Edward IV, who allowed the Exeter inheritance to pass into the hands of the queen's family. He had thus had a vested interest in the fall of the Woodvilles and the Greys in 1483. In the event, by act of parliament in 1484, the king dispossessed his rivals only to resume the Exeter lands for the crown.[104] It is hard to believe, too, that the king's occupation of the lordship of Raby was entirely to Neville's liking. Exactly when Richard III took possession, and on what pretext, is not known, but it seems that the king took advantage of the second earl's enfeoffment to his councillors to secure control of the estate and perhaps also the person of Neville's infant son. Even before the old earl died, the king was assigning some of its revenues for the support of his new council at Sandal, and in 1485 he appointed his own receiver, Geoffrey Frank, to manage it.[105] In effect Raby was added, if only temporarily, to Richard's personal estate in the county palatine.

Thus, Neville's gains from the accession of the new king were not as he might have anticipated. Indeed, in his own county, where he might have expected that he would be given room to resume the dominance which his ancestors had once enjoyed, he found himself in reduced circumstances. Nor, as he might also have hoped, did he find himself more fully employed in the affairs of the border. The west march, once his great-grandfather's, remained in the king's hands, administered by Humphrey, Lord Dacre. And he served in only one commission of many appointed during the reign to negotiate with the Scots or to conserve the truce.[106] By August 1485, he may well have been regretting his earlier enthusiasm for the king. If he did not engage in the battle of Bosworth, as seems the case, he certainly had cause enough to stand by to await its result.[107]

In Neville's place, the king preferred to rely on his household servants, first among whom was Sir Richard Ratcliffe. Ratcliffe, sheriff of Westmorland since the death of Sir William Parr, played a prominent role in the negotiations at Nottingham in September 1484 and served on all the subsequent commissions in the west march.[108] But he was also a familiar figure in the county palatine. He was the constable of Barnard Castle and probably also the master forester of Teesdale – offices he probably held in 1475 when, as of Barnard Castle, he was admitted to the Corpus Christi Guild of York.[109] He was active in his master's affairs in the bishopric, especially those touching the Nevilles. He was one of the councillors to receive Lord Neville's quitclaim for Middleham and Sheriff Hutton, and was a feoffee of Raby. In 1477 and 1478, with his fellow ducal servants, Geoffrey Frank and John Kendal, he was a witness to deeds executed by Ralph Brackenbury settling lands in School Aycliffe on his younger son Robert.[110] Ratcliffe was already, Robert Ebbchester later revealed, highly enough regarded as a confidant of the duke of Gloucester before February 1478 to be promised the nomination to Merrington by Prior Bell.[111] A commissioner of array in the bishopric in 1480, he was knighted before the abortive siege of Berwick in 1481. It was he, too, it is to be noted, who rode north to the bishopric in June 1483 to summon Lord Neville to London 'enstructed with all my mynde and entente'.[112] Precisely what position he held in the palatinate during Richard III's reign is impossible to tell for lack of episcopal records. He held a lease of Evenwood Park,[113] and he became linked by two marriage alliances with local families. His younger brother Edward married Anne, one of the grand-daughters of Sir Robert Claxton of Horden, and his daughter Isabel married Roger, the second son of Sir George Lumley.[114] More might have been revealed by the missing membranes of the patent roll and the receiver-general's accounts. But we do have Prior Ebbchester's testimony, which there is no reason to doubt, to 'the grete rewll that he berith under the kynges grace in oure cuntrey'.[115]

The county palatine formed an integral part of Richard III's great northern dominion. Indeed, on the eve of his accession to the throne he probably enjoyed greater authority in Durham than he did in any other part of the north except the west march.[116] Building from his base in the lordship of Barnard Castle, at first frustrated by Bishop Booth but after 1476 taking advantage of the compliance of Bishop Dudley, he became the *de facto* ruler of the bishopric several years before he became its *de jure* king, and he absorbed its leaders into his affinity. After his accession he revealed a determination, as he did elsewhere in the north, not to surrender this power to others. In the palatinate the episcopal council may well have been employed in much the same way as the new council of the north at Sandal. The king's principal agents were his 'overmighty household men', the steward, Richard Danby, and his knight of the body, Sir Richard Ratcliffe.[116] So as to maintain local control, like Henry VII after him, Richard turned to his trusted servants and councillors rather than to the heads of old-established local families. By August 1485, he may already have given the earl of Westmorland cause to regret the support he had offered in 1483. And the same earl was to discover that what Richard had initiated his successor intended to continue. After 1483 the palatinate was rarely again to fall under the sway of a mighty layman. Indeed, if any year was a turning point in its late-medieval political history, it was not 1485 but 1483 when, it seems, the poacher turned gamekeeper.

10

ONE SUMMER AT
MIDDLEHAM

Among the many documents transcribed in the Signet Docket Book of 1483-85 known as BL Harleian MS 433, there is one particularly unusual item: a warrant issued to the auditors of the king's lordship of Middleham to allow the receiver there, Geoffrey Frank, to offset in his forthcoming account the sum of £196 10s., largely spent by him between the beginning of May and 25 September 1483.[1] This brief document, supplemented by material in the York House Books, enables us to reconstruct, in part, the activities and movements of Edward of Middleham and the household in which he lived over the four months in which his father became King Richard III and he Prince of Wales. The document is well known, and has been used in histories of Prince Edward,[2] but it repays the detailed analysis to which it has not, hitherto, been subjected.

The warrant lists 59 items (see appendix).[3] It would have been presented by Frank at the audit in October and attached to his final account for the year Michaelmas to Michaelmas 1482-3.[4] The account itself has been lost. We owe it to the exceptional circumstances of 1483 that the authorisation was made by the signet office; in 1482 the duke/king's own sign manual, as happened in 1473, would have been given; in 1484 it is likely to have been the clerk of the Council of the North.[5] The exceptional circumstances are also reflected in the scale and character of the expenses incurred by Frank from May until September. In but a third of the accounting year he spent, on the duke/king's business, approximately one-fifth of the estate's income.[6] Some expenditure was on routine estate management, matters for which warrants were normally issued: 'works' (no. 46), the keeping of one of the parks at Middleham (no. 45), the purchase of lead (no. 11) and the maintenance of the hunting establishment at the castle (no. 43). But most, over 75%, would seem to have been consumed on the 'lord prince', Edward of Middleham, his household costs and servants, and other related matters. Two items seem to have been ordered by the king in September 1483; one a payment to a 'wife besides Doncaster' (no. 52) and the settlement of £6 18s. owed to Sir Thomas Gower for the period when Anthony, Earl Rivers was in his custody at Sheriff Hutton. Other payments, especially of wages for two quarters, for a half year (nos 25, 57, 26, 42) and in one instance the whole year, while possibly made between May and 25 September, clearly extend beyond the summer.

Frank's claims are neither dated nor listed in a strict chronological order. One imagines that he presented himself at Pontefract to the clerk of the signet, or even to John Kendal himself, clutching a bundle of acquittances, receipts and other slips of parchment, which were summarised in the warrant in the order in which they were assembled by him and handed over. The clue that there was some coherence, some order, to Frank's documentation is provided by entries nos 37, 38 and 39. These authorise expenditure on my lord prince's household for three

53. Document bearing the sign manual of King Edward V ('RE' top left) and countersigned by his 'entirely beloved uncle', Richard, duke of Gloucester (centre right).

periods: St Ellenmass to midsummer's day; midsummer to 2 August and 2-22 August. The feast of St Ellen would seem to be that of the obscure St Helen of Carnaervon on 22 May, rather than St Helen the mother of Constantine, which in the west was celebrated on 18 August. It is not certain whether midsummer is 21 June or 24 June, which one might have expected to have been identified as the feast of the Nativity of John the Baptist. These would seem to represent three separate monthly payments, fitting into an annual cycle running from Michaelmas to Michaelmas, but with the June/July payment extended and the July/August reduced. I will return to a possible explanation for this unequal division in the payment of the salary bills for these two months. However, it is possible that these entries, with one or two possible exceptions, separate the expenditure borne before midsummer (nos 1-36) from those incurred after midsummer (nos 40-58). This is clearly indicated by two separate payments for a quarter's wages to five named servants, one for the quarter ending midsummer, the other for the quarter ending Michaelmas (nos 25, 57). Furthermore, expenditure related to the upkeep of George Neville and Sir Richard Grey (the lord Richard) at Middleham, both of whom were dead by 25 June, occurs only before this section (nos 1, 12, 18, 24); and expenditure related to events and journeys after 26 June, when Richard III ascended the throne, are listed after this section. The only items relating to expenditure by commandment of the 'king' fall in the second half (no. 52). One exception would seem to be the recording of the costs of the burial of Sir Richard Grey in the first half; another might be the recording of the purchase for the prince of a feather, perhaps even the Prince of Wales' badge of three ostrich feathers, which was sometimes called 'the feather', in the first half (no. 10). However, the broad chronological division is sufficient to allow a general reconstruction of the prince's activities.

Yet, since none of the entries is dated and some are clearly out of sequence, for instance one item of expenditure on George Neville who died on 4 May is noted after expenditure on the burial of

Sir Richard Grey who was executed on 25 June (nos 18, 13), the detailed chronology eludes us. In particular, significantly different reconstructions are possible for the weeks after 26 June. Furthermore, there is an inconsistency in the manner to which the 'lord' is identified, leading sometimes to potential confusion as to which specific household is meant, that of the prince or his father. In the central entries concerning household payments (nos 37-9), the first entry refers to 'the lord prince's household ', the second to 'the same house' and the third to 'my said lordes household', which is plain enough. In other entries 'my lord prince' is usually identified, but in four clustered together, it is merely 'my lord' (nos 27, 30, 33, 34): my lord's virga, my lord's drinking, my lord's alms and a primer for my lord. These could be references to Duke Richard himself, but in the context of the duke being absent in London, and comparable entries concerning my lord prince drinking or giving alms, it seems most likely that they refer to the lord prince, implied in the sense of 'my said lord's' household above (no. 39). Bearing in mind these inconsistencies and uncertainties, it is nevertheless worth endeavouring to tease a pattern out of these apparently random items, for they reveal, if never conclusively, tantalising suggestions as to how Edward of Middleham spent the summer of 1483, both in the six weeks or so immediately before his father became king and in the following ten leading to his investiture as Prince of Wales on 8 September.

The evidence of the warrant suggests that Edward was seven years old in 1483, supporting the supposition that he was born in 1476. There is uncertainty over the date of his birth because John Rous, while recording that he was born at Middleham, did not give a date, merely stating in his *Historia* that at his investiture he was aged seven years or a little more.[7] The Tewkesbury Chronicle gives the date of birth of an unnamed son at Middleham as 1476, but there is a possibility that this might have been a younger brother who subsequently died.[8] The warrant reveals that Prince Edward was still in the care of women in the early summer of 1483. Jane Collins who received the substantial annual salary of £5 (no. 42), bought 'stuff' (household goods or cloth) and made offerings on his behalf (no. 23), may have been one of his nurses. There were at least two others: Isabel Burgh, who was granted a pension after his death and Anne Idley, 'maistress of our nurcery' in *c*.1479. Could it be that nurses served in rota, as did the esquires and knights of an adult household? Jane was probably assisted by Agnes Cooper, whose fee was 2 marks (£1 6s. 8d., no. 6). She too, a widow, received an annuity after the death of the prince, £2 for life charged to the revenues of Middleham.[9]

The boy seems to have been attended by a bodyguard of five persons – Oliver Camer, John Vaughan, Rukes Metcalfe, Anthony Peacock, Dennis, and John Marlar – who were paid 18s. each per quarter (nos 25, 57). Metcalfe and Peacock were paid extra for running on foot beside my lord prince; presumably acting as his postillions when young Edward was travelling in his carriage (no. 41), upon the keep of which Frank spent over 7s. (nos 27, 51, assuming the 'virga' and 'charyot' are the same vehicle). The prince, it seems did not ride; he was conveyed in a carriage. Edward made many visits, one assumes in his carriage, mostly it would seem before midsummer, to neighbouring shrines and religious houses where, chaperoned by Jane Collins, he made offerings. These were to Our Lady of Coverham, just over the hill, Our Lady of Wensleydale, twice at Jervaux, just down stream, and at Fountains (nos 17, 20, 21, 23). It may well have been that all these visits were undertaken in preparation for his first communion, for which a chaplain, Thomas Brownlees, gave him instruction (no. 33) and for which also a primer, costing 13s. 4d. was bought, and covered, along with a psalter, in black

54. *Yorkist badges of the fetterlock, white rose and 'Prince of Wales' feathers, on the choir stall in Tansor Church, originally from Fotheringhay, Northamptonshire.*

satin (nos 34, 35). The boy's life was not all religious instruction. He might have watched the hounds at work in the parks (he was still too young to learn to hunt himself). It being early summer, he was taken along to the local May Games, generous donations being made in his name towards the choosing of the kings of both Middleham and West Witton (nos 4, 16). He was also entertained by Martin the Fool (no. 28); one is reminded that Yorick died when Hamlet was but seven, yet the grown man remembered well how the fool had borne him a thousand times upon his shoulders.[10]

Household employees apart, Edward was not alone in the castle. Until early May he had the eighteen-year-old George Neville, disinherited son of John Neville, Marquis Montagu – plain Master Neville in the warrant – for his company.[11] They were both fitted out in gowns of green cloth, possibly for the celebration of floriala at the beginning of May (nos 1, 2); and other 'stuff' was bought for George (no. 18). George sadly died on 4 May, but Edward was soon joined by another companion, Sir Richard Grey, his half-cousin, the son of the queen mother, Elizabeth Woodville, who had been seized by the duke of Gloucester at Stony Stratford on 30 April. Grey was an unwilling house guest, but the expenses of his servants and horses were met by Frank (no. 15, 24); and more 'stuff' was bought for his minder, Edward Pilkington, an illegitimate member of the Yorkshire family in Gloucester's service (no. 19).[12]

Grey's presence in the castle was a reminder of the uncertain political world beyond the idyllic tranquility of an early summer in Wensleydale. His expenses and the expenses of Prince Edward's household were accounted for jointly by Frank from St Ellenmas to Midsummer's day (no. 37). But then Grey was taken down to Pontefract, and on 25 June was summarily executed alongside his uncle, Earl Rivers. The costs of his journey and of his burial (£2 6s. 4d.) (nos 12, 13) were paid by Frank. Was the eight penny trussing cord (no. 31) bought in association with the same grisly purpose?

One reading of the warrant could be that that Prince Edward accompanied Sir Richard on his last journey. Costs were paid for the lord prince's drinking at Kippax (no. 36), just two or three miles north of the town, and again at Dringhouses (no. 30), just south of York, while his household incurred expenses at both Wetherby and Tadcaster (no. 39), all indicating the route taken there and back. He made an offering there (at the Friary) of 4s. (no. 22). The journey was not without its difficulties: men had to be hired for 'sheren', or grass cutting, by the way (no. 28), suggesting a section of the road so choked with vegetation in high summer that it was difficult for the prince's carriage to pass. It is not easy to construct an itinerary out of these entries. The order in which they occur suggests a journey via York, with stops at Dringhouses and Kippax; the return via Tadcaster and Wetherby (it would have to be in that order). The places at which the the items occur in the warrant could also fit in with the supposition that the journey down occured before midsummer; the return afterwards. However one would have expected stops at Dringhouses and Tadcaster on one route; Kippax and Wetherby on the other. It may be too that the contribution to the St Christopher Guild at York (no. 9) was incurred during this journey. There are no other entries relating to York in the first half of the list, but several in the second half. Nevertheless, a journey which took the prince via York, where he joined the earl of Northumberland and contingents of the army about to converge on London, is not implausible.

It is possible, therefore, but no more than a possibility, that young Edward was taken to witness the executions of Rivers, Grey and Vaughan, a brutal rite of passage to the adult world and a symbolic, political blooding appropriate to his imminent status as heir to the throne of England. If so, we may guess that he and his minders already knew what was afoot. But we cannot know precisely when the prince and his household heard that his father had actually become king of England: probably not until the very end of June. Edward's new status was marked by the visit to Middleham of a delegation from the city of York led by its mayor, John Newton, between 12 and 19 July. The citizens themselves put on a banquet for the prince, supplying six cygnets, six heronsaws, two dozen rabbits and two barrels of wine (young creatures for a young boy?). They took their own cook too, for he was subsequently compensated for the loss of his horse on the journey.[13]

By 31 July, the citizens were preparing for the first visit of their new king.[14] It may be that the prince travelled once more to York to take up residence for three weeks. This might explain the separate payment of the household between 2 August (leaving Middleham) and 22 August (arriving at Pontefract). In this reading the keep of the prince's horse at York, the bating (parking) of the chariot there and the subsequent expenses of the journey from York to Pontefract were all incurred then (nos 49, 50, 51, 53, 54). Alternatively, Peter Hammond has placed all these expenses after 29 August, the day upon which the king and prince made their ceremonial entry to the city. He proposes that the costs of the prince's household travelling from York to Pontefract were incurred after the investiture in the Minster on 8 September when the royal party began its return south, arriving at Pontefract by 22 September, three days before Frank presented his claim for expenses. By implication, all the listed expenses at York would thus have fallen after the arrival of the royal party in the city. In the warrant, these items are interspersed with entries concerning the supply of black velvet, fustyane and 'stuff' from Barnard Castle (nos 55, 56, 58), all suggesting preparations for the investiture.

This may be so. but the warrant implies that the independent household of the prince ceased to exist on 22 August, suggesting that on that date it was absorbed into that of the king. But when, and where, did the prince join his father? The king was still at Nottingham on 23 August. Did Edward meet him there? Were they both at Nottingham when he was created Prince of Wales on 24 August?[15] Yet the expenses, including three wains, were incurred only as going as far as Pontefract and staying there. No expenses were claimed for going further. The royal itinerary from Nottingham is also a matter of speculation. Peter Hammond suggests the entourage reached Pontefract on 24 August, but surely that is too early. Pamela Tudor-Craig plumps for 27 August, the day the king had set for supporters to join him there. He ought to have arrived in time. Indeed, 22 August might even be an accounting convenience, the date subsequently agreed when the charge for the payment of the Prince's household was transferred to another source of revenue. We just do not have enough evidence to be sure of the chronology. However, we do know for certain that on 29 August the royal entourage, the Prince at the king's side, was formally and ceremonially welcomed to York.[16]

On the evidence of an order sent from York, two days later, on 31 August, to Piers Curteys, Keeper of the Wardrobe to despatch clothing and trappings for the investiture, Peter Hammond has further suggested that the ceremony had not been pre-planned.[17] The logistics of the messenger riding to London, and for the materials to be loaded and transported to York in no more than eight days, seem extremely tight. Geoffrey Frank was also despatched to London to fetch 'the Jewelles', possibly in late August. He was paid five marks for his expenses there for eight days and for returning with them (no. 47). Were these the regalia for the investiture of the Prince of Wales? He also paid £10 to the 'lyutens' (no. 48) Was this the Lieutenant of the Tower, Sir Robert Brackenbury? Was the payment made for the surety of the 'the Jewelles? Or was it for some other purpose at the Tower on behalf of his master, the king? We do however know that he stayed for eight days, and is unlikely to have spent less than four days riding post haste there and four days back. To have returned in time for the investiture he would have had to have left Pontefract or Nottingham not much later than 24 August, the day on which Edward was created Prince of Wales. An alternative reading would be that this journey, in the company of the earl of Northumberland's army, was made in late June to attend the coronation.[18] But returning with the jewels after the coronation in July would presuppose that plans for the investiture had already been laid. This is a matter which cannot easily be resolved.

The chronology of the prince's movements is impossible to disentangle, especially after Richard III's accession to the throne. But the exceptional circumstances of the summer of 1483 have led to the survival of a document which enables us to see something of what was going on in Yorkshire as the seven-year-old was propelled from a domestic and private world of aristocratic childhood dominated by the company of women into the ceremonial and public world of the heir to the throne under the guidance of men. In his case the normal transition at this age was overtaken by the impact of his father's sudden and violent accession to the throne. In the event he had but six more months to live, but in the months documented by Frank's warrant his short life had been transformed. Geoffrey Frank, the man who, as both councillor and financial officer, seems to have been responsible for the prince during these months (no reference is made to his mother) continued to prosper in his new king's service, becoming an esquire of the body by March 1484. He survived Bosworth to join a resistance group in the Lake District. He made his peace in August 1486, and lived the last fifteen years of his life at Escrick in quiet country obscurity. 'Sic transit gloria mundi'.[19]

Appendix

Warrant to the Auditors of Middleham to allow Geoffrey Frank, receiver of the same, the sum of £196 10s.

1. 22s. 9d. (1) for grene clothe for my lord prince and Maistre Nyville (2)
2. 20d. for making of gownes of the same clothe
3. 13s. 4d. to the Gld of Alverton (3)
4. 5s. to chesing of the king of Westwittone (4)
5. 5s. 9d. for Rushes
6. 26s. 8d. for Augnes Couper
7. 9s. for a Clothe sak (5)
8. 23s. 4d. for a horsse boughte for William Litille Scott
9. 8d. to seint Christofire gild at York
10. 5s. for a fethere to my lord prince
11. £10 for 3 fodere of lede boughte of Thabbot of Coverham
12. 13d. for the lord Richard Costes from Middleham to Pountfret
13. for the lord Richard Berialle
14. 14s. 4d. to Dyryk Shomakere for stuff foe my lord prince
15. 6s. 8d. to the lord Richard servauntes
16. 6s. 8d. for the chesing of the king of Middleham
17. 15s. For my lord prince offering to oure lady of Gervaux Coverham and Wynsladale
18. 17s. 9d. for certene stuff boughte for Maister Neville
19. 15s. 9d. for stuff boughte of (6) Edward Pilkington
20. 20d. for my lordes prince offering at Gervaux
21. 2s. 6d. for offering at Founteyns
22. 4s. for his offering at Pountfret
23. 46s. To Jayne Colyns for offeringes & othere stuff by hire boughte
24. 21s. 6d. for thexpenses of the lord
Richard servauntes & the horses at Middelham
25. £4 l0s. to Olyver Camer, John Vachane, Rukes Metcalf, Anthony Pacok, Dennys, John Marlar (7) for there quartere wages at Midsomere
26. 33s. 4d. to Henry Forest (8) for his halff yere wages
27. 12d. to yeft for mending of my lordes virga (9)
28. 12d. for Martyn the fole
29. 12d. to Sheren (10) by the way
30. 20d. for my lordes drynkyng at Rynghouses (11)
31. 8d. for trussing Corde
32. 8d. for a bridille bit
33. 15s. 9d. to Sir Thomas Brounles for my lordes Almus
34. 13s. 4d. for a prymmere (12) for my lord
35. 7s. for blak Satane for Coveryng of it & of a Sawtere (13)
36. 2s. for my lordes prince drynkyng at Kyppes (14)
37. £37 16s. 11d. for thexpenses of my lord prince household and the lord Richard from Seint Elynmesse to Midsomer day
38. £31 11d. for thexpenses of the same house from Midsomer day to the 2nd day of August
39. £37 17s. $\frac{1}{2}$d. for my said lordes household fro the 2nd day of August to the 22nd day of the said moneth
40. 50s.$\frac{1}{2}$d. for my said lordes houshold at (Ta) Wedderby and Tadcaster
41. 6s. 8d. to Metcalf and Pacok for Rynnyng on fote by side my lord prince

42. 100s. to Jane Colyns for hire hoole yere wages ending at Michelmese
43. £10 for costes of houndes and theire wages that kepes them
44. £6 13s. 4d. for household wages
45. 43s. 8d. for keping of Sonscewghe (15)
46. 40s. to Michelle Whartone for warkes
47. 5 marcs for lieng at Londone 8 dayes & for comyng with the Jewelles from Londone
48. £10 to the lyutens
49. 33s. 4d. for thexpenses of my lord prince Chariot from York to Pountfret and there
50. 10s. fro 3 wayne from York to Pountfret
51. 6s. 5½d. for thexpenses of my lord prince Chariot from York to Pountfret and there
52. To a wiff besides Dancastre by the kinges commandement
53. 2s. 11d. for theire bating of the Chariot at York
54. 8s. 2d for the expenses of my lord prince horsse at York
55. 22s. 1d. for bringing of stuff from Barnardes Castelle
56. £5 6s. 8d. for 8 yards of blak velvet
57. £4 10s. to Olyver Cambre, John Vaghn, Rukes Metcalff, Pacok, Dennys, John Marlere for there quarter wages from Midsomere to Michille
58. 3s. 6d. for fustyane boughte of Thomas Fynche
59. £6 18s. for money paied to Sir Thomas Gowere by him laid out for thexpenses of the lord Rivers.

Yevene the 25 day of Septembre Anno primo (1483)

Notes to Appendix

1. All sums of money have been rendered in arabic numerals.
2. Horrox and Hammond transcribed this as Nigel. Nyville seems to me to be the correct transcription, being a corruption of Neville. I am grateful to Peter Hammond for providing me with a photocopy of the original text and for discussing with me the problem of reading the original letter forms.
3. West Witton, three miles upstream from Middleham.
4. Northallerton.
5. Sackcloth.
6. This might be an error made by the copyist, which should correctly read 'for'.
7. It would seem that 'Dennys' lacked either a Christian or a surname. Many Metcalfes and Peacocks were employed as park and forest officials in Wenslydale.
8. Forest may have been a relation of Miles Forest of Barnard Castle, later identified by Sir Thomas More as one of the murderers of the Princes in the Tower.
9. a chariot or litter.
10. Grass cutting? I am grateful to Felicity Riddy for advice on the possible meaning of this word.
11. Dringhouses.
12. a first religious instruction book.
13. Psalter.
14. Kippax.
15. Sunskew, one of the parks of Middleham. Horrox and Hammond transcribed the word as Souscewghe.

Notes

Introduction

1. A.J. Pollard, *North Eastern England during the Was of the Roses: Lay Society, War and Politics, 1450-1500* (Oxford, Clarendon Press, 1990); idem., *Richard III and the Princes in the Tower* (Stroud, 1991).
2. A.J. Pollard, 'The Northern Retainers of Richard Neville, Earl of Salisbury', *Northern History*, 11 (1976).
3. Charles Ross, *Richard III* (1981), pp.44-59; M.A. Hicks, *Richard III as Duke of Gloucester: a Study in Character* (York:Borthwick Paper, 70, 1986); R.E. Horrox and others, *Richard III and the North* (Hull, 1986) and others; idem, *Richard III: a* Study of Service (Cambridge, 1989), pp.39-72. See also the proceeedings of the fourth Richard III Society triennial conference in A.J. Pollard, ed., *The North of England in the Age of Richard III*, (Stroud, 1996).
4. A.J. Pollard, *North-Eastern England*, pp.2-4 and references there.
5. Horrox, Richard III, pp.178-205 ; Pollard, *North-Eastern England*, pp.346-53.
6. J.H. Burns, *Lordship, Kingship and Empire: the Idea of Monarchy, 1400-1525* (Oxford, 1992); J.L. Watts, *Henry VI and the Politics of Kingship* (Cambridge, 1996), pp.16-38.
7. C.M. Barron, 'The Tyranny of Richard II', *Bulletin of the Institute of Historical Research*, 41 (1968).
8. Horace Walpole, *Historic Doubts on the Life and Reign of Richard III*, 2nd edition 1768 with an introduction by Peter Hammond (Gloucester, 1987), esp. pp.12, 121-7, 127.
9. A.J. Pollard, 'The Characteristics of the Fifteenth-Century North', in J.C. Dalton and P. Dalton, eds., *Government, Religion and Society in Northern England*, 1000-1700 (Stroud, 1997), pp 131-43; Pollard, *North of England*, ix-xx.
10. H.M. Jewell, *The North-south Divide: the Origins of Northern Consciousness in England* (Manchester, 1994); F. Musgrove, *The North of England: a History from Roman Times to the Present* (Oxford, 1990), pp.155-82. Jeremy Potter, *Good King Richard?* (1983), p.46.
11. M.J. Bennett, 'A County Community: Social Cohesion among the Cheshire Gentry, 1400-1425', *Northern History*, 8 (1973).
12. M.M. Condon, 'Ruling Elites in the Reign of Henry VII', in Charles Ross, ed., *Patronage, Pedigree and Power in Later Medieval England* (Gloucester, 1979).
13. M.C. Carpenter, in *English Historical Review, XCVII (1982), 179.*
14. M.C. Carpenter, 'Gentry and Community in Medieval England', *Journal of British Studies*, 33 (1994): A.J. Pollard, *Late Medieval England, 1399-1509* (2000), pp.248-51.
15. A.J. Pollard, 'Lord FitzHugh's Rising in 1470', *Bulletin of the Institute of Historical Research,* vol. 52, no. 126 (1979), 170-5; idem., *North-Eastern England*, pp.303-14.
16. Pollard, 'Characteristics', passim.
17. Pollard, *North-Eastern England*, pp.401-5.
18. A.J. Pollard, 'The Crown and the County Palatine of Durham, 1437-94', in Pollard, ed., *North of England*, pp.84-7.
19. H. Summerson, *Medieval Carlisle* (Cumberland and Westmorland Antiquarian and Architectural Society, Extra Series, 25, vol 2, 1993), pp.467-75; idem, 'Carlisle and the West March in the Later Middle Ages', in Pollard, ed., *North of England*, pp.103-13;

S.G. Ellis, 'A Border Baron and the Tudor State: the Rise and Fall of Lord Dacre of the North', *Historical Journal,* 35 (1992). For the borders in general see the work of C.J. Neville, especially 'Keeping the Peace on the Northern Marches', *English Historical Review,* 109 (1994); 'Local Sentiment and the National Enemy in Nothern England', *Journal of British Studies,* 35 (1994) and *Violence, Custom and Law the Anglo-Scottish Borders in the Later Middle Ages* (Edinburgh, 1998) and A.E. Goodman, 'The Anglo-Scottish Marches in the Fifteenth Century: a Frontier Society' in R.A. Mason, ed., *Scotland and England, 1286-1815* (Edinburgh, 1987) and 'Religion and Warfare in the Anglo-Scottish Marches', in R. Bartlett and A. Mckay, eds, *Medieval Frontier Societies* (Oxford, 1989).

20. PRO, Durh 3/228/3, 9, 12-13, 17-18 and below.

21. John Weaver, *Middleham Castle* (English Heritage, 1993), pp.301; Anthony Emery, 'Greater Medieval Houses of England and Wales', vol. 1, *Northern England* (Cambridge, 1996), pp.368-72.

22. It is also after the birth of Edward of Middleham that Gloucester began to take steps to protect his title to the Neville estates in Yorkshire from other potential claimants. See M.A. Hicks, *Richard III and his Rivals*; pp.291-6, 331-2; Pollard, 'St Cuthbert and the Hog', below, pp.126-7.

23. Revenue from Middleham, along with the other Yorkshire estates, was used for funding the Council of the North established in July 1484. See Pollard, *North-Eastern England,* pp.353-8.

24. Pollard, *North-Eastern England,* pp.342-6.

25. M.A. Hicks, 'Richard, Duke of Gloucester and the North', in Horrox, *Richard III and the North,* 11-26.

26. D.M. Palliser, 'Richard III and York', in Horrox, *Richard III and the North,* pp.51-81.

27. As for instance in the matter of the York fee farm, for which see L.C. Attreed, 'The King's interest: York's Fee farm and the Central Government, 1482-92', *Northern History,* 17 (1981).

28. Ross, *Richard III,* pp.53-5.

29. P.W. Booth, 'Richard Duke of Gloucester and the west march towards Scotland', 1470-1483,*Northern History*, vol. 36, 2(2000), pp.233-46. It is to be noted, nevertheless, that Parr was retained by the duke. On 6 March 1474 Gloucester authorised the payment by the Reiceiver of Midleham of £10 to Parr for his wages as his lieutenant of the town and castle of Carlisle (PRO, Duchy of Lancaster 29/648/10485, payments by warrant).

30. But see 'The Political Legacy of Richard III in Northern England', in Griffiths and Sherborne, *Kings and Nobles,* pp.205-27.

Chapter 1: The Tyranny of Richard III

1. I would like to record my gratitude to Professor R.B. Dobson for reading a draft of this paper and to acknowledge my debt to his valuable comments on it.

2. Jacob 1961:645. See also Holmes 1967:223-6; Keen 1973:483-9; Lander 1969:98; Loades 1974:86-94; but Wilkinson (1964:297-304) strikes a more traditional note. Kendall's vigorous apology for Richard III (1955) is undoubtedly an over-favourable portrait.

3. Sylvester 1963 :lxxix-lxvii, c, ciii-civ. This is not the place to discuss Dr Hanham's provocative and ingenious argument (1975:156-90) that More's History is a 'spoof'. But it is worth noting that neverthe-less she too concludes (1975:195) 'In the History he [More] put his gift for scurrility to joyous use because he saw King Richard as a personification of that tyranny which he loathed with an intensely personal hatred. In

his creative purpose he became the symbolic figure in a moral tale.'

4. I am much indebted to Mr Nicholas Pronay for discussing the continuation with me. It is his view that the author was not Bishop John Russell as has been sometimes claimed and that the continuation was indeed the work of one man put together in the last ten days of April 1486. His detailed reasoning must await the publication of his forthcoming edition of the text. [See now N. Pronay and J. Cox, eds., The Crowland Chronicle Continuation: 1459-1486 (Alan Sutton for the Richard III and Yorkist History Trust, 1986) pp.78-98]. For contrary views see Edwards 1966; Ross 1974:430; Hanham 1975:74-95.

5. Riley 1854:453, 505. I have used Riley's translation, in spite of its occasional inaccuracies, because of its greater accessibility.

6. Riley 1854:509 (my italics); see also 1854:489,490, 495, 499 for other passages showing the author's prejudice.

7. Smith 1583:6. The first draft was written in about 1565.

8. Thomas and Thornley 1938:238; compare Dr Hanham's comment that 'Richard's unforgiven crime was the boy's dispossession' (1975:196).

9. See the works cited above in note 2 and also Kendall 1955:312-13,314-15.

10. Kendall 1955:319. Langton's eulogy ('God has sent him to us for the weal of us all') is in a letter written by him to the prior of Christ Church, Canterbury, in September 1483 (Sheppard 1877:46).

11. Raine 1939:119; see also the description in October 1485 of Richard as 'the most famous prince of blessed memory' (1939:126).

12. Raine 1939:23. The most comprehensive discussion of Richard's relationship with York is Miller 1961:61-5. See also Dr Hanham's discussion of her claim that 'ordinary citizens of York were never

unanimous in his [Richard's] praise' (1975:60-4).

13. Raine 1939:34-5, 38-9, 83, 117, 118.

14. Pugh 1972:110-12. For the troops present at the coronation see Armstrong 1969: n. 104, pp.132-33.

15. Lander 1961; Chrimes 1972:328-9; Ross 1974:66-8. Compare Dr Wolffe's comment, 'lands were seized and redistributed on a scale unprecedented since Richard II disinherited his opponents in 1398' (1971:193).

16. Wolffe 1971:193; BL MS. Harley 433, f. 284. *Calendar of Patent Rolls* 1476-85:476; Kendall 1955:277.

17. *Calendar of Patent Rolls* 1476-85: 418, 435, 485; BL MS. Harley 433, fos. 31v lbs. 284, 9 Iv; Kendall 1955:312.

18. Calendar of Patent Rolls 1476-85: 368,482-3,MS. Harley 433, fos. 3Iv, 45.

19. BL MS. Harley 433, lbs. 63, 92.

20. BL MS. Harley 433, f. 144; Wolffe 1970:126 (my italics).

21. Calendar of Patent Rolls 1476-85: 392, 393, 397, 398,400, 489, 490, 492.

22. BL MS. Harley 433, fos. 30, 35v, 132,286, 289; *Calendar of Patent Rolls* 1476-85: 399, 412, 480, 491, 514.

23. BL MS. Harley 433, fos. 169, 285; Calendar of Patent Rolls 1476-85: 370, 371, 397, 490, 556, 558, 572.

24. BN MS. Harley 433, f. 283; *Calendar of Patent Rolls* 1476-85: 371, 399, 488, 577; Coles 1961: Appendix B, 12, 17. Wedgwood 1936:709.

25. BN MS. Harley 433, fos. 30, 131, 282, 285, 285v, 286, 287, 288, 289; Calendar of Patent Rolls 1476-85: 398, 413, 427, 429, 478, 483, 559, 572; Coles 1961: Appendix B.

26. BN MS. Harley 433, fos. 44, 85, 282; Coles 1961: Appendix B.

27. BN MS. Harley 433, f. 285; *Calendar of Patent Rolls* 1476-85:472.

28. Thomson 1972: 238, 240, 243, 244; Complete Peerage: 945; BN MS. Harley 433,

fos. 282v, 285v.

29. Wright 1861:262-3; Gairdner 1872:541.
Clement wrote to his brother John on 23
January 1461: 'The pepill in the northe robbe
and styll, and ben apoyntyd to pill all thys
countre, and gyffe a way menys goods and
lufflods in all the southe countre.'

30. But note McFarlane (1965:98), 'These were
neither wars between north and south nor
between the lowland south-east and the dark
corners of the north and west.'

LITERATURE

Armstrong, C.A.J. (ed.) 1969. Dominic Mancini.
The usurpation of Richard III. Second
edition. Oxford.

Calendar of Patent Rolls, 1476-85. 1901. London.

Chrimes, S.B. 1934. Sir John Fortescue's theory
of dominion. Transactions of the Royal
Historical Society 17:117-47.

Chrimes, S.B. 1936. English constitutional ideas
in the fifteenth century. London.

Chrimes, S.B. (ed.) 1942. Sir John Fortescue. De
laudibus legum anglie, London.

Chrimes, S.B. 1972. Henry VII. London.

Coles, G.M. 1961. The lordship of Middleham.
M.A. thesis. Liverpool University.

Complete peerage 12, 2. 1959. London.

Edwards, J.G. 1966. The second continuation of
the Crowland chronicle. Bulletin of the
Institute of Historical Research 34:117-29.

Ellis, H. (ed.) 1809. Edward Hall. The union of
the noble houses of Lancastre and Yorke.
London.

Ellis, H. (ed.) 1844. Polydore Vergil. Three books
of Polydore Vergil's English history. Camden
Society, London.

Gairdner, J. (ed.) 1872. Paston letters, 1. London.

Gairdner, J. (ed.) 1875. Paston letters, 3. London.

Gairdner, J. 1898. History of the life and reign of
Richard III. Revised edition. London.

Gewirth, A. (ed.) 1956. Marsilius of Padua, 2. The
defender of the peace. New York.

Hanham, A. 1975. Richard III and his early historians. Oxford.

Hay, D. 1952. Polydore Vergil: Renaissance
historian and man of letters. Oxford.

Hay, D. (ed.) 1950. Polydore Vergil. The 'Anglica
Historia' of Polydore Vergil. Cainden Society,
London.

Hicks, M.A. 1971. The career of Henry Percy,
Fourth earl of Northumberland. M.A. thesis.
Southampton University.

Holmes, G.A. 1967. The later middle ages. London.

Jacob, E.F. 1961. The fifteenth century. Oxford.

Keen, M.H. 1973. England in the later middle
ages. London.

Kendall, P.M. 1955. Richard III. London.

Lander, J.R. 1961. Attainder and forteiture, 1453-
1509. Historical journal 6: 120-51.

Lander, J.R. 1969. Conflict and stability in
fifteenth-century England. London.

Levine, M. 1959. Richard III – Usurper or lawful
king. Speculum 34:391-401.

Loades, D.M. 1974. Politics and the nation, 1450-
1660. London.

McFarlane, K.B. 1965. The Wars of the Roses.
Proceedings of the British Academy 50:87-119.

Miller, E. 1961. Medieval York. In: The Victoria
history of Yorkshire: the city of York. P.N.
Tillot (ed.), 25-116. London.

Myers, A.R. 1954. The character of Richard III.
History today 4:511-21.

Myers, A.R. 1968. Richard III and historical
tradition. History 53:181-202.

Nichols, J.G. (ed.) 1854. Grants from the Crown
during the reign of Edward V etc. Camden
Society, London.

Pugh, T.B. 1972. The Magnates, knights and
gentry. In: Fifteenth-century England. S.B.
Chrimes, C.D. Ross, R.A. Griffiths (eds.),
88-128. Manchester.

Raine, A. (ed.) 1939. York Civic Records I.
Yorkshire Archaeological Society, Record
series. York.

Raine, A. (ed.) 1941. York Civic Records II.
Yorkshire Archaeological Society, Record

series. York.

Riley, H.T. (ed.) 1854. Ingulph's Chronicles.
London.

Ross, C.D. 1974. Edward IV. London.

Sheppard, J.B. (ed.) 1877. Christ Church letters.
Camden Society. London.

Smith, T. 1583. De republica anglorum. London.

Smith-Fussner, F. 1970. Tudor history and historians. New York.

Sylvester, R.S. (ed.) 1963. St Thomas More. The
history of King Richard Ill. In: The complete
works of St Thomas More, 2. New Haven.

Thomas, A.H. and I.D. Thornley (eds.) 1938.
The Great Chronicle of London. London.

Thompson, J.A.F. 1972. The Courtenay family in
the Yorkist period. Bulletin of the Institute of
Historical Research 45:230-46.

Wedgwood, J.C. 1938. History of parliament:
biographies of the members of the
Commons house, 1439-1509. London.

Wilkinson, B. 1969. The later middle ages.
London.

Wolffe, B.P. 1970. The Crown lands, 1461-1536.
London.

Wolffe, B.P. 1971. The royal demesne in English
history. London.

Woodward, G.W.O. 1972. King Richard Ill.

Wright, T. (ed.) 1861. Political poems and songs,
2. RS. London.

Chapter 2: Dominic Mancini's Narrative of the Events of 1483

1. Dominic Mancini, *The Usurpation of Richard
   III,* ed. C.A.J. Armstrong (2nd edn., Oxford,
   1969). Since Armstrong's translation of the
   original title is contested in some quarters
   (see Jeremy Potter, *Good King Richard: an
   Account of Richard III and His Reputation, 1483-
   1983,* 84-5), I have throughout referred to
   the work by its shortened Latin title.
   Armstrong's edition is abbreviated as
   Mancinin in all further references, which are
   given to the English translation unless

otherwise indicated.

2. Charles Ross, Richard III (London, 1981),
   p.xlii

3. A. Hanham, *Richard III and his Early Historians*
   (Oxford, 1975), 65. Commentaries on
   Mancini other than those already cited are to
   be found in A. Gransden, *Historical Writing in
   England, II, c.1307 to the Early Sixteenth
   Century* (London, 1982), 300-7 and A.J.
   Pollard, *Richard III and the Princes in the Tower*
   (Stroud: Alan Sutton, 1991), 5, 7-9.

4. Michael Hicks, *Richard III: the Man behind the
   Myth* (London, 1991), 161. [See now the
   revised 2nd edition, Richard III, (Tempus,
   2000)]

5. Ibid, 95-108.

6. Mancini, 1-14.

7. Michael K. Jones and Malcom G.
   Underwood, *The King's Mother: Lady Margaret
   Beaufort, Countess of Richmond and Derby*
   (Cambridge, 1992), 63*;* Ian Arthurson,
   'Espionage and Intelligence from the Wars of
   the Roses to the Reformation', *Nottingham
   Medieval Studies*, xxxv (1991), 134-54, esp.
   145-6.

8. Mancini, 3, 6-7.

9. Gransden, *Historical Writing,* 301.

10. Ibid., 302-3; Hicks, *Richard III,* 76.

11. See also Ross, *Richard III,* xlii, 'he may be
    seen as a reporter of other mens' opinions'.
    An earlier unpublished version of this paper,
    delivered to a conference of the Richard III
    Society in 1985, was entitled 'From Our
    Foreign Correspondent'. This appears to be
    the basis for Dr Hicks' remark that Mancini
    'has been sneeringly dubbed as 'our foreign
    correspondent' (*Richard III*, 77). I am at a loss
    to know what prompted the use of 'sneeringly'. The analogy is aposite and, I would
    have thought, uncontroversial, even complimentary.

12. Mancini, 93. For Argentine see D.E. Rhodes,
    'The Princes in the Tower and their Doctor',
    EHR, lxxvii (1962); *John Argentine, Provost of*

King's: his Life and Library (Amsterdam, 1967), 304-6; A.B. Emden, *A Biographical Register of the University of Cambridge to AD 1500* (Cambridge, 1963), 15-16.

13. Mancini, 71.
14. Ibid , 67.
15. Ibid, 75.
16. Ibid, 77.
17. Ibid, 83.
18. Ibid, 93.
19. Ibid 71, 73, 75.
20. Ibid, 89.
21. Ibid, 93, 103. Chancery administration virtually ceased on 15 June. See Rosemary Horrox, *Richard III: A Study of Service* (Cambridge, 1989), 117-18.
22. Mancini, 19. Antonia Gransden has suggested (*Historical Writing,* 301) that through Carmeliano, Mancini met Robert Brackenbury, who was to become constable of the Tower, and thus had access to court circles. It is, however, unlikely that Brackenbury held any position of influence until after Richard III's accession.
23. Mancini, 73.
24. Ibid, 81-3.
25. Ibid, 91, 95-7.
26. Ibid, 81, 85. See also the comment by Hicks, *Richard III,* 103.
27. *The Cely Letters, 1472-1488,* ed. Alison Hanham (*Early English Text Society*, 1985).To judge by the garbled nature of George Cely's memorandum, it would seem that Mancini was better informed.
28. Mancini, 61, 108-9.
29. Ibid, 63.
30. Ibid, 71, 81.
31. Ibid 61, 71, 73, 81.
32. Ibidm 85, 91.
33. Ibid, 85-7.
34. Ibid, 93.
35. Ibid, 95.
36. Ibid, 65.
37. Hicks, *Richard III,* 103; Horrox, *Richard III,*

108-9 and 'Financial Memoranda of the Reign of Edward V', *Camden Miscellany,* xxix (Camden Fourth Series, xxix, 1987.), 208-13.
38. A.J. Pollard, *North-East England during the Wars of the Roses: Lay Society, War, and Politics 1450-1500* (Oxford, 1990), 338-9.
39. Hicks, *Richard III,* 103, 99-100.
40. Mancini, 65, 67, 69.
41. Ibid, 67-9. Hicks (*Richard III,* 85-6), however, in claiming that Mancini was 'wholly critical' of the Woodvilles, overlooks this difference in attitude.
42. Mancini, 61.
43. Ibid, 43 .
44. Ibid, 61-3. Hicks (*Richard III,* 107-8), on the other hand, argues that this propaganda was believed by 'innocent newcomers like Mancini'.
45. Mancini, 57, 61.
46. Ibid, 77, 93.
47. Ibid, 63 (bis), 73, 83.
48. lbid, 63-65. The word used by Mancini (64, 1.2) is *artibus*, translated in this context by Armstrong as 'arts'. On 1, l.2 it is translated as 'machinations'. It seems to me that 'machinations' brings out more clearly the sense that Richard was manipulating public opinion for his own self-advantage. Hicks (Richard III, 85) interprets Mancini as stating that Richard was devoting himself to the good government of the north. But see also 59-60 where he stresses the manner in which the passsage emphasises Richard's self-conscious promotion of himself.
49. Mancini, 73.
50. Mancini, 83, 91, 95.
51. Ibid, 61, 63-5, 77.
52. See Pollard, Richard III, 17-20. Hicks (*Richard III,* 77) is reluctant to recognise the literary nature of the work, or indeed of history itself. He castigates Richard III's modern supporters for viewing Mancini as 'a purveyor of literature rather than history'. One suspects that he has fiction in mind. For

discussion of the literary character of histor-
ical narrative see H. White, *The Content of the
Form; Narrative Discourse and Historical
Representation* (Baltimore, 1987), esp. pp.ix-x.

53. Mancini, 91.

54. Ibid. See also Armstong's comments (12) on
Mancini's moralism in his *De Quatuor
Virtutibus.* Mancini's views on public moralty
were highly conventional.

55. For the view that it is not a 'moral treatise on
over-ambition and tyranny', see Hicks,
Richard III, 77.

56. As eloquently put by Hicks, *Richard III*, 107.

57. Hicks, *Richard III*, 163.

58. For recent discussion of Richard's years in
the north as duke of Gloucester see Hicks,
Richard III, 53-68; Horrox, 39-72; and
Pollard, *North-Eastern England*, 333-8, 316-41.

59. Mancini, 57

60. Pollard, *Richard III*, 9-17. It seems to me that
Hicks himself (*Richard III*, 108-11), notwithstanding his criticism of Mancini, gives very
much the same version of the story in a
section entitled 'The Verdict of History'.

61. Rhodes, *John Argentine*, 14.

62. St Thomas More, *The History of King Richard
III*, ed. R.S. Sylvester (New Haven:Yale
University Press, 1976), 9.

CHAPTER 3: NORTH, SOUTH AND RICHARD III

1. This is a slightly revised version of a paper
given at the Society's seminar at Trinity
College, Oxford on April 4, 1981. I would
like to record my thanks to the Society for
inviting me to participate.

2. C.D. Ross, *The Wars of the Roses* (London
1976), pp.98-100; A.J. Pollard, The Tyranny of
Richard III, *Journal of Medieval History*, 3
(1977), pp.147-166; Rosemary Horrox, *The
Extent and Use of Crown Patronage under Richard
III*, unpublished Cambridge University PhD.
thesis (1977) and *The Household of Richard III*,

paper delivered to the Trinity College
Seminar. Professor Ross' forthcoming study
of the reign will contain a further discussion
of the subject. [See now Horrox, *Richard III: a
Study of Service* (Cambridge, 1989) and Ross,
Richard III (1981)].

3. I am grateful to Pat Hairsine for permission
to cite this information presented at the
Trinity College seminar. This information
was originally given to Mrs. Hairsine by
Miss M.E. Holmes, County Archivist of
Dorset, from the Pitt Rivers Papers at the
Dorset Record Office: D396/L3.

4. *St Ingulph's Chronicles*, ed. H.T. Riley (Bohn's
Library 1854), pp.422-3.

5. C.L. Scofield, *The Life and Reign of Edward the
Fourth*, I (London 1923), pp.135-6; *The Paston
Letters*, ed. J. Gairdner, I (London 1872),
p.541.

6. Verses on the Battle of Towton, *Archaeologia*,
29 (1842), pp.344-7.

7. Dominic Mancini, *The Usurpation of Richard
III*, ed. C.A.J. Armstrong, (Oxford 2nd ed.,
1969), pp.132-3.

8. See Pollard, Tyranny, p.149 and n.4.

9. *Ingulph's Chronicles*, p.509.

10. *The Anglica Historia of Polydore Vergil*, ed. D.
Hay (Camden Society, 1950), p.11.

11. R.L. Storey, The North of England, in
Fifteenth-Century England, ed. S.B. Chrimes et
al (Manchester, 1972), p.129. R.S. Schofield,
The Geographical Distribution of Wealth in
England, 1334-1649, *Economic History Review*,
2nd series, 18 (1965), pp.483-510.

12. I am grateful to Mr R.D. Linacre for
allowing me to cite the early results of his
research on the distribution of wealth in the
North Riding between 1301 and 1334.

13. C. Phythian-Adams, *The Desolation of a City:
Coventry and the Urban Crisis of the Later
Middle Ages,* (Cambridge 1979), p.16; D.M.
Palliser, A Crisis of the Later Middle Ages?
The Case of York, 1460-1640, *Northern
History*, 14 (1978), p.115.

14. Storey, North of England (cited n.11 above), *passim* and The Wardens of the Marches towards Scotland, *English Historical Review*, 72 (1957), pp.593-615; J.A. Tuck, Richard II and the Border Magnates, *Northern History*, 3 (1968), pp.27-52.

15. R.L. Storey, *The End of the House of Lancaster* (1968), *passim*; R.A. Griffiths, Local Rivalries and National Politics: the Percies, the Nevilles and the Duke of Exeter, 1452-55, *Speculum*, 43 (1968), pp.589-632.

16. D.A.L. Morgan, The King's Affinity in the Polity of Yorkist England, *Transactions of the Royal Historical Society,* 5th series, 23 (1973), pp.l-26. C.D. Ross, Edward IV (London 1975), especially pp.331-341.

17. *Christ Church Letters*, ed. J.B. Sheppard (Camden Society 1877), p.46.

18. *Ingulph's Chronicles*, p.481.

19. *York Civic Records*, ed. A. Raine (Yorkshire Archaeological Society 1939), I, p.126; see also E. Miller, Medieval York, in *The Victoria History of Yorkshire*: the City of York, ed. P.M. Tillot (1961), pp.61-5.

20. Sir George Buck, *The History of King Richard III* (1619), ed. A.N. Kincaid (Alan Sutton, Gloucester 1979).

21. A.R. Myers, Introduction to Sir George Buck, *The History of the Life and Reign of Richard III, (*reissue 1973), p.vii.

22. Buck, *History*, ed. Kincaid, pp.20-1.

23. A. Hanham, *Richard lll and his Early Historians, 1483-1535* (Oxford 1975), especially pp.191-5.

Chapter 4: The Richmondshire Community of Gentry During the Wars of the Roses

1. *The 'Anglica Historia' of Polydore Vergil*, ed D.Hay (CS, 1950), p.11.

2. J.Warkworth, *A Chronicle of the First Thirteen Years of the Reign of King Edward the Fourth*, ed. J.O. Halliwell (CS, 1839), p.6; 'The Chronicle of the Rebellion in Lincolnshire, 1470', *Camden Miscellany*, I (CS, 1847), p.17; *DNB*, XVI, p.1319.

3. CP, VII, p.481; *Wills and Inventories from the Archdeaconry of Richmond*, ed.J. Raine (SS, 1853), pp.5-6.

4. Camden Miscellany, I, p.12.

5. *Ibid*, p.16.

6. *Ibid*, p.17.

7. *PL*, V (1904), p.80.

8. *CPR, 1467-77*, pp.215-16. For a fuller discussion of the involvement of the Richmondshire gentry in this rising see my 'Lord FitzHugh's Rising in 1470', forthcoming in *BIHR* [lii, no. 126 (1979); 170-5].

9. *Historie of the Arrival of King Edward IV*, ed. J.Bruce (CS, 1838) pp.31-2.

10. Especially the Clervaux Cartulary belonging to Mr.W.D.Chaytor and the Lawson of Brough Papers deposited in the North Yorkshire County Record Office.

11. A.H.Thompson, 'The Register of the Archdeacons of Richmond, 1442-77', *YAJ*, XXX (1931) and XXXII (1936).

12. NYRO, Lawson of Brough Papers, ZAL 3/17.

13. *VCH, North Riding*, ed. W. Page, I (1914). The following two paragraphs are based on an analysis of the parochial and manorial histories, pp.36-390. (See Map 2).

14. PRO, SC 6/1085/20.

15. H.L. Gray, 'Incomes from land in England in 1436'. *EHR*, XLIX (1934), p.617. The figures given by Gray are generally accepted to be underassessed.

16. For ministers' accounts of Snape see M.Y. Ashcroft, 'Snape in the late fifteenth century', *North Yorkshire County Record Office Journal*, 5 (June 1977), 20-58.

17. According to a rental of 1478-9 the Harcourt moiety of Bedale was worth £49 (see NYRO, ZBA 11/8/1/23).

18. H.B.McCall, *The Family of Wandesforde of Kirklington and Castlecomer* (1904), p.319.

19. A.J. Pollard, 'The Burghs of Brough Hall, c.1270-1574', *North Yorkshire County Record Office Journal*, 6 (April 1978) pp.9-10 [below p.83]

20. A.J.Pollard, 'Richard Clervaux of Croft: a North Riding Squire in the Fifteenth Century', *YAJ*, L (1978), p.154 [below pp.104].

21. Quoted by A.R. Wagner, *Heralds and Heraldry in the Middle Ages* (2nd ed.,1959), p.79.

22. *CPR, 1429-36*, p.379; K.B. McFarlane, *The Nobility of Later Medieval England* (1973), p.25; PRO, C. 218/17/1 Part 1/34.

23. NYRO, Clervaux Carulary, fly leaf; Lawson of Brough Papers, ZRL 1/53; PRO, SC6/1085/20; DL 29/648/10485.

24. Calculated from *VCH Yorks, North Riding*, I.

25. J.S. Purvis, 'Monastic Rentals and Dissolution Papers', *Miscellanea,* III (Yorkshire Archaeological Society, Record Series, LXXX, 1931), p.42.

26. *Valor Ecclesiasticus*, V, ed. J. Caley and J. Hunter (1834), p.235. The gross income was £188 16s. 2d. Its sister house at Egglestone held property worth £65 5s. 6d. gross in 1535 (*Ibid*, p.236).

27. For example, the holding of Jervaulx Abbey in the vill of Brough. See Pollard*, North Yorks. Journal*, p.9 [below pp.79-80]

28. R.B.Dobson, 'The Later Middle Ages, 1215-1500' in *A History of York Minster*, ed. G.E. Aylmer and R. Cant, (Oxford, 1977) pp.55-6.

29. In Yorkshire about a quarter of the chantries dissolved in the middle sixteenth century were established after 1480 (C.Haigh, *Reformation and Resistance in Tudor Lancashire* (1975), p.71). A good example of Richmondshire foundations is provided by the Burgh family who founded three chapels in 1474, 1491 and 1505 which were endowed with property to the value of £8 of rent p.a. (Pollard, *North Yorks. Journal*, 6, p.9 [below p.92])

30. R.S. Schofield, 'The geographical distribution of wealth in England, 1334-1649'.

31. H.L. Gray, 'Incomes from Land', *EHR*, XLIX, pp.635-6. One wonders whether the incomes of knights and esquires were not as underassessed for taxation as those of the baronage. See T.B. Pugh & C.D. Ross. 'The English Baronage and the Income Tax of 1436', *BIHR*, 26 (1953).

EcHR, 2nd series, XVIII (1965), p.504.

32. M.J. Bennett, 'A county community: social cohesion amongst the Cheshire gentry, 1400-1425', *Northern History*, VIII (1973), pp.24-44, reveals a very similar pattern in another northern county earlier in the century.

33. Pollard, *YAJ*, L, p.160 [below p.83]; *North Yorks. Journal*, 6, p.26 [below p.106].

34. Ibid.

35. *A Visitation of the North of England*, c.1480-1500 ed. C.H. Hunter-Blair (SS, 1930), pp.106-7; Pollard, *YAJ*, L, p.160-1 [below p.106].

36. *Visitation*, ed. Hunter-Blair, pp.92-4; J. Raine, 'Marske in Swaledale', *YAJ*, VI (1879-80), p.54.

37. *Ibid*; J.W. Clay, *The Extinct and Dormant Peerage of the Northern Counties of England* (1913), p.32.

38. McCall, *Wandesforde*, p.198.

39. University of York, Borthwick Institute of Historical Research, Probate Register, Vol 5, f. 133v; T. Horsfall, *Notes on the Manor'of Well and Snape* (Leeds, 1912), p.31, from the Inquisition Post Mortem. Mr. Keith Dockray has pointed out to me that Inquisitions Post Mortem of the North Yorkshire gentry are generally a fruitful source of information on enfeoffments.

40. NYRO, Lawson of Brough Papers, ZRL 1/33; *Testamenta Eboracensia*, II, ed. J. Raine (SS, 1855), p.246; *Testamenta Eboracensia*, III, ed. J. Raine (SS, 1864), p.265.

41. NYRO, Clervaux Cartulary, ff. 147-7d.

42. McCall, *Wandesforde*, p.99.

43. NYRO, Lawson of Brough Papers, ZRL 1/48.

44. NYRO, Clervaux Cartulary, f.146d.

45. Thompson, YAJ, xxxii, pp.127-8.

46. McCall, *Wandesforde*, p.327.

47. NYRO, Clervaux Cartulary, ff. 155-6.

48. See Raine, *Testamenta Eboracensia*, III, p.292.

49. *Plumpton Correspondence*, ed. T. Stapleton (CS, 1889) esp. pp. lxv-xciv.

50. A.Gooder, *The Parliamentary Representation of the County of York*, 1258-1832, II (Yorkshire Archaeological Society, Record Series, XCI, 1935), pp.3-6.

51. *Plumpton Correspondence*, ed. T.Stapleton, pp.31, 33.

52. I am grateful to Dr R.A.Griffiths & Professor Ross for pointing this out to me.

53. Pollard, *YAJ*, L, pp.164 [below p.110].

54. NYRO, Clervaux Cartulary, fly-leaf; PRO, SC6/1085/20.

55. A.J.Pollard, 'The Northern Retainers of Richard Neville, earl of Salisbury', *Northern History*, XI (1976 for 1975), p.54.

56. PRO, DL 29/648/10485.

57. Pollard, *North Yorks. Journal*, 6, pp.13-15 [below pp.86-9].

58. PRO, SC6/1085/20; DL29/648/10485; see also below pp.63-4.

59. W.C. Metcalffe, *Book of Knights Banneret, Knights of the Bath and Knights Bachelor* (1885), 6-7.

60. NYRO, Clervaux Cartulary, f. 154.

61. Ibid. ff. 167d, 155-6.

62. BL. Harley MS. 433 f. 118; *CPR, 1477-85*, p.482.

63. BL, Harley MS. 433, if. 93,287 (Sir John Conyers), 50d (Richard Conyers), 85 (Markenfield), 53d, 61d (Mountford).

64. Hay, *Anglica Historia*, pp.11, 39; *York Civic Records*, II, ed. A.Raine (Yorkshire Archaeological Society, Record Series, 1941), pp.9-10. For the most recent discussion of the disturbances created by some of Richard III's followers see M.A. Hicks, 'Dynastic Change and Northern Society: the career of the fourth earl of Northumberland', *Northern History*, XIV (1978), esp. pp.96-7.

65. *Plumpton Correspondence*, p.xcvi; NYRO,

Clervaux Cartulary, f. 150-50d; *CPR, 1485-94*, p.175; CP, III, p.404.

CHAPTER 5: THE MIDDLEHAM CONNECTION

1. *Rotuli Parliamentorum*, eds J. Strachey and others (1767-77), vol 6, pp 124-5.

2. *Chronicle of the Rebellion in Lincolnshire*, 1470, ed J.G. Nichols (Camden Society, 1847), pp 12, 16-17.

3. *Historie of the Arrivall of King Edward IV*, ed J.Bruce (Camden Society, 1838), pp 31-2.

4. from a privately owned document. I am grateful to Dr Lorraine Attreed for providing me with a transcript in advance of its forthcoming publication in Speculum. [An Indenture between Richard, Duke of Gloucester and the Scrope Family, of Masham and Upsall, *Speculum*, 58 (1983)].

5. *York Civic Records*, ed A. Raine, vol 1 (Yorkshire Archaeological Society, Record Series, 98, 1939), pp 73-4.

6. British Library, Harleian Ms, 793.

7. *British Library Harleian Manuscript* 433, eds Rosemary Horrox and P.W. Hammond, vol 2 (1980), p 24.

8. Ibid, p 29.

9. Ibid, p 25.

10. *The Itinerary of John Leland*, ed L. Toulmin Smith, vol 4 (1909), p86.

11. The *Anglica Historia* of Polydore Vergil, ed D. Hay (Camden Society, 1950), p 11.

12. Sir George Buck, *The History of King Richard III* (1619), ed A.N. Kincaid (1979), p 20.

CHAPTER 6: THE BURGHS OF BROUGH HALL, 1270-1574

1. The Lawson of Brough Papers now deposited in the North Yorkshire County Record Office, reference ZRL.

2. ZRL 1/46.

3. See H.B. McCall, *The Family of Wandesforde* (1904) and the Clervaux Cartulary, belonging

to Mr. W.D. Chaytor and deposited in the North Riding Record Office.

4. Especially Feet of Fines, Close Rolls and Patent Rolls.

5. The exception in Yorkshire is the Plumpton Family. See T. Stapleton, ed, *The Plumpton Correspondence* (Camden Soe. old series, iv, 1839) and J. Taylor, 'The Plumpton Letters, 1416-1552'. *Northern History*, x (1975), 72-87.

6. The best reproductions are to be found in T.D. Whitaker, *A History of Richmondshire* (1823) vol. II, following 28. The fullest descriptions are to be found in M. Stephenson, 'Monumental Brasses in the North Riding', *Yorkshire Archaeological Journal*, xvii (1903), pp.268-72.

7. Ibid; J. Raine, *Catterick Church* (1834), plates XI & XII, H.B. McCall, *The Churches of Richmondshire* (1910), 27: C.S. Perceval, 'Notes on the Documents of Sir John Lawson of Brough Hall', *Archaeologia* xlvii (1882), 194; ZRL 1/33; anon, 'Catterick Brasses', YAJ xx (1909), p.490.

8. In addition to the works cited above, see L.S. Salzman, *Building in England down to 1540* (2nd ed 1967), Appendix B, Nos. 53 & 59; *Archaeological Journal*, vii.

9. *Kirkby's Inquest*, ed R.H. Skaite (Surtees Society, xlix for 1867), 162; *Feet of Fines, Yorks. 1272-1300*, ed F.H. Slingsby (Yorkshire Archaeological Society, Record Series, cxxi, 1956), 115; ZRL 1/3, 9.

10. *Kirkby's Inquest*, 336; ZRL 1/9; Perceval, *Notes*, 184.

11. ZRL 1/33.

12. ZRL 1/3,9; *Feet of Fines, Yorks., 1272-1300*, 115.

13. *The Yorkshire Lay Subsidy, 30 Edward I (1301)*, ed. W. Brown (YAS, RS, xxi 1897 for 1896), 91.

14. *Feet of Fines, Yorks, 1246-72*, ed, J. Parker (YAS, RS, lxxxii, 1932), 145; Feet of Fines,

15. ZRI. 1/6.

16. ZRL 1/9, 13, 3/19; John de Marmion's confirmation of the sale (ZRL 1/10) is tran-

scribed in *YAJ*, xx, 217.

17. ZRL 1/15, 16.

18. ZRL 1/12, 23, 25. The exchange of 1376 (ZRL 1/12) is transcribed in *YAJ*, xx, 215-6.

19. ZRL 1/7, 8, 3/41, 42-4.

20. *Feet of Fines, Yorks 1347-77*, ed. W.P. Balldon (YAS, RS, lii, 1915), 187; ZRL 1/19, 24, 43,:1/43.

21. ZRL 1/24.

22. ZRL 1/16; *The Victoria History of the County of York: The North Riding*, ed. W. Page, i (1914), 24.

23. ZRL 1/56.

24. ZRL 1/25, 41, 48, 51.

25. ZRL]/2.5.

26. ZRL 1/56, 3/48-50. For a brief note on the history of the Richmond mills, which were held until the reign of Henry V by the alien priory of Begar in Normandy see C. Clarkson, *The History and Antiquities of Richmond (1821)*, 31-2. There is in the Lawson Papers an extent of the Richmondshire property of the priory dated 1482 (ZRL 3/77).

27. See illustration 40. ZRL 1/24, 39, 40; McCall, *Churches*, ch. 2 passim.

28. ZRL 1/19 21, 38, 48, 3/50.

29. ZRL 1/33. For Danby see T. Horsfall, *The Manor of Well and Snape* (1912), 79; for Pigot see *Testamenta Eboracensia, III*, ed. J. Raine (Surtees Society, xlv for 1864), 156-7.

30. *Calendar of Close Rolls, 1422-9*, 342-3; Ibid, *1429-35*, 267; Ibid *1435-41*, 59; McCall, *Wandesforde*, 198, 99, 201.

31. ZRL 1/23. Transcripts of the contract are to be found in *Archaeological Journal*, vii and in Salzman, *Building in England*. 497-9.

32. ZRL 1/26, 46; McCall, *Wandesforde*, 203, 327; Clervaux Cartulary, ff. 155-6; A.H. Thompson 'The Register of the Archdeacons of Richmond, 1422-77, Part 2' *YAJ* xxxii (1936) 127-8. For the dispute over the Burgh inheritance see below, pp.29-31 [p.93-4].

33. *Calendar of Patent Rolls, 1385-89*, 82; *1388-92*, 138; *1396-9*, 64, 96, 160, 236, 365, 509; *1399-*

1401, 567; *1401-05*, 520, *1405-8*, 500; *1408-13*, 487; ZRL 1/17. John was on many other royal commissions after 1399 including commission of array issued for Yorkshire during the Percy rebellion of 1403 (*Calendar of Patent Rolls 1401-05*, 284, 89, 91).

34. For the early quarrels of the Nevilles of Middleham see E.F. Jacob, *The Fifteenth Century* (1961) 321-3, and R.A. Griffiths, 'Local Rivalries and National Politics', *Speculum*, xliii (1968).

35. A.J. Pollard, 'The Northern Retainers of Richard Neville, earl of Salisbury' *Northern History*, xi (1976 for 1975), 68. For Danby's links with Salisbury, *The Paston Letters*, ed. J. Gairdner (1906) vol. iii, 121-2 and *Testamenta Eboracensia*, II, J. Raine (Surtees Society, xxx for 1855), 239-46. McCall, *Wandesforde*, 198; *Calendar of Patent Rolls, 1452-61*, 568. Among the other Richmondshire men to receive pardons were Christopher Conyers and Thomas Mountford. Sir John Conyers was attainted for his part in the rebellion (*Rotuli Parliamentorum*, v, 348-9).

36. *Calendar of Patent Rolls, 1461-6*, 30, 66, 576.

37. For a detailed account of the war in Northumberland between 1461 and 1464 see C.L. Scofield, *The Life and Reign of Edward the Fourth* (1923) vol. I, Book II, ch. V-XI. A less detailed but more modern interpretation is to be found in Charles Ross, *Edward IV* (1975) pp.45-63.

38. ZRL 1/27.

39. ZRL 1/28, 29; Perceval, *Notes*, 189.

40. A first hand account of the campaign is to be found in *Paston Letters*, iv, 59-61.

41. ZRL 1/30; Perceval, *Notes*, 190.

42. *Calendar of Patent Rolls, 1454-61*, 310.

43. ZRL 1/32; P.R.O. SC 6/1085/20, reprinted In G.M. Coles, 'The Lordship of Middleham' (University of Liverpool M.A. Thesis, 1961) Appendix B, 13. For the treason in Newcastle see 'Gregory's Chronicle' in *The Historical Collections of a Citizen of London*, ed.

I. Gairdner (Camden Society, 1876) 223. The grant of the orchard is transcribed by Perceval, *Notes*, 193.

44. Scofield, *Edward the Fourth*, I, 330-7.

45. ZRL 1/31, 33; Perceval, *Notes*, 191-2; A.H. Thompson, 'Register', *YAJ*, xxxii, 112.

46. *Calendar of Patent Rolls, 1461-6*, 450, 576.

47. Ross, *Edward IV*, 119-20; ZRL 1/34.

48. Ross, *Edward IV*, 126-32, 439-40. [see above, p.51, for my identification of 'Robin' as Sir John's brother, William of Marske.]

49. *Calendar of Patent Rolls, 1476-77*, 215. Also among those pardoned were Roger Aske, Henry and John Conyers, Thomas and Edward Frank, Rowland Pudsay and Alan Fulthorpe.

50. *Ibid*, 637.

51. *Ibid*, 260, 266.

52. PRO DL 29/648/10485, abstracted in Coles, 'Middleham', Appendix B, 17-8; McCall, *Wandesforde*, 1,51; ZRL 1/35. The contract of indenture and the warrant for payment are transcribed by Perceval, *Notes*, 195-6.

53. Clervaux Cartulary, ff. 155-64; *Calendar of Patent Rolls, 1477-85*, 401, 92. For Richard III's reliance on his northern men see A.J. Pollard, 'The Tyranny of Richard III', *Journal of Medieval History*, 3 (1977) [above ch.1].

54. ZRL 1/16, 23. The contract for the Church (ZRL 1/23) is transcribed in Raine, *Catterick Church*; McCall, *Churches*, 37-40, and Salzman, *Building in England*, 487-90. Raine's work provides fine architectural drawings set alongside the plans laid down in the contract.

55. McCall, *Churches*, 62; Salzman, *Building in England*, 482-3, 505-9. M.G.A. Vale, *Piety, Charity and Literacy among the Yorkshire Gentry, 1370-1480* (Borthwick Paper No. 50, 1976), pp.8-10.

56. ZRL 1/38, 42, 43, 45; *Certificates of the Commission to survey Chantries in County York*, i, ed. W. Page (Surtees Society, xci for 1892), 113-4. The endowment of the chapel on the bridge (ZRL 1/38) is transcribed in YAJ, xx,

218-9. In Yorkshire about a quarter of the chantries dissolved in the middle sixteenth century were established after 1480. Lancashire too witnessed this late revival of lay piety. On the other hand, the evidence of wills made by the Yorkshire gentry in the century before 1480 suggests that foundations were rare in that period and that there was a tendency instead to concentrate on bequests to existing foundations. See C. Haigh, *Reformation and Resistance in Tudor Lancashire* (1975) p.71 and Vale, *Piety, Charity and Literacy*, pp.22-3.

57. ZRL 1/54; *Calendar of Patent Rolls 1494-1509*, 522.

58. ZRL 1/46, 7.

59. ZRL 1/48, 50, 1.

60. ZRL 1/53, 55-8. In the sixteenth century the word 'Inn' was used to describe a dwelling place as well as a hostelry. Although it would be nice to think that there was a hostelry on the site of the Catterick Bridge Hotel from the mid-sixteenth century, unfortunately one cannot be sure about this.

61. ZRL 1/59-61; *Wills and Inventories from the Registry of the Archdeacon of Richmond*, ed. J Raine (Surtees Society xxvi for 1853), 243-5.

62. M.H. & R. Dodds, *The Pilgrimage of Grace, 1536-7*, (1915) i, 203. Christina Burgh, perhaps Christopher's daughter, was the last prioress of Nunkeeling in Holderness. Giles held the stewardship of all its manors, at a fee of 56s. 8d. at the time of the Dissolution. See J.W. Clay, ed. *Yorkshire Monastries, Suppression Papers* (YAS, RS, XLVII for 1912), 144.

63. C. Sharp, *Memorials of the Rebellion of 1569* (1840), 54, 57, 61, 100; *Wills and Inventories*, 248.

64. *Wills and Inventories*, 243-4, 249-50. For a discussion of the significance of wills in revealing the commitments of Englishmen in the mid-sixteenth century see A.G. Dickens, *Lollards and Protestants in the Diocese of York*,

1509-1558 (1959), 171, 215-7, 238. For the development of catholicism in the North Riding see J.C.H. Aveling, *Northern Catholics: Recusancy in the North Riding 1558-1791* (1966).

Chapter 7: Richard Clervaux of Croft

1. The Paston Letters are of course the single most important source for the history of the fifteenth-century gentry. H.S. Bennett *The Pastons and their England* (2nd ed., 1932) and F.R.H. Du Boulay, *An Age of Ambition* (1970) make excellent use of them. C.L. Kingsford, 'Social life and the Wars of the Roses', in *Prejudice and Promise in Fifteenth Century England* (1925) is a necessary starting point for other sources and for modern assessments of the role of the gentry in the fifteenth century. Amongst more recent studies the following are particularly valuable: M.J. Bennett, 'A county commmnity: social cohesion amongst the Cheshire gentry', *Northern History*, 8 (1973), pp.24-43; C. Dyer, 'A small landowner in the fifteenth century', *Midland History*, 3 (1972), pp.1-14; and J. Taylor, 'The Plumpton Letters, 1416-1552', *Northern History*, 10 (1975), pp.72-87.

2. The Clervaux Cartulary belongs to Mr. W.D. Chaytor of Croft and is deposited in the North Yorkshire Record Office, Northallerton. I would once again like to record my gratitude to Mr. Chaytor for allowing me to borrow the Cartulary whilst preparing this essay.

3. W.H.D. Longstaffe, *The History and Antiquities of the Parish of Darlington* (1854), pp.lxix-lxxx; A.H. Thompson, 'The Clervaux Chartulary', *Archaeologia Aeliana*, 3rd series, xvii (1920), pp.2-44. For Cartularies in general see G.R.C. Davies, *Medieval Cartularies of Great Britain* (1954). Only 159 secular cartularies have

survived compared with 1,185 ecclesiastical cartularies. A good example in print of a cartulary similar to the Clervaux cartulary is provided by H.E. Salter, *The Boarstall Cartulary* (Oxford 1930). This was compiled in 1444 and the following years by Edward Rede of Boarstall, near Brill, Oxon, a man of similar wealth and standing to Richard Clervaux.

4. Thompson, *Arch. Ael*. xvii, p.7. My comments here expand and correct the brief remarks I made on the composition of the Cartulary in 'The northern retainers of Richard Neville, Earl of Salisbury', *Northern History*, II (1976 for 1975), p.56.

5. Cler. Cart., f.39d

6. *The Victoria County History of the couonty of York, North Riding,* ed. W Page, i (1914), p.167.

7. See Joan Thirsk, ' The Origins of the common fields', *Past and Present*, 29 (1964), pp.3-25. This article together with the debate it stimulated is usefully reprinted in *Peasants, Knights and Heretics*, ed. R.H. Hilton (1976).

8. Cler. Cart. f.153; (D)urham (R)ecord (Office), Chaytor Papers, D/Ch/D200; Longstaffe, *Darlington*, p.Ixix.

9. Cler. Cart. ff. 5-7. The problem of land measurement in fifteenth-century England is discussed briefly in Appendix 1.

10. See the discussion following.

11. Cler. Cart. ff. 145-6d, 33d-4, 156d, 157; D.R.O., D/Ch/D198.

12. Cler. Cart. ff. 146, 148, 158, 159d.

13. Cler. Cart. ff. 113d-4, 145, 146-6d, 161.

14. Clef. Cart. ff. 147-7d, 151d; D.R.O. D/Ch/d196, 7. The final latin deed transcribed on f. 152 includes one more holding in Croft than the initial indenture in English on f. 147. In the original of these, preserved amongst the Chaytor papers deposited at Durham Record Office, this holding is included in the indenture in English.

15. Cler. Cart. if. 145d, 157d-8, 159, 159d.

16. Cler. Cart. ff. 145, 157d-8d

17. Cler. Cart f. 154d

18. Cler. Cart. ff. 147, 152

19. Cler. Cart. f. 149.

20. M.M. Postan, *The Cambridge Economic History of Europe*, vol. 1, *The Agrarian Life of the Middle Ages* (2nd ed. 1966), pp.610-13; C. Dyer, *Midland History*, 3. p.1.

21. Cler. Cart. f. 143.

22. Cler. Cart. ff. 152d, 155d, 157.

23. Cler. Cart. f. 164d.

24. D.R.O. D/Ch/D 201, 210, 218. In 1548 the demesne was described as being 'nowe inclosyd with dyges and hedges' into three fields of arable land. In the same year, two farms called Fatt Hill and Crossfield were sold to Christopher Chaytor. Forty years later, the Clervaux possessions in Croft were described in an extent as being six farms of land.

25. Cler. Cart. ff. 154d, 155d. See also below p.108.

26. Cler. Cart. f.149.

27. Cler. Cart. ff. 66d-7. When the extent was made the demesne of 216 acres was valued at the low sum of £1 13s. 4d. *per annum*.

28. Cler. Cart. ff. 138d-9; Thompson, *Arch. Ael*, xvii, p.37.

29. Cler. Cart. f. 143; Thompson, *Arch. Ael*, xvii, p.39.

30. Cler. Cart. ff. I44-4d.

31. For example in I447 (f. I44; Thompson, *Arch. Ael*, xvii, p.39-40) and I457 (f. I44d; Longstaffe, *Darlington*, p.lxviii, where the date is wrongly transcribed as 25 Henry VI).

32. A.H. Thompson, 'The Register of the Archdeacons of R.ichmond, I422-77', *Y.A.J,* 30 (193I) pp 108, 110. In 1453 Richard received a licence to have masses celebrated *voce submissa* for one year. Many of his neighbours had private chapels: see for examples, *ibid*, pp. 92, 111, 115, 130. It is possible that Clervaux also put up a new porch to his house. According to the herald's visitation of 1666 there was a full coat of arms and the

letters R.C. set in stone above the porch. (T.D. Whitaker, *A History of Richmondshire in the North Riding of the County of York* (London, 1823), i, pp.241-2.)

33. Cler. Cart. f 142d; Longstaffe, *Darlington*, p.lxvi.
34. Cler. Cart. f. 55; Longstaffe, *Darlington*, p.lxviii.
35. Cler. Cart. ff. 145-5d, 157d, 158d, 159-9d, 161.
36. Cler. Cart.ff.159d, 160, 161, 167d. Thompson, *Y.A.J.* 30, p.110.
37. Cler. Cart. f.149d.
38. See R.H. Hilton, *The Decline of Serfdom in Medieval England* (1969); M.M. Postan, *Cambridge Economic History*, i, pp.617-28.
39. Cler. Cart. ff.147, 158d. It is of particular interest that the cartulary contains evidence of the word 'yeoman' being used to describe both social status and official function in the same community at approximately the same date. See R.B. Dobson and J. Taylor, *Rymes of Robyn Hood* (1976), pp.34-5.
40. Cler. Cart. ff. 147, 159d; R.P. Littledale, *The Pudsay Deeds* (Y.A.S. Record series, 56, 1916), p.41.
41. Cler. Cart. ff. 160, 167d. For the most recent discussion of the fifteenth-century franchise see D. Hirst, *The Representative of the People?* (1975), pp 29-30.
42. These details and those that follow are from Longstaffe's authoritative pedigree of the Clervaux which has no pagination.
43. For Vincent see Cler. Cart., f. 131d; *V.C.H., Yorks, I,* p.198; for Tailboys see Cler. Cart. f. 128; R. Surtees, *The History and Antiquities of the County Palatine of Durham,* 4 vols. (1816-40), III, pp.221-2; for Headlam see Surtees, *Durham*, I, pp.98-9 and *Testamenta Eboracensia*, ii, ed. J. Raine (Surtees Society, 30 for 1855), p.247.
44. For Strangways, see J.S. Roskell, 'Sir James Strangeways of West Harlsey and Whorlton', *Y.A.J.*, 34 (1958), pp.455-81 and *The Commons and their Speakers in English Parliaments, 1376-1523* (1965), pp.271-5; for

FitzHenry see *V.C.H., Yorks*, I, p.91; for Laton see *V.C.H., Yorks*, I, pp.151-2; for Aske see V.C.H., Yorks, I, p.91; and for Conyers of Wynyard see *V.C.H., Durham*, III, p.252 and *Surtees*, Durham, III, p.79. It is to be noted that Conyers of Hornby was lord of the manor of Solberge and Strangways was lord of a moiety of the manor of Warlaby, in both of which places Clervaux held property.

45. Cler. Cart. ff. 145, 145d, 146d, 158, 160, 161; Littledale, *Pudsay Deeds*, pp.38, 353 Thompson, *Y.A.J.*, 30, pp.127-8.
46. Cler. Cart., ff. 158, 160, 161, 161d.
47. Cler. Cart., ff. 158 (Henry Tailboys); 158, 161, 161d (William Vincent); 146d, 157, 159, 160, 161d (Killinghall); 145,147, 159, 160 (Conyers); 159, 160 (Thomas Tailboys); 147 (Roger Vincent); 146d, 160, 161 (Strangways); 146d, 151, 160, 161d (Laton); and 158d (Aske).
48. Cler. Cart., ff. 146d, 160, 161, 160d (Frank); 145d, 146d (Catterick); 147, 159, 160 (Surtees); 146d, 161d (Conyers of Hornby); 145 (Metham); 145d (Wycliff); 146d (Mountford); and 152d (Boynton).
49. Cler. Cart., ff. 158-8d, 148, 146d.
50. Cler. Cart., ff. 155-6d; Longstaffe, *Darlington*, pp.lxix-xx; Whitaker, *Richmondshire*, I, 239-40.
51. Cler. Cart., ff. 143-4d; Longstaffe, *Darlington*, p.lxvii; Thompson, *Arch. Ael.*, xvii, pp.39-40.
52. Tailboys' career is discussed in detail by R. Virgoe, 'William Tailboys and Lord Cromwell: Crime and Politics in Lancastrian England', *Bulletin of the John Rylands Library*, 55 (1973), pp 459-82. His misdeeds are also referred to by R.L. Storey in 'Lincolnshire and the Wars of the Roses', *Nottingham Medieval Studies*, 14 (1970), pp.64-82.
53. Cler. Cart., f. 154; Longstaffe, *Darlington*, p.lxviii
54. Pollard, *Northern History*, 11, pp.57-8.
55. Cler. Cart., f. 148; Longstaffe, *Darlington*, p.lxvi. The Pudsays' involvement on the

Percy side in the private wars of 1453-5 is described by R.A. Griffiths in 'Local Rivalries and National Politics: the Percies, the Nevilles and the Duke of Exeter, 1452-55', *Speculum,* 43 (October 1968).

56. Clef. Cart., f. 144d; *(C)alendar of (P)atent (R)olls, 1452-61*, pp.368, 540-1, 543, 547, 564, 647, 683.

57. Cler. Cart., f. 154. See also above p.oo-oo.

58. Public Record Office, Special Collections 6/1083/20, and Duchy of Lancaster 29/648/10485; G.M. Coles, 'The Lordship of Middleham' (unpub. M.A. thesis, Liverpool Univ. 1961), Appendix B, pp.12-18.

59. Cler. Cart., f. 167d; K.B. McFarlane, *The Nobility of Later Medieval England* (1973), pp.107-8; J.C. Wedgwood, *History of Parliament, Biographies of the Members of the House of Commons 1439-1509* (1936), p.904.

60. Cler. Cart., ff. 155-6.

61. British Library, Harleian mss. 433, f. r18; Cler. Cart., f. 150; *C.P.R.*, 1477-85 p.482. *Paston Letters*, ed. J. Gairdner, Vol. 3 (1875), p.306.

62. See Charles Ross, *The Wars of the Roses* (1976), p.98. This facet of Richard III's reign is explored more fully in Charles Ross's *Richard III* and Pollard 'The Tyranny of Richard III *Journal of Medieval History*, 3 (1977), pp.157-62 [above ch.1].

63. 'Croyland Chronicle', ed. H.T. Riley in *Ingulphs Chronicles* (1854), p.509; *York Civic R.ecord,s,* II, ed. A. Raine (Yorks. Arch. Soc. Record series, 1941), pp.9-10; *The Anglica Historia of Polydore Vergil*, ed. D. Hay (Camden Society, 1950), pp.11, 39. See also the brief discussion in M.A. Hicks 'The career of Henry Percy, 4th earl of Northumberland' (unpublished MA Thesis, University of Southampton, 1971), pp.69-74.

64. Cler. Cart., f. I50-50d; *C.P.R. 1485-94,* pp.175, 266. Clervaux's nephew, John Vavasour, was another who rallied quickly to Henry VII.

65. See Appendix 2, below, pp.115-16.

66. Kingsford, *Prejudice and Promise*, p.63.

67. Longstaffe, *Darlington*, p.lxviii.

68. See K.B. McFarlane, 'The Wars of the Roses', *Proceedings of the British Academy*, L (1965), pp 117-19 and Ross, *Wars of the Roses*, pp.151-7 for discussion of the craven mood of the political nation as a whole by 1485.

69. The Clervaux died out in the male line in 1591 and Croft passed to Anthony Chaytor in right of his mother, Elizabeth Clervaux (d. 1584). His descendants have occupied the estate ever since. The later history of the family is to be found in brief in Longstaffe, *Darlington*, pp.lxxii-xxix and *V.C.H., Yorks.*, I, p.165. A full study of the Chaytors is yet to be undertaken. The materials for this exist in collections of family papers in the Durham Record Office and the North Yorkshire Record Office. The Durham Record Office has compiled a useful calendar of the Chaytor Papers which contains much that is relevant to Croft in the seventeenth and eighteenth centuries.

70. Cler. Cart. ff. 149; 127d-28: N. Sutherland, *Tudor Darlington*, I, (1974), p.22.

71. Cler. Cart. f. 64.

72. e.g. Cler. Cart. f. 35d.

73. F.W. Maitland, *Domesday Book and Beyond* (Fontana Library, 1960), p.442.

74. I am grateful to Mr. H.MacL. Currie for his advice on the latin in the epitaph.

75. This is as inscribed and is a correction of Longstaffe's transcription which gives the proper form of the word.

76. Longstaffe, *Darlington*, p.lxxii.

77. Thompson, Arch. Ael., xvii, p.5.

78. See the discussion above, p.113.

Chapter 8: Richard III, Henry VII and Richmond

1. *The Great Chronicle of London*, ed. A.H. Thomas and I.D. Thornley (1938), pp.238-9;

George Cavendish, *The Life and Death of Cardinal Wolsey*, ed. R.S. Sylvester, (1959), pp.131-2.

2. A.J. Pollard, *North-Eastern England during the Wars of the Roses*, (Oxford, 1990), pp.318-9.

3. *Victoria History of the County of Yorkshire: North Riding*, ed. W. Page, i (1914), pp.9-10, *Calendar of Patent Rolls, 1441-6*, pp.96, 108, 191,429, 458; *1446-52*, pp.281, 544; Public Record Office, E199/50/32. The account given in the VCH is not entirely accurate.

4. Pollard, *North-Eastern England*, pp.258-9, 288; PRO, SC 6/1085/20.

5. Pollard, *North-Eastern England*, pp.318-9, 321; *Calendar of Patent Rolls , 1461-7*, pp.121-3; *1467-77*, pp.342-3.

6. The analysis is based on two Receiver's accounts for the joint lordships for 1473-4 and 1488-9 (PRO, DL 29/648/10485; 649/10500) and a review of the revenues of the lordship of Richmond alone from Michaelmas 1483 to Whitsun 1486, compiled, it would seem, to provide Henry VII with a summary of the revenues due from it (PRO, DL 28/31/14).

7. This information is drawn from a number of surviving ministers' accounts for 1436-7, 1439-40, 1465-6 and 1468-9 (PRO, SC 6/1085/18, 20; E 199/50/32; and Lancashire County Record Office, DD Ma 228). The material exists for a fuller study of the economic history of Richmond than attempted here..

8. *Calendar of Patent Rolls, 1436-41*, 452, 509-10; PRO, E 199/50/32; DL 28/31/41; North Yorkshire County Record Office, ZRL 1/48. The agrarian crisis is discussed in A.J. Pollard, 'The North-Eastern Economy and the Agrarian Crisis of 1438-40', *Northern History*, 25 (1989), pp.88-105.

9. Pollard, *North-Eastern England*, pp.72-3, 74-5.

10. PRO, DL 28/31/14; NYCRO, ZRL 1/7, 8, 49, 50.

11. A.J. Pollard, 'Richard Clervaux of Croft',

Yorkshire Archaeological Journal, 50 (1978), p.161, [above p.106]; Lancs CRO, DD Ma 228, m 7d.

12. For Conyers, see Pollard, *North-Eastern England*, pp.90-1, 323,344,357,373,375,385. Conyers was first granted the office of Bailiff of the wapentakes of Richmondshire jointly with his father as early as 1435. They were retained in office by Salisbury in 1444. Sir John is known to have presided over courts held at Ellerton on Swale, Richmond, Bedale and Leeming between 4 October 1443 and 9 October 1445 (PRO, E 199/51/1). He succeeded his father to the offices of steward and Constable of the joint lordships of Middleham and Richmond *c*.1463.

CHAPTER 9: ST CUTHBERT AND THE HOG: RICHARD III AND THE COUNTY PALATINE OF DURHAM, 1471-85

1. Durham, Dean and Chapter, Reg. Parv. III, f. 188v. The copy of Ebbchester's letter is undated. However, the king can only have been Richard III and Ebbchester died on 24 June 1484. John Le Neve, *Fasti Ecclesiae Anglicanae, 1300-1541: Northern province* (1963), p.111 (henceforth Le Neve, *Fasti*).

2. Aspects of Richard Ill's relationship with Durham have been discussed by Charles Ross, Richard III (1981), p.53; M.A. Hicks, 'Dynastic Change and Northern Society: the career of the fourth earl of Northumberland, 1470-89', *Northern Hist.*, XIV (1978), 85-86; M.O'Regan, 'Richard III and the monks of Durham', *The Ricardian*, IV (1978), 19-22; and R.B. Dobson, 'Richard Bell, Prior of Durham and Bishop of Carlisle', *Trans. Cumberland and Westmorland Antiq. and Archaeol. Soc.*, LXV (1965), 182-221. This discussion concentrates on the main body of the county palatine which lay between the Rivers Tyne and Tees and was commonly

called the bishopric to distinguish it from the Yorkshire enclaves of Howden, Crayke and Northallerton to the south and the Northumbrian enclaves of Bedlington and Norham (North Durham) to the north.

3. W. Hutchinson, *The History ard Antiquities of the County palatine of Durham*, I (1785), 362. Hutchinson, a native of Barnard Castle who was not enamoured of Richard III, underestimated his local importance. 'The dreadful machinations', he wrote, 'by which Richard duke of Gloucester was opening his passage to the throne, do not seem to have had any particular influence on the northern parts of the kingdom.'

4. PRO, Durh.3/49/4. The text is printed by G.T. Lapsley, *The County Palatine of Durham*, I , study in constitutional history (Harvard, 1900), p.46.

5. For the genesis of this dispute, see *Records of Antony Bec*, ed. C.M. Fraser (Surtees Soc., CLXII, 1953 for 1947), passim, and C.M. Fraser, *The History of Antony Bek* (Oxford, 1957), pp.203-5, 208.

6. PRO, Durh. 3/48/5,6,7; *Memoirs of Ambrose Barnes*, ed. W.D. Longstaffe (Surtees Soc., L, 1867 for 1866), p.95. The king's claim was that since Barnard Castle was excluded from the palatinate it therefore lay within Northumberland. For a contemporary royal grant describing Barnard Castle as being in Northumberland, see *CPR, 1436-41*, p.408.

7. *CPR, 1467-77*, p.330. In March 1472 reference was specifically made to a previous grant to Clarence of all the Countess Anne's estates.

8. M.A. Hicks, 'Descent, Partition and Extinction: the Warwick Inheritancc', *BIHR*, LII (1979), esp. pp.120—22.

9. Charles Ross, *Edward IV* (1974), p.192; Durham, Church Comm., Bishopric Estates, 189820 (audit). £7 12s. 4d. was paid to the sheriff and others for their expenses incurred in riding to Hartlepool to seize Thomas

Clifford and others in his company, being rebels of the king.

10. Ross, *Edward IV*, p.199; Hicks, 'Dynastic Change', pp.82-84.

11. Durham, Church Comm., Bishopric Estates, 189883. The reeve of Crayke delivered some of the issues of the manor to his lord at Sheriff Hutton during the financial year 1472-73.

12. The chancellor's fee alone was worth more than twice the revenue of Barnard Castle (see below p.113).

13. PRO, DL29/648/1048, receiver, payments by warrant.

14. Ibid., fees and wages. Roger Conyers of Wynyard and Thomas Blakeston of Blakeston, from near Stockton-On-Tees, were retained for life on 3 September 1473.

15. Durham, Dean and Chapter, Reg. 4, f. 214.

16. Hicks, 'Descent, Partition and Extinction', p.122.

17. See Map 6. For five years, between 14 January 1476 and 12 Decembcr 1480, by virtue of a contract with Elizabeth, Dowager Lady Scrope of Masham, Gloucester also enjoyed the service of all her tenants of Winston, which lies on the north bank of the Tees, between Whorlton and Gainford (see L.C. Attreed, 'An Indenture, between Richard duke of Gloucester and the Scrope family of Masham and Upsall', *Speculum*, LVIII [1983], 1018-25).

18. R. Surtees, *History and Antiquities of the County Palatine of Durham*, IV, part 1 (1840), p.8.

19. PRO, SC6/1303/11, 12; BL, Egerton Charter 8773. I am grateful to Dr Alexandra Sinclair for drawing my attention to these estate records.

20. PRO, DL29/637/10357.

21. These figures are drawn from an analysis of privy seal letters in *British Library, Harleian Manuscript 433*, ed. R.E. Horrox and P.W. Hammond, vols. 1, 2 (1979, 1980), passim. There can be little doubt that after 1483 Richard Ill exploited the revenues of Barnard

Castle for the purpose of patronage. In 1484-85 extraordinary fees totalled £145.

22. See Map 6.

23. PRO, DL29/648/10485; Library of Congress, Collection John Boyd Thatcher 1004; *Harleian Manuscript 433*, II, 132.

24. David Austin, 'Barnard Castle Excavations', *JBAA*, CXXXII (1979), 21-22, 82-83, 86-96 ('A dinner in the Great Hall'); *Harleian Manuscript 433*, II, 30.

25. Ibid., p.28.

26. *Rot. Parl.*, VI, 172-73; William Dugdale, *Monasticon Anglicanurn*, 11I, part 2 (1673), pp.203-4; Ross, Richard Ill, p.131.

27. As well as in the castle and on the church, badges of the white boar are to be seen at Blagraves House, The Bank and in the Bowes Museum from a house in Newgate.

28. *CPR, 1436-85*, p.372; Durham, Church Comm., Bishopric Estates, 189831; Surtees, *Durham*, IV, 73.

29. PRO, DL41/34/1/107; *Harleian Manuscript 433*, I, 202. I am grateful to Dr. R.E. Horrox for information on these men.

30. Ibid., II, 160.

31. PRO, Durh. 3/55/5d, 6d.

32. See R.L. Storey, 'The North of England', in *Fifteenth-century England, 1399-1509*, ed. S.B. Chrimes, C.D. Ross and R.A. Griffiths (Manchester, 1972), pp.139-40.

33. Ibid., pp.140-41; Dobson, 'Richard Bell', p.205.

34. Fees totalled £233 6s. 8d. in 1453-54 (Durham, Church Comm., Bishopric Estates, 189812). Richard Neville, earl of Salisbury, however, continued to serve on the commission of the peace and retained his tenancy of Stanhope Park until his attainder in 1459 (North Yorkshire Record Office, Clervaux Cartulary, fly-leaf, dorse).

35. Durham, Church Comm., Bishopric Estates, 189814-29, passim.

36. PRO, Durh. 3/48/2. In December 1457 William, Lord Fauconberg was replaced as steward by Thomas Neville of Brancepeth.

37. Storey, 'The North', p.140. The key to Booth's political allegiance between 1461 and 1471 lies in his antipathy towards the Middleham Nevilles rather than in dynastic preference.

38. Between 1461 and 1482 Norham was the only defensible fortress in English hands on the north-east frontier.

39. *Rotuli Scotiae in Turri Londinensi*, II (RC, 1819). 430-31, 433, 443-45, 446-48; N.F. McDougall, *James III: a political biography* (Edinburgh, 1982), p.116.

40. *Rot. Scot.*, II, 437; *Calendar of Documents relating to Scotland*, ed. James Bain, IV (1884), nos. 1409, 1414; McDougall, *James III*, p.113.

41. BL, Cotton, Vesp.CXVI, f. 121v-126.

42. Durham, Dean and Chapter, Reg. IV, f. 174v-175.

43. PRO, Durh. 3/49/8, 11; DL29/648/10485. Ashton was replaced by another of Gloucester's servants, Edward Gower, in 1478 (Durham, Church Comm., Bishopric Estates, 189885).

44. See below p.117.

45. PRO, Durh. 3/49/5, 6; CP, XII, ii, 551; J. Petre, 'The Nevills of Brancepeth and Raby, 1429-99, Part 11', *The Ricardian*, 76 (1982), 44.

46. PRO, Durh. 3/49/15. It is possible that Booth was attempting by this appointment to secure Neville's future role in the affairs of the palatinate after his departure.

47. The move seems also to have enabled Booth and Gloucester to come to a more lasting understanding, for shortly after his transla-tion the new archbishop appointed the duke his steward of the liberty of Ripon (Borthwick Institute of Historical Research, Register Neville and Booth, f. 290v).

48. Emden, *Oxford*, I (Oxford, 1957), 600.

49. K. Emsley and C.M. Fraser, *The Courts of the County Palatine of Durham* (Durham, 1984), p.92.

50. *Cal. Docs. Scotland*, II, 410-11; PRO, Durh. 3/54/1.

51. Durham, Church Comm., Bishopric Estates,

189831, m.4. The receiver general was charged with the expenses of the royal commissioners. The activities of the commission provide yet another example of the bishop's inability to preserve his franchise (see Lapsley, *County Palatine*, pp.307-8; Storey, 'The North', p.141). This flurry of activity also seems to imply that Richard III's later claim that bishops before Shirwood had neglected the defences of the castles of the palatinate was directed at Booth's pontificate (see *Harleian Manuscript 433*, III, 67-68).

52. Wedgwood, p, 562; PRO, Durh. 3/54/7.
53. Durham, Church Comm., Bishopric Estates, 190240 (Howden receiver's account), audit. Pilkington was paid £8 12s. 0d. Such a sum would be consistent with a fee of £10 paid up to his death in early 1479 (see Wedgwood, p.685).
54. *Rot Parl.*, VI, 172-73; Dugdale, *Monasticon*, I11, part 2, p.203. Contrast this with the episcopal licence granted by Dudley for Lord Neville to found a chantry in the parish church of St Brendan, Brancepeth, on 20 September 1483 (PRO, Durh. 3/54/21). A privy seal warrant of 1484 also describes Barnard Castle as being in the bishopric (*Harlieian Manuscript 433*, I, 202). After 1485, however, it was unequivocally annexed to the royal demesne. An episcopal inquisition post mortem on Richard 'late king of England' reported that the only land held by him of the bishop had been seventy acres and a capital messuage in Darlington (PRO, Durh. 3/168/8).
55. PRO, Durh. 3/54/11.
56. Ibid., 2; Durham, Church Comm., Bishropic Estates, 189831, m.5.
57. PRO, Durh. 3/54/9. This superseded the grant of an annuity of £100 made the preceding day, Richard Neville, earl of Salisbury had received the rents from the park, totalling £61 6s. 8d. From 1449 to 1459

(Ibid., 44/4; J.L. Drury, 'Early Settlement in Stanhope Park, Weardale, c.1406-79', *Archaeologia Aeliana*, fifth ser., IV [1976, 145).

58. PRO, Durh. 3/54/17; Durham, Church Comm., Bishopric Estates, 190031, m.2. A total of six fees were paid by the king to tenants of the forest in the last year of his reign, four to members of the Emerson family (see also J.L. Drury, 'Westgate Castle in Weardale', *Trans. Architect. and Archaeol., Soc. of Durham and Northumberland*, new ser., IV [1978], 31).
59. PRO, Durh. 3/54/11.
60. Durham, Church Comm., Bishopric Estates, 189816 m.21. Pigot became second justice in 1465-66 (ibid., 189819). For Pigot's connections with Gloucester, see PRO, DL 29/648/10485, warrants for issue, and *Yorkshire Deeds*, ed. W. Brown, 111 (Yorks. Archaeol, Soc., Record Ser., LXIII, 1922), 143-44.
61. Durham, Church Comm., Bishopric Estates, 189831. Metcalfe was paid the regular fee of £l0, together with a supplement of £3 16s. 8d. during the lifetime of William Racket, his fellow and senior auditor. In 1481, after Racket's death, Metcalfe went to the length of having the confirmation of his fee registered at the priory (PRO, Durh. 3/54/14; Durham, Dean and Chapter, Reg. IV, f. 217v).
62. Durham, Church Comm., Bishopric Estates, 189831.
63. PRO, Durh. 3/54/1, 3, 5, 6, 11, 13.
64. *Gower*, keeper of Crayke castle, forester and parker, October 1478 (PRO, Durh. 3/54/7, 9; Durham, Church Comm., Bishopric Estates, 189 885); *Tunstall*, annuity of £2 10s. (ibid. 189 831); *Conyers*, annuity of £4, November 1480 (PRO, Durh. 3/54/13); *Strangways*, annuity of £5, March 1481 (ibid., 12); Kendal, by agreement between the bishop and the duke, the issues of North Duffield, Howdenshire, during the minority of Anne

Salvin, c.1482 (*Harleian Manuscript 433*, III, 103-4); *Scrope*, chief forester of Weardale and supervisor of the parks of Auckland and Evenwood, February 1483, with a fee of £6 13s. 8d. (PRO, Durh. 3/54/17). The scale of fees in Gloucester's favour does not compare with the scale of those granted by Bishop Neville to his family (see above p.165 n.34).

65. Dobson, 'Richard Bell', pp.205-6, 209-11, provides an excellent discussion of Gloucester's relationship with the priory until 1478, on which the above is based.

66. Durham, Dean and Chapter, Reg. Parv., III, f. 182-183v.

67. R.B. Dobson, *Durham Priory, 1400-1450* (Cambridge, 1973), p.164.

68. Durham, Dean and Chapter, Reg. Parv. III, f. 184-184v.

69. Ibid., f. 184v,

70. Ibid., f. 183v.

71. Ibid., f. 185v; *Historiae Dunelmensis Scriptores Tres*, ed. James Raine (Surtees Soc., IX, 1839), cclxxxvii, p.366. For the Coldingham dispute, see R.B. Dobson, 'The last English monks on Scottish soil', *ScotHR*, XLVI (1967) and N.F. McDougall, 'The Struggle for the Priory of Coldingham', *Innes Review*, XXIII (1972).

72. *Account Rolls of the abbey of Durham*, ed. J.T. Fowler, I (Surtees Soc., XCIX, 1898), 96.

73. Durham, Dean and Chapter, Bursar's account, 1480-81, m.6d.; *York Civic Records*, ed. Angelo Raine, I (Yorks. Archaeol. Soc. Record Ser., XCVIII, 1939), 34-35. The letter to York, given under the duke's signet, was written on 8 September and called for troops to muster at Durham 'on Thursday next coming'.

74. Durham, Dean and Chapter, Bursar's account, 1482-83, m.5. Gloucester and Northumberland were entertained by the priory, and their servants were rewarded by the cellarer, during the same year and presumably on the same occasion (ibid.,

Cellarer's account, 1482-83).

75. Ibid., 1483-84; *Rites of Durham*, ed. J.T. Fowler (Surtees Soc., CVII, 1903), p.69; M. O'Regan, 'Monks of Durham', p.20. Richard's cooks usually received six ells of cloth on the occasions of their master's visits; in 1483-84, when he was king, they received thirty ells and cash rewards of 7s. 10d. In his *Accounts of Durham*, Fowler did not publish this extract or that cited in n.74 above.

76. Durham, Church Comm., Bishopric Estates, 189830. Thomas Middleton was restored.

77. *Historiae Scriptores Tres*, cclxxiv, p.359.

78. Durham, Church Comm., Bishopric Estates, 189831. The annuity was £4.

79. Surtees, *Durham*, III, 289; Durham, Dean and Chapter, Halmote Rolls, 1466-96, passim.For the role of the prior's steward, see Dobson, *Priory*, pp.125-29. Thomas Langton. (steward, 1416-36) was an esquire of Ralph, first earl of Westmorland; William Hoton (steward in 1437-46) was steward to Ralph, the second earl; and Robert Rodes (steward in 1446-60) was a servant of Sir Thomas Neville. Claxton's successor, William Bulmer, was receiver general of Ralph, Lord Neville as third earl (Westminster Abbey Muniments 6052).

80. Durham, Church Comm., Bishopric Estates, 189820-22; PRO, Durh. 3/54/I. He was also the widower of Eleanor Scrope, daughter of John, Lord Scrope of Masham (d. 1455).

81. PRO, CP25(1)/281/164/32.

82. PRO, Durh.3/168/14. The enfeoffment is cited in the inquisition post mortem of the second earl (1484). It is undated, but from internal evidence it can be placed during the eighteen months between the collation of Robert Booth, one of the feoffees, as dean of York and the death of another, Sir John Pilkington (Le Neve, *Fasti*, p.8; and above p.166 n.53).

83. The six common to both were Sir John Pilkington, Sir James Tyrell, Thomas

Barowe, clerk, William Hopton, Thomas Middleton and Richard Ratcliffe, esquires. Thomas Metcalfe was not a party to the quitclaim, but was a feofee of Raby. The same six councillors of the duke or their survivors also took the quitclaim of Elizabeth, Lady Latimer in 1480 and were, as feoffees of Middleham, parties to land trans-actions on the duke's behalf in 1479 and 1484 CPRO, CP [2511]/281/165/23; William Atthill, *Documents of the collegiate church of Middleham* [Camden Soc., XXXVIII, 1847], pp.84-85; *CPR, 1476-85*, p.505). Were these men, one wonders, to assume responsibility for the child's upbringing?

84. *York Civic Records*, l, 29; Library of Congress, Washington DC, Thatcher Collection, 1004; James Raine, *An Historical Account of the Episcopal Castle of Auckland* (Durham, 1852), pp.55-56.

85. *The Paston Letters, 1422-1509*, ed. James Gairdner, VI (1904), 71-72.

86. It will be clear from the preceding paragraphs that I cannot accept James Petre's judgement that it was the Nevilles and not Richard of Gloucester 'who were the real masters of the palatinate' ('The Nevilles', p.5).

87. All three were knighted while campaigning against Scotland m 1481 (Hicks, 'Dynastic Change', p.105; W.E. Hampton, *Memorials of the Wars of the Roses* (Upmmster, 1979), pp.245-46). Bowes sold the advowson of Seaham to Gloucester in 1476; Gloucester gave it to Coverham abbey (Durham RO, D/Bo/D22). He became chief chamberlain of Durham in 1481 and sheriff in 1482 (PRO, Durh. 3/54/14, 17).

88. Surtees, *Durham*, IV, part 2, 114-15. The original was once in the Salvin papers at Croxdale, but disappeared between the early nineteenth century (when it was transcribed by Surtees) and 1964, when the papers were deposited in the Durham Record Office. It is hard to believe that Salvin was as alone in the

world as he made out, for in 1476, the year before he inherited Croxdale, he married Eleanor, the daughter of Gloucester's retainer, Sir Roger Conyers of Wynyard (ibid.).

89. Library of Congress, Washington DC, Thatcher Collection, 1004. I am extremely grateful to Mr Geoffrey Wheeler for making available to me a photocopy of this document. The final settlement of this dispute, delayed for two further years, may well be marked by the deed of gift and quitclaim issued by Claxton to Randson on 24 September and 4 October 1482 concerning one messuage and eighty acres of arable land in Burntoft; these deeds were witnessed by two of Gloucester's local retainers, Sir Roger Conyers and William Blakeston and by their sons (Durham RO, Miscellaneous Papers, D/X/209/I, 2).

90. His bastard son Lionel was retained by Gloucester before 1473; his third daughter, Elizabeth, married Richard Conyers of Ulshaw (the second son of Sir John of Hornby). PRO, DL 29/648/10485; Surtees, *Durham*, I, 28.

91. Compare Gloucester's settlement of a dispute between Selby Abbey and the parishioners of Snaith in 1481 (*The Register of Thomas Rotherham, Archbishop of York*, ed. E.E. Baker, I Canterbury and York Soc., LXIX, 1976), pp.194-95; Ross, *Richard III*, p.55). For the role of baronial 'councils learned' in the arbitration of disputes, see C. Rawcliffe, 'The Great Lords as Peacemaker: arbitration by English noblemen in the later middle ages', in *Law and Social Change*, ed. J.A. Guy and H.G. Beale (Royal Hist. Soc., 1984), pp.37-38.

92. Although Dudley sang a requiem mass at Edward IV's funeral, he showed no apparent reluctance to support Richard Ill's usurpa-tion, officiating at the coronation and sitting on the king's right hand, in the archbishop of Canterbury's place, at the banquet (A.F.

Sutton and P.W. Hammond, *The Coronation of Richard III* [Gloucester, 1984], pp.14, 36-45).

93. Le Neve, *Fasti*, p.109; Emden, Cambridge, p.524; *Harleian Manuscript 433, III*, 58, 61. See also the letters of Prior John Aukland to Bishop Shirwood in Rome (Durham, Dean and Chapter, Reg. IV, f. 3ff, printed in *Historiae Scriptores Tres*, cclxxiv-w).

94. *Foedera*, XII, 224; *Harleian Manuscript 433*, III, 66-68.

95. CPR, 1476-85 p.412; *Harlean Manuscript 433*, I, 102, 113, 167, 169, 207-8; II, 86-87. For Hoton, see W.E. Hampton, 'John Hoton of Hunwick and Tudhoe, county Durham, esquire for the body to Richard III', *The Ricardian*, VII, no. 88 (1985), 2-17.

96. PRO. Durh. 3/54/17; J.L. Drury, 'Westgate Castle', p.31; 'Stanhope Park', pp.142, 145. See above n 64.

97. Durham. Church Comm., Bishopric Estates, 189820-31 passim; *Plumpton Correspondence*, ed. Thomas Stapleton (Camden Soc., 1839), pp.lxxxii; *CIPM, Henry VII*, I (1898), 202; Petworth House Archives, MAC D/9/8/2; *York City Chamberlain's Account Rolls*, ed. R.B. Dobson Surtees Soc., CXCII, 1980), pp.136, 15I, 168, 184; Durham, Dean and Chapter, Bursar's Accounts, (fees', 1478-79 et seq.; *CPR, 1467-77*, pp.572, 635; *1475-6*, pp.50, 345, 580. In March 1483 Roland Ludworth was appointed joint steward, but Middleton continued to preside over halmote courts until replaced by Danby (PRO, Durh. 3/17/118d; 18/1;54/18). He died in 1492, his will being proved on 5 November (Borthwick Institute of Historical Research. Probate Register V, f. 422) and his epitaph is to be seen in Spofforth Parish Church.

98. PRO, SC6/1085/20; CP25(1)/281/164/32; 165/23; Atthill, *Middleham,* pp.84-85; J. Nicholson and R. Burn, *The History and Antiquities of Westmorland and Cumberland*, I (1777), 253-54. He died before 26 May 1481, when his widow received dispensation to

marry Geoffrey Frank, another councillor and servant of the duke (*C. Pap. R.*, 1471-84, p.271)

99. Attorney-general for Bishop Neville in 1438-39, Danby rose to be first justice of the county palatine by 1453 (Durham, Church Comm., Bishopric Estates, 189811-12). He was retained by Gloucester after he was dismissed as chief justice by Edward IV (PRO, DL29/648/10485; E.W. Ives, *The Common Lawyers of Pre. Reformation England* [Cantbridge, 1983], p.233). He died after 1 October 1474, when he executed a deed of enfeoffment in the county palatine (PRO, Durh. 3/166/14), but before 1 February 1475, when his widow took the veil (*Testamenta Eboracensia*, ed. James Raine, III [Surtees Soc., XLV, 1864], p.34).

100. Hicks, 'Dynastic Change', p.106; *CPR, 1476-85*, p.438.

101. Ibid., pp.371, 579; *Harleian Manuscript 433*, II, 51-52; PRO, Durh. 3/18/5. Danby succeeded Middleton between the end of the February circuit of the halmote court and the beginning of the July circuit.

102. *Paston Letters*, VI, 1-2.

103. *Harleian Manuscript 433*, I, 169; CPR, *1476-85*, pp.427-28.

104. *Rot. Parl.*, V1, 242-44; T.B. Pugh, 'The Magnates, Knights and Gentry', in *Fifteenth-Century England*, pp.111-12; Petre, 'The Nevilles', pp.2-3, 6.

105. *Harleian Manuscript 433*, II, 205; 1II, 114-15. In this context Henry VII's assumption of the keeping, rule and marriage of Neville's heir on 5 December 1485 takes on a new significance; it seems more probable that Henry inherited custody from Richard III and did not, as is usually suggested, take the boy as a hostage (see Petre, 'The Nevills', p.6).

106. *CPR, 14764-5*, pp.485-86; *Foedera*, XII, 241; the one commission was to keep the truce on 20 September 1484.

107. There is no evidence, other than the Ballad

of Bosworth Field, that Westmorland was present at the battle (Ross, *Richard III*, p.159; Petre, 'The Nevills', p.6).

108. *Rot. Scot.*, II, 464-66; *Cal. Docs. Scotland*, IV, 309-10.

109. *The Register of the Guild of Corpus Christi, York*, ed. R.H. Skaife (Surtees Soc., LVII, 1871), p.98; North Yorks. R.O., Clervaux Cartulary, f. 167v. In 1459 Sir John Neville was granted the offices of constable and forester, each carrying a fee of 10 marks (PRO, Durh. 3/48/6).

110. See above p.123; PRO, Durh. 3/55/15d.

111. Durham, Dean and Chapter, Reg. Parv. III, f. 188v.

112. PRO, Durh. 3/54/11; Hicks, 'Dynastic Change', p.106; *Paston Letters*, V1, 71—72.

113. Durham, Church Comm., Bishopric Estates, 190031. He paid a rent of £14 per annum.

114. Surtees, *Durham*, I, 32.

115. See above p.000.

116. Compare R.E. Horrox, 'The Extent and Use of Patronage under Richard III' (unpublished Cambridge University PhD thesis, 1977), p.222.

CHAPTER 10: ONE SUMMER AT MIDDLEHAM

1. British Library, Harley MS 433, fos 118-118v, printed in R.E. Horrox and P.W. Hammond, *British Library Harleian Manuscript 433*, vol II (1980), pp.24-5.

2. P.W. Hammond, *Edward of Middleham, Prince of Wales* (Cliftonville, 1973). See also my forthcoming entry in the *New National Dictionary of Biography*.

3. See Appendix pp.144-5, in which the warrant is set out item by item. The numbers in parenthesis in the text which follow refer to this appendix. I am grateful to the editors for permission to reproduce the text.

4. Geoffrey Frank was a son of Cuthbert Frank of Knayton, North Riding, who emerged in the service of Richard of Gloucester in the

1470s. He was a councillor and feoffeee for the duke by 1478, at which date he was probably already receiver of Middleham. See W.E. Hampton, *Memorials of the Wars of the Roses* (Upminster, 1999), pp 253-4 and A.J. Pollard, *North-Eastern England during the Wars of the Roses* (Oxford, 1990), pp.166, 357, 361, 372-3 and 'St Cuthbert and the Hog', above p.135.

5. PRO, Duchy of Lancaster 29/648/10485. There were nineteen payments by signed warrant of the duke authorising the payment of fees and wages (the majority), the settlement of debts (including £153 6s. 8d. for part payment of the purchase of silver and jewels), and the costs of the duke's household at Pontefract in April 1474 and at Middleham and Barnard Castle in October (£113 11s. 6d.). The full sum allocated, including these payments, was £397 12s. 10d. For the Council of the North and its finances see Pollard, *North-Eastern England,* pp.355-6.

6. In 1473-4 the expected receipts were £931 13s. 6d., and in 1488-9, £938 15s. 10d. (PRO, DL29/648/10485;29/649/10500).

7. Hammond, *Edward of Middleham*, n. 14, pp 35-6; M.A. Hicks, 'One Prince or Two? The family of Richard III', *The Ricardian*, 122 (1993), pp.467-8.

8. Hicks, 'One Prince or Two', passim.

9. Horrox and Hammond, *Harleian MS 433,* vol II, p.144; Hammond, *Edward of Middleham*, p.15.

10. R. Hutton, *The Rise and Fall of Merry England: the Ritual Year, 1400-1700* (Oxford), pp.28-31, 115-17.

11. M.A. Hicks, 'What Might Have Been: George Neville, Duke of Bedford, 1465-83: His Identity and Significance', in *Richard III and His Rivals* (Hambledon Press, 1991), pp.291-6.

12. For the Pilkingtons see R.E. Horrox, *Richard III: a Study of Service* (Cambridge, 1989), 45-6; R.C.E. Hayes, 'Ancient Indictments for the

North of England', in A.J. Pollard, ed., *The North of England in the Age of Richard III* (Stroud, 1996), pp.37-44 and especially 39 where Edward is identified as an illegitimate son of Edmund, the third son of the head of the family, Sir John Pilkington. Edward was one of the members of his family indicted for his involvement in disturbances in the West Riding in 1478. He was imprisoned, but escaped. He was presumably protected by Gloucester, who had himself presided over the proceedings of a commission of oyer and terminer which had condemned him.

13. *The York House Books,* ed. L.C. Attreed (Richard III and Yorkist History Trust, 2 vols, 1991), I, pp.286-7, 299.

14. *Ibid,* p.287.

15. The question remains as to who was responsible for the finances of the Prince's houshold before 22 May.

16. Hammond, *Edward of Middleham,* pp.15-18; P. Tudor-Craig, 'Richard III's Triumphant Entry into York', in R.E. Horrox, *Richard III and the North* (Hull, 1986), pp.109-10.

17. Hammond, *Edward of Middleham,* p.17, citing Harley 433, fo 126.

18. Pollard, *North-Eastern England,* pp.342-3.

19. Hampton, *Memorials,* pp.253-4.

LIST OF ILLUSTRATIONS

MAPS

COLOUR SECTION

Copyright and picture research: Geoffrey Wheeler, unless otherwise stated.

MAPS

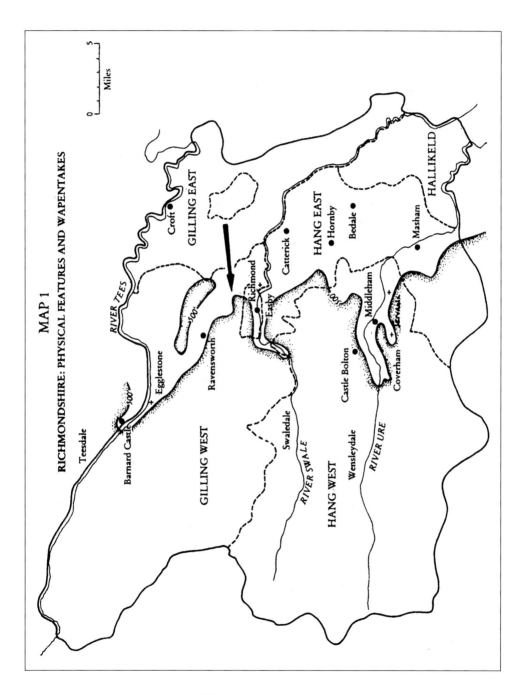

Map 1. Richmondshire: Physical Features and Wapentakes.

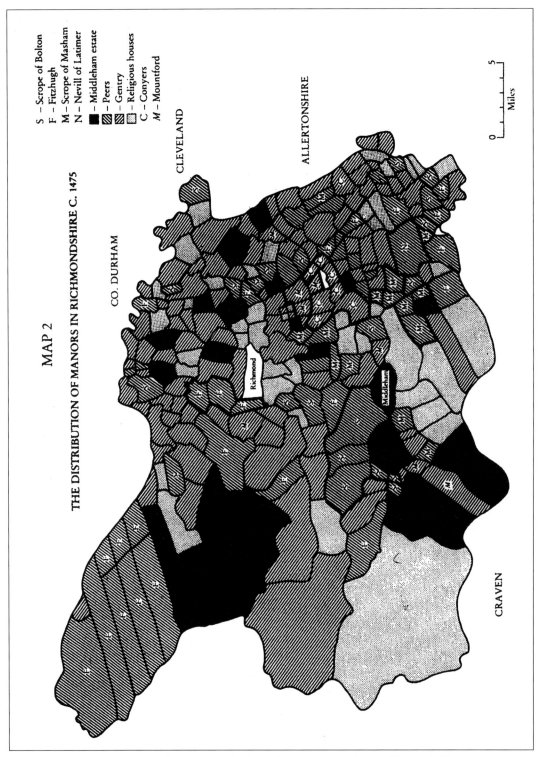

MAP 2

THE DISTRIBUTION OF MANORS IN RICHMONDSHIRE C. 1475

S – Scrope of Bolton
F – Fitzhugh
M – Scrope of Masham
N – Nevill of Latimer
– Middleham estate
– Peers
– Gentry
– Religious houses
C – Conyers
M – Mountford

CLEVELAND

ALLERTONSHIRE

CO. DURHAM

CRAVEN

Richmond

Middleham

0   5
Miles

Map 2. The Distribution of Manors in Richmondshire *c.*1475.

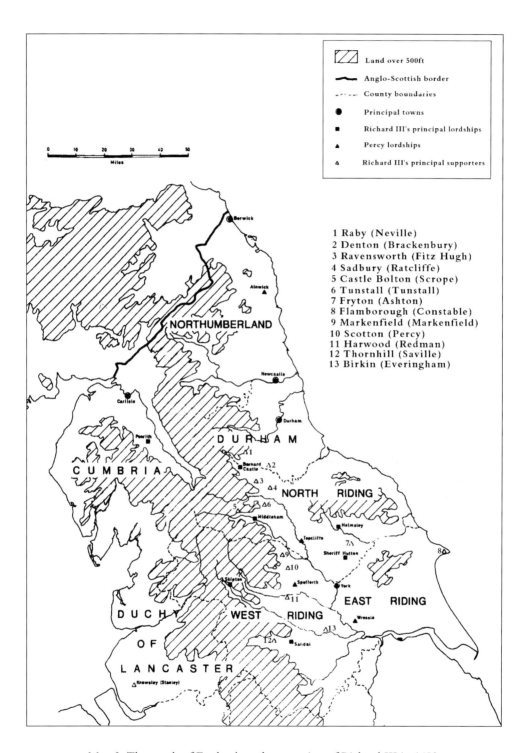

1 Raby (Neville)
2 Denton (Brackenbury)
3 Ravensworth (Fitz Hugh)
4 Sadbury (Ratcliffe)
5 Castle Bolton (Scrope)
6 Tunstall (Tunstall)
7 Fryton (Ashton)
8 Flamborough (Constable)
9 Markenfield (Markenfield)
10 Scotton (Percy)
11 Harwood (Redman)
12 Thornhill (Saville)
13 Birkin (Everingham)

Map 3. The north of England on the accession of Richard III in 1483.

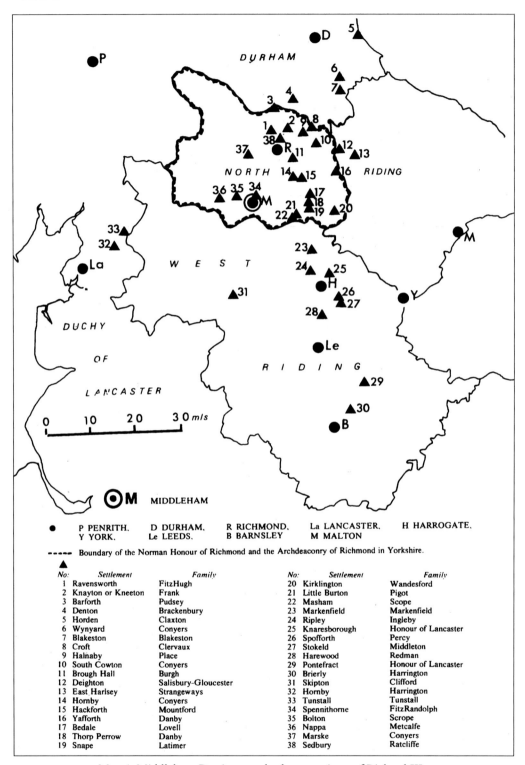

No:	Settlement	Family	No:	Settlement	Family
1	Ravensworth	FitzHugh	20	Kirklington	Wandesford
2	Knayton or Kneeton	Frank	21	Little Burton	Pigot
3	Barforth	Pudsey	22	Masham	Scope
4	Denton	Brackenbury	23	Markenfield	Markenfield
5	Horden	Claxton	24	Ripley	Ingleby
6	Wynyard	Conyers	25	Knaresborough	Honour of Lancaster
7	Blakeston	Blakeston	26	Spofforth	Percy
8	Croft	Clervaux	27	Stokeld	Middleton
9	Halnaby	Place	28	Harewood	Redman
10	South Cowton	Conyers	29	Pontefract	Honour of Lancaster
11	Brough Hall	Burgh	30	Brierly	Harrington
12	Deighton	Salisbury-Gloucester	31	Skipton	Clifford
13	East Harlsey	Strangeways	32	Hornby	Harrington
14	Hornby	Conyers	33	Tunstall	Tunstall
15	Hackforth	Mountford	34	Spennithorne	FitzRandolph
16	Yafforth	Danby	35	Bolton	Scrope
17	Bedale	Lovell	36	Nappa	Metcalfe
18	Thorp Perrow	Danby	37	Marske	Conyers
19	Snape	Latimer	38	Sedbury	Ratcliffe

Map 4. Middleham Retainers and other associates of Richard III.

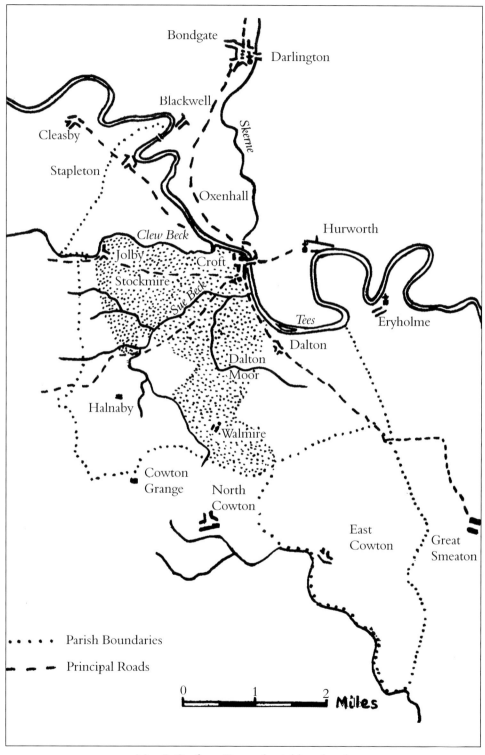

Map 5. Croft on Tees and neighbourhood.

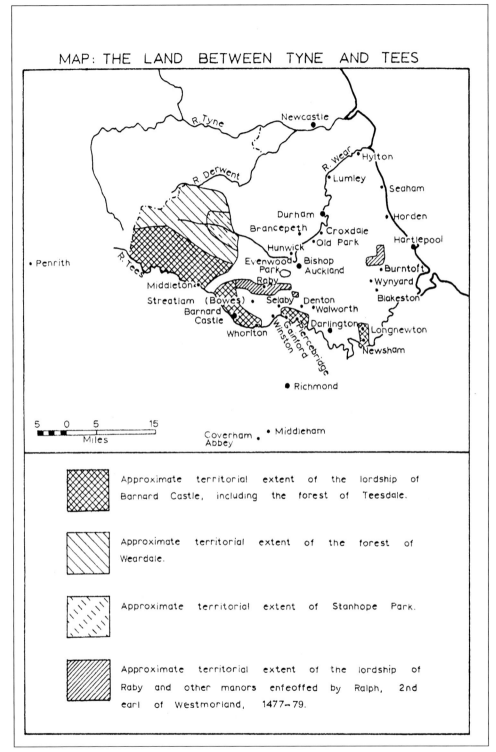

Map 6. The Land between Tyne and Tees.

INDEX

Richard, 11, 54, 59-61, 63-4, 71-2, 83-4, 91, 97-116 *passim*, 121;
  his tomb, *98*
Richard, the younger, 100
Robert, 106
Thomas, 100, 106
William, 114
Cleseby, Elizabeth, 57
family of 57
Clifford, family of, 26
  Henry, Lord, 59
  Robert, 69, 72
  Thomas, lord, 59
Coldingham, 130
Collins, Jane, 139
Colville, family of, 56
  William, 81
Condon, Margaret, 9
Constable, Sir Marmaduke, 29
Conyers, Christopher, of Hornby, 57, *58*, 59, 84, 86
  Christopher, of Sockburn, 107
  Elizabeth, dau of Robert of Sockburn, 106
  Elizabeth, dau of Christopher, 83
  family of, 54, 57, 61, 95, 109
  John, father of Christopher of Hornby, 83, 92
  John, grandson of Sir John, 61, 69
  John, son of sir John. 72
  Sir John, 51-2, 57, *58*, 59, 61, 64, 68-69, 72-4, 83, 86, 89, 90, 106, 108, 110-11, 121
  Sir Richard, of South Cowton, bro of Sir John, 53, 61, *62*, 64, 69, 71, 74
  Richard, son of Sir John, 61, 69
  Robert, of Sockburn, 196
  Sir Roger, of Wynyard, bro of Sir John, 11, 57, 70 61, 111, 130
  William, 1st lord, 57, 64, 73-4, 83, 93, 122
  William, of Marske, bro of Sir John, 51, 57, 61, 68-9, 74
Cook, John, 121
  Thomas, 118
Cooper, Agnes, 139

Copeland, Edward, 121
Courtenay, family of, 30
Coverham Abbey, 56, 72, 128, 139
Cow, Dun, the badge of the earldom of Richmond, 117, *119*, 122
Cracall, Richard of, 91
Crayke, 128
Cressi, a scribe, 97
Croft, North Yorks, 11, 84, 97-116, *passim*
Croft, John de, 105
Cromwell, Oliver, 32
Croyland Chronicle Continuator, 18-20, 22, 26, 30, 33, 47, 50
Curteys, Piers, 142

Dacre, Humphrey, Lord, 26, 135
Dalton, 99-100
Danby, 118
Danby, Sir James, 72, 134
  Ralph, 73
  Richard, 133-4
  Robert, father of Sir Robert, 84
  Sir Robert, 59-60, 69, 72, 83, 86
Darcy, Margery, 57
Darlington, 11, 99, 101
  Bondgate, 114
Daubeney, Sir Giles, 30
De La Pole, John, earl of Lincoln, 28, 112
Deighton, 73, 66, 110
Dennis, a postillion, 139
Dereham, Gilbert, 121
Dernlove, John, 105
Dinham, John Lord, 30
Dishforth, 118
Dockray, Keith, 9, 13
Doncaster, 99
Dorset, marquis *see* Grey
Dringhouses, 141
Drury, William, 95
Dudley, William, bishop of Durham, 10, 128-33, 135
Dunstanburgh Castle, *82*, 87
Durham, bishops of, *see* Booth, Dudley,

NEW IN PAPERBACK
RICHARD III
Michael Hicks

'a most important book by the greatest living expert on Richard…
fluently written and forcefully argued, it makes for compulsive reading.
A must for anyone even remotely interested in Richard.'

BBC HISTORY MAGAZINE

'important… where early historians simply accepted the Tudor myth and later
ones denied it, Michael Hicks returns to the original sources.'

THE INDEPENDENT ON SUNDAY

'important'

HISTORY TODAY

The modern biography of the most vilified English king, from model of nobility, to murderer and monster.

240pp 125 illus (25 col)   Paperback £12.99/$19.99   0 7524 2302 9

UK ORDERING

Available from all good bookshops or direct from Tempus Publishing Ltd with free postage and packing
(within the UK only).

Simply write, stating the quantity of books required and enclosing a cheque for the correct amount, to:
Sales Department, Tempus Publishing Ltd, The Mill, Brimscombe Port, Stroud, Glos. GL5 2QG, UK.
Alternatively, call the sales department on 01453 883300 to pay by Switch, Visa or Mastercard.

USA ORDERING

Please call Arcadia Publishing, a division of Tempus Publishing, toll free on 1-888-313-2665